Praise for
Rhythms of Faith

"I want—no, I *need*—this book by my nightstand, on my dinner table, in my church pew! Claude Atcho saves us from giving our time to Caesar, returning it rightfully to Christ. Walking us through the cycles of light, life, and love, Atcho shows us how to measure our days by Christ so that we might gain wisdom."

—JESSICA HOOTEN WILSON,
Fletcher Jones Chair of Great Books at
Pepperdine University and author of several books,
including *The Scandal of Holiness*

"We all need a sense of time. Let this book be your guide."
—JUSTIN WHITMEL EARLEY,
business lawyer and author of *Habits of the Household*
and *The Body Teaches the Soul*

"Claude Atcho is an eloquent, excellent guide to the Christianity of the church year. This wise, well-crafted, and generous book is the best answer I have seen to the ever-relevant question: 'How do I start practicing time in a Christian way?' Here is an artful, accessible resource the church has badly needed for many years. I thank God for *Rhythms of Faith*."

—S. D. SMITH,
author of *The Green Ember* series

"Claude Atcho's *Rhythms of Faith* pastorally guides readers toward the roots of the liturgy: the words and acts of Jesus. This book is a wise, accessible invitation to marking time by the evergreen movement of God in our lives, instead of by achievement, consumption, or even the weather. A rich resource for both those unfamiliar with the liturgical year and those wishing to deepen their practice of holy timekeeping."

—DR. GRACE HAMMAN,
author of *Ask of Old Paths: Medieval Virtues and Vices for a Whole and Holy Life*

Rhythms of Faith

Rhythms of Faith

A Devotional Pilgrimage
Through the Church Year

Claude Atcho

WaterBrook

WaterBrook

An imprint of the Penguin Random House Christian Publishing Group,
a division of Penguin Random House LLC

1745 Broadway, New York, NY 10019

waterbrookmultnomah.com
penguinrandomhouse.com

Library of Congress Cataloging-in-Publication Data

Names: Atcho, Claude, 1986- author
Title: Rhythms of faith : a devotional pilgrimage through the church year / Claude Atcho.
Description: New York, NY : WaterBrook, [2025] | Includes bibliographical references.
Identifiers: LCCN 2025008182 | ISBN 9780593601990 hardcover |
ISBN 9780593602003 ebook
Subjects: LCSH: Church year meditations | Devotional calendars—Anglican
Communion | Christian life—Anglican authors
Classification: LCC BV30 .A89 2025
LC record available at https://lccn.loc.gov/2025008182

Printed in Canada on acid-free paper

1 3 5 7 8 9 6 4 2

First Edition

The authorized representative in the EU for product safety and compliance is Penguin
Random House Ireland, Morrison Chambers, 32 Nassau Street, Dublin D02 YH68,
Ireland. https://eu-contact.penguin.ie

BOOK TEAM: Editor: Jamie Lapeyrolerie • Production editor: Jessica Choi •
Managing editor: Julia Wallace • Production manager: Maggie Hart •
Copy editor: Tracey Moore • Proofreaders: Bailey Utecht, Karissa Silvers

Book design by Susan Turner

For details on special quantity discounts for bulk purchases, contact
specialmarketscms@penguinrandomhouse.com.

To Kelsey,

Thank you for keeping sacred time with me.

Contents

LENT
A Bright Sadness   103

HOLY WEEK
The Journey to Redemption   145

EASTER
Resurrection Life   169

ORDINARY TIME
Walking the Way of Christ   213

Introduction

What, then, is time? If no one asks me, I know
what it is. If I wish to explain it to him who
asks me, I do not know.

—Augustine, *Confessions*

Were you there when they crucified my Lord?
Were you there?

—Negro spiritual

A t my first Easter Vigil, a single word set my mind rac-
ing. The darkened sky, a moody blue–black mixture
with the Blue Ridge Mountains in the background,
seemed a perfect setting for a weighty theological phrase to
strike. But as the story of redemption was read aloud from the
Old Testament Scripture, all throughout the outdoor service
my mind fixated on one simple word: *this*.

The liturgy for Easter Vigil, the long meditative service on
Saturday evening before Easter Sunday, begins with these
words: "On this most holy night, in which our Lord Jesus
passed over from death to life . . ."[1] As I stood near the communion table, listening and experiencing the near culmination
of my first immersion into the fullness of Holy Week, I was

struck by the choice of *this* over *that*. I had known my pastoral transition from a nondenominational megachurch to a liturgical tradition would require some shifts. (That's why I desired to make the change.) But one month into my new ecclesial home, was I really ready for this sort of disorientation? Was I prepared to trade "*that* most holy night"—how I would have phrased it—for "*this* most holy night"? I had not misheard the liturgy, nor had I been authorized to approve the supremacy of *that* over *this*. The purposeful use of *this* represented a different orientation to worship, to Christ, and subsequently to time itself.

Days before, on Maundy Thursday, I had heard these words as the service, which centers on Jesus's Last Supper according to John's gospel, began:

> *This* is the night that Christ the Son of Man gathered with his disciples in the upper room.
>
> *This* is the night that Christ our Lord and Master took a towel and washed the disciples' feet, calling us to love one another as he has loved us.
>
> *This* is the night that Christ our God gave us this holy feast, that we who eat this bread and drink this cup may here proclaim his perfect sacrifice.
>
> *This* is the night that Christ the Lamb of God gave himself into the hands of those who would slay him.[2]

The language of *this* reminded me I was truly, terrifyingly, and gloriously caught up in this story of Jesus—foot washing, betrayal, false accusations, crucifixion, despair, and ultimately the undoing of death. This realization came not primarily through the power of the preached word but through, in part, the temporal emphasis of that single word: *this*.

This suggests that time is something in which we participate. That some things are so real, so present, so deep, they don't just pass like the breeze. Some parts of time summon us to partake of them, and like a holy echo, they reverberate through the ages with sacred ramifications that grip the present. The notion of "*that* time" (as in "on that most holy of nights") suggests that time is strictly linear, detached. It's a thing that goes by and is done and gone. "*This* time" suggests the opposite—that certain events defy our common grasp of time. Embedded in each phrase is a different sense of time, one common and memorial and one holy and participatory.

Time in the Hands of a Gracious God

What is time? If the question left a true luminary like Saint Augustine confounded, it's no surprise that whatever answer just popped into your mind feels like grasping at straws. In our confusion we often disregard the question entirely. Who has time for such philosophical musings? Or in the words of a wonderful meme, ain't nobody got time for that.

Whether or not we take up the inquiry, each of us lives by some notion of time. All around us are competing ideas on what time is, what it's for, and why it matters. The pseudo-maxims are well known. According to some, time is money. It's the one resource billionaires can't buy even if they can fund treks to outer space. According to others, time is short. It is defined by its scarcity—it's the one resource perpetually slipping through our clenched hands. Even as you read this, you are "losing" time.

Time is by God and for God. But for what reason? In part, time is formative. Psalm 90:12 says, "Teach us to number our days that we may get a heart of wisdom." Sounds a bit like the whole "time is short" ethos, doesn't it? Yet there's more. If time is God's, then it serves a greater purpose than being an ever-constant reminder of death. After all, death comes from sin and is, according to the apostle Paul, our great enemy (1 Corinthians 15:26). There must be more to time in God's mind than to remind his creatures that our funerals are right around the corner.

Time is a creative tool in the hands of a gracious God. From the very beginning, God has revealed himself as "merciful and gracious" (Exodus 34:6), and the fullness of his revelation in Jesus authenticates that he is "full of grace and truth" (John 1:14). It is no shock, then, that our gracious God uses time to draw us deeper into life with him. Among its many features, time is a gift, a means of drawing us nearer to our deepest purpose: knowing and enjoying God in exultant fullness.

Christians across the centuries have experienced time as a spiritually formative gift through the church year, or the church calendar. The church year is a gift, not a restraint. If "how we spend our days is . . . how we spend our lives," as Annie Dillard writes,[3] then the church year offers us the sacred task of spending our living in Jesus Christ. As we keep sacred time—spending our days, personally and corporately, rooted in the cycle of his life—the church year guides us to tangibly experience our spiritual unity with Jesus in our minutes, hours, days, and years.

Robert Webber described this dynamic of the church year through the concepts of objective and subjective spirituality. Webber defined objective spirituality as "a *given* spirituality." It is the gift of salvation in Christ that none of us can secure or merit (Ephesians 2:8–9). But subjective spirituality is participatory; it "arises out of our response to God's grace."[4] Whether we define and distinguish these two realities as justification and sanctification or as union and communion, what matters most is the recognition that there are both an *objective* basis and *experiential* reality to our faith. And it is in the church year that we find a structure that deepens and intensifies our subjective experience of living with, in, and for Christ. In the church year, God gifts us a subjective way of going deeper in the objective truth of our salvation—Christ himself. Time is a formational tool in the hands of a gracious God.

The Church Year: Living into Higher Time

The church year is a call to live out the higher time of the kingdom in our so-called ordinary lives. Think of the church year as a metaphorical U-turn, a return to the recognition that time possesses a higher purpose than pushing us toward productivity or simply reminding us of our finitude. Time is a means of drawing close to Christ, eternal life, and the way of the kingdom. More specifically, the church year draws us in as participants in the life of Jesus, the world's one true Lord. The church year, then, is a journey further up and into the "unsearchable riches of Christ" (Ephesians 3:8). It's one more step, one more cycle into the hope of glory, which is Christ in us (Colossians 1:27).

By contrast, think about the nature and purpose of the civic year. The civic year possesses its own formative goal: Its aim is to mold us into its definition of conscientious consumer citizens who march along to the drumbeat of society. The cadence of the American civic year is alluring. We know its rhythms by heart: Make goals and resolutions at New Year's, get hyped for a new round of ads on Super Bowl Sunday, buy Hallmark cards at Valentine's, ache for the leisure of summer vacation by late April, grow melancholy as fall returns and normal rhythms of the ordinary accompany the turning of the leaves, try not to overspend on Black Friday, and wage war against the onslaught of our basest consumer impulses come December. Then we rest for a few weeks. And we do it all over again.

There are few things blatantly evil about the civic calendar. In fact, what makes it such a dangerous frame for living is the absence of anything overtly sinister. Its discipleship by time silently conforms us not to the life of the kingdom but to the life of the state—a life of banality and consumption, a life untethered from Christ's holy truths and counterintuitive rhythms.

The civic year offers us a life lived in lower time, ordered toward blind notions of progress, an inhumane ethos of productivity, and an addictive lust for autonomy, pleasure, and products. At a certain point, all of us must ask whose time we wish to live by—Caesar's or Christ's. We render our taxes to Caesar, but let us render ourselves to Christ by living into the church's time.

The Church Year: Formation for Spiritual Zeros Who've Tried Everything Else

One aspect that drew me to a liturgical tradition was the formative power of the church year for people like me—easily distracted and undisciplined types. In *A Praying Life,* Paul Miller remarks that a life of prayer is less about self-discipline and more about neediness.[5]

His point is that if you want to pray more, get in touch with your needs, and the prayers will flow in either words or groans. It's not the spiritual elite so much as the spiritually needy who pray without ceasing. I feel similarly about the church year. It's not the elite who keep sacred time; it's the spiritual zeros.

I was drawn to the church year for its beauty, yes, but also for its gracious structure. It mitigated my devotional weakness by supplying clear tracks on which my life and heart could run, even if slowly and clumsily, toward Christ in every season. In the church year, it felt as though I received an heirloom, a long-lost family gift that enabled me to walk in the deep desire of my heart. One can live a holy life by the civic year, but I've found the effort required is herculean. If you find yourself yearning to walk more closely with Jesus but wavering in commitment and vigor, the church year can be a gracious guide into a vibrant spirituality. It is not for the strong and trendy but for the hungry and needy. In the church year, God employs time as our teacher, forming us in the curriculum of Christ's very life. Time becomes a deep immersion into the life of Jesus.

The Cycles of the Church Year: Experiencing the Saving Life of Christ

The church year invites us to experience the saving life of Christ in three cycles or movements:[6]

1. **The Cycle of Light:** Advent, Christmastide, Epiphany
2. **The Cycle of Life:** Lent, Holy Week, Eastertide, Pentecost
3. **The Cycle of Love:** Ordinary Time

The Cycle of Light is God *with* us in the Incarnation, the Cycle of Life demonstrates God *for* us in the gift of salvation, and the Cycle of Love is God working *through* us in love, service, and mission. In a sense, Ordinary Time is less extraordinary in contrast to the Cycle of Light and the Cycle of Life, as evidenced by its fewer special days like Christmas or Palm Sunday. A fuller perspective, however, recognizes that Ordinary Time is the season in which all the cycles that have gone before form our daily lives.[7]

Entering the Cycle: How to Use This Book

Because this book introduces you to the church year, at some level to use this book is to follow the church year. I suggest entering each season by reading the introductory orientation that prefaces it. From there, I suggest partaking of the Scripture readings and devotions for each season.[8] Try praying the collect prayer (the themed prayer) over multiple days. This slower, prayerful pace will help the themes of each season sink and settle into your soul. Approaching this differently than a daily devotional encourages you to engage the scriptures, prayers, and devotionals slowly and reflectively—and communally. Consider reading on your own and then connecting with a group to discuss both the Scripture passages and devotional readings. Note that depending on the date of Easter, there will be more or fewer weeks for some seasons in this book. Advent, which is the beginning of the church year, always starts on the fourth Sunday before Christmas. From there, you can find the length of particular seasons with a Google search or at claudeatcho.com.

That said, you've bought this book, so you own it; it doesn't own you. Use it in whatever way is most life-giving and edifying for you. Here are some possible approaches:

- **Daily devotional approach.** If you're the type who yearns for a daily devotional, read one of the Scripture passages each day. Once you've read through all the passages, read the devotional that draws from them. This approach gives you a chance to mediate on the Scripture readings and the devotional reflection over the course of five days, with two makeup days in case you get behind.

- **Weekly approach.** Say you already have a regular daily devotional practice. Use this book weekly to go deeper into each season of the church year. In one sitting, read the Scripture passages, pray the collect prayer, and read the devotional. This method works well as part of a Sunday or Sabbath routine, a tool for family devotions, or a way for preacher folks to get filled up after Sunday. An alternative approach could entail slowly reading the Scripture texts and prayer one day, engaging with the devotional sections on another, and concluding with a day of reflection on the discussion questions.

- **Communal approach.** As alluded to earlier, this book works well for group study and reading. Gather a group of friends for a season to read and discuss together the texts and the devotional. Keeping time with others represents the communal nature of our faith.

Whatever strategy you take, be assured that the Word will do its work.

Blessed Lord, who caused all Holy Scriptures to be written for our learning: Grant us so to hear them, read, mark, learn, and inwardly digest them, that by patience and the comfort of your holy Word we may embrace and ever hold fast the blessed hope of everlasting life, which you have given us in our Savior Jesus Christ; who lives and reigns with you and the Holy Spirit, one God, for ever and ever. Amen.[9]

THE CYCLE OF LIGHT

THE CYCLE OF LIFE

THE CYCLE OF LOVE

ADVENT

CHRISTMAS

EPIPHANY

LENT

GOOD FRIDAY

EASTER

PENTECOST

ORDINARY TIME

NOV DEC JAN FEB MAR APR MAY JUN JUL AUG SEP OCT

ADVENT

The Lord Who Arrives Thrice

Advent is the time when God breaks in on
us with new surprises and touches us with a
renewing and restoring power.

—ROBERT WEBBER, *Ancient-Future Time*

Before we begin our Advent devotions, I want to provide some insight into this season and what it means. Few things frustrate and challenge us quite like waiting. Yet waiting is the first note of the church calendar. The church year begins with Advent, which means it begins with waiting—or better yet, anticipation. Anticipation is waiting flavored by hope, and this is at the center of Advent.

In Advent, we gaze backward to the Incarnation, Christ's first coming at his birth in Bethlehem. At the same time, we gaze forward to Christ's second coming, when he will judge, save, and usher in God's new creation in full. Just as the Israelites longed for a savior before the birth of Christ, we wait with the church across the ages for the second coming of our King.

At times, Advent has suffered from a slight case of mistaken identity. Advent is not Christmas extended. They are sibling seasons, but Advent has its own distinct personality.

The preparation of Advent launches us into the celebration of Christmas.

Advent Spirituality: How Advent Shapes Us

How does Advent shape our discipleship to Jesus? Advent summons us to align and ready our lives and hearts for the arrival of our Lord. At a basic level, the logic is intuitive. When guests plan to come for an extended stay in your home, you no doubt take essential and sometimes rather elaborate measures to prepare. Often, the anticipated arrival of a guest will produce in us fresh waves of motivation. Knowing they are coming may energize us to fix what we might otherwise leave broken, like a janky kitchen drawer, or to straighten up rooms we would have lazily left cluttered. The guest's anticipated presence ends up elevating the state of the whole house. Jesus spoke about his arrival in similar terms, comparing his second coming to the return of the master of the house at a time unknown:

> Therefore stay awake—for you do not know when the master of the house will come, in the evening, or at midnight, or when the rooster crows, or in the morning—lest he come suddenly and find you asleep. And what I say to you I say to all: Stay awake. (Mark 13:35–37)

Advent spirituality is about the holy work of anticipation: watching, waiting, and staying awake.

Wherever we have been sluggish in our faith, apathetic toward Christ's return, and bored with seeking Christ's kingdom, Advent is a gracious wake-up call. In this season, the Lord wakes us from our slumber, calls us to stay alert, and beckons us to live under the truth that will soon transform every square inch of reality: the fullness of the kingdom at the return of Jesus.

The "Three Advents" of Christ

- Christ's coming at Bethlehem to be our savior
- The longing for Christ to come anew into our lives and hearts
- The expectation of Christ's second coming at the end of history to rescue, judge, and establish his rule

When Christians speak of Christ's coming, we speak of a truth that bends time. The advent of our Lord is a past, present, and future gift and reality. In this way, Advent centers on the Lord who arrives thrice. In the Incarnation, we marvel at the Lord's first advent among us as the Word became flesh (John 1:14). We anticipate the Lord's second advent in his future return at the end of history (Revelation 22:20). And in the present, we seek the Lord's third advent—his continual in-breaking work in our lives. These three comings of Christ form us as we live in faithful anticipation.

Following Jesus in Advent is a deeply formative way to walk the peculiar path of discipleship. Advent is a time to watch, wait, and stay awake (Mark 13). It's a season in which we take a hard look at the world's darkness, injustice, and longing and say with the psalmist, "How long, O Lord?" (Psalm 13:1). This understanding of Advent chafes against the way we're used to spending the weeks leading up to Christmas. Let's be real: It can feel odd to sit in waiting and lament during the early weeks of December, while the fanfare of shopping and Mariah Carey's Christmas anthems are all around us. (It will feel equally odd to insist on continuing to celebrate and feast for twelve days following Christmas Day.) By inhabiting this peculiarity, we follow Christians of the past who embraced the rhythms of sober preparation and patient waiting, rhythms we can offer to a busy and broken world by embracing them first ourselves. In Advent, waiting leads to the gift of Christlike formation in the present and fullhearted celebration in due time.

Advent Practices

What are the particular practices that mark worship and discipleship in Advent? We could name several, but these few form a helpful starting place for individuals and communities.

Count down to Christmas in anticipation. There are a variety of ways to prayerfully count down to Christmas. One is the use of an Advent wreath, an embodied practice focused on the coming light of Christ. Each week, on Sunday, a purple candle is lit, with a pink or rose candle lit on the third Sunday of the season. (Traditions do vary across denominations, and it is fine to use purple candles on the third Sunday.) The candles enact light overcoming darkness. The fifth candle—the white Christ candle—is lit on Christmas Eve. Make the Advent wreath the centerpiece of your dining table, and engage in Scripture and prayer as you light a candle each Sunday in anticipation of Christ's advent.

Make room for lament. For many, the approach of Christmas is a time not of rejoicing but of sadness due to tragedy and loss. Since Advent begins in the dark, make room to lament. Where are you disappointed or experiencing loss? Bring these things before the Lord in prayer. Consider using the language of

Psalm 13 and lighting a candle as you do so, letting the dancing flame remind you of the presence of God.

Immerse yourself in Advent hymns and music. Christmas music rejoices while Advent music vocalizes the longing of a world in need of rescue. Create a playlist of Advent hymns and music, and don't turn too quickly to the joy of your favorite Christmas anthems. Hymns such as "Let All Mortal Flesh Keep Silence," "O Come, O Come, Emmanuel," "Come, Thou Long Expected Jesus," and "Lo! He Comes with Clouds Descending" are classics for good reason.

Consider the threats to keeping an intentional Advent. Because Advent is such a countercultural season in its call for reflection when the rest of our world calls for consumption and busyness, it's worth assessing what will keep you from embracing Advent the way you want to. Most of us will face these three threats: hurry, perfection, and noise. Here are helpful tips to overcome them:

1. **Hurry.** For many, late November and December are among the busiest times of the year. Busyness and hurry are enemies of the spiritual life. *Remedy:* Plan before the season starts. Consider doing Christmas shopping early—even before Advent begins. Pick your activities, traditions, family worship rhythms, and so forth ahead of time. This will add a sense of calm to your Advent experience.
2. **Expecting perfection.** The truth is you won't have a perfect Advent, nor will you live up to all your Advent plans. That's both fine and to be expected. *Remedy:* Reject attempts to "perform" at Advent. Simply do

something with intention, try to stick with it, trust God's grace, and expect God to make this season meaningful in ways seen and unseen.

3. **Noise.** For those who live in a house with many room-mates or children, the prospect of eliminating noise is a pipe dream. While few of us can eliminate noise, many of us can limit it in various ways. *Remedy*: Decide in advance to limit noise, media, and consumerism to attend to God and others.

Advent Feast Days

Finally, each season has notable feast days in which the church is called into a deeper experience of the life of Christ together. Feast days are days of celebration and remembrance that point us to God's redemptive story and work in and through his church. Some include special church services while many can be noted and celebrated at home through specific prayers, meals, or Scripture readings.[1] Here are some notable feasts during Advent:

The Feast of Saint Nicholas (December 6). This day celebrates Saint Nicholas, a fourth-century bishop in Asia Minor who was deeply concerned with the poor. Tradition states Nicholas secretly came at night and left gold at the home of a family in grave need, providing the means to keep the daughters from entering slavery. Because the stories of Saint Nicholas have morphed into various secular forms of Santa Claus, our gift giving on Christmas can trace its lineage to this saint and feast. However, this feast day reminds us of our call to reflect the generosity of God through sacrificial giving and caring for the needy and offers a great opportunity to engage in this traditional Advent practice.

The Feast of Saint Lucia (December 13). This day celebrates Saint Lucy (or Lucia), a third-century Christian in Sicily who was martyred. According to church tradition, Saint Lucy, whose name means "light," often brought food to suffering Christians who were hiding in catacombs to avoid persecution. It is believed Saint Lucia wore a wreath of candles on her head to light her path in the dark. This day thus celebrates the light of Christ that shines in the dark and offers a time of feasting amid the longing of Advent.

Gaudete Sunday (Third Sunday of Advent). *Gaudete* means "rejoice" in Latin. In the midst of Advent's sober call to wait and watch, Gaudete Sunday is a call to rejoice and anticipate in hope, knowing that the promise of the Incarnation at Christmas approaches. It is common to light a rose or pink candle on the Advent wreath or in the home to mark this day in representation of the coming celebration. In liturgical churches, this service infuses a jolt of joy into Advent in anticipation of Christmas.

Reading Advent Texts and Devotions

As you read the following Scripture texts and devotions, you'll encounter riveting passages from Isaiah, the central Old Testament prophet of our readings. Isaiah confronts us with humanity's brokenness and God's gracious promises while our New Testament readings from James and Romans show how Christ's return is transformative news for the vulnerable. These emphases highlight Advent's focus on the coming of the Lord in power and glory. May these reflections enable you to set your hope on the Lord and to live in such a way that you are regarded by Jesus as one who "stays awake."

First Week

Light and Dark

Isaiah 2:1–5
Psalm 122
Romans 13:8–14
Matthew 24:29–44

The people who walked in darkness have
seen a great light; those who dwelt in a land of
deep darkness, on them has light shone.

—Isaiah 9:2

Almighty God, give us grace to cast away the works
of darkness, and put on the armor of light, now in the
time of this mortal life in which your Son Jesus Christ
came to visit us in great humility; that in the last day,
when he shall come again in his glorious majesty to
judge both the living and the dead, we may rise to the
life immortal; through him who lives and reigns with
you and the Holy Spirit, one God, now and for ever.
Amen.[1]

Advent is a gracious but demanding season. It is a season that "begins in the dark."[2] Which is to say, Advent challenges us to see ourselves and the entire world as broken and in need of rescue and healing. Our Scripture readings graciously draw us into this essential work by shattering our unhealthy idealism. Our Isaiah and Romans readings highlight the contrast between the themes of light and dark, demanding that we attend to the harsh shadows of reality while believing that the light of hope has invaded and prevailed and, at the right time, will again. In this way, Advent calls us to be faith-filled realists, seeing things as they really are, without becoming despairing pessimists, believing no hope is on the way. Advent guides us into the serious work of hoping in God alone, trusting in the light even when it seems we are surrounded only by darkness.

Rival Advent Voices: Hebrew Prophets and American Celebrities

For these reasons, Isaiah is an essential Advent text, concerned with warning, preparation, judgment, and salvation. Isaiah prophesied several centuries before Christ's birth when things were especially dark for God's people. In Isaiah 1, we find that they are unfaithful and idolatrous. In Isaiah 8:22, we hear that this people "will look to the earth, but behold, distress and darkness, the gloom of anguish. And they will be thrust into thick darkness." The people of God, Isaiah declares, have chosen suffocating darkness over life-giving light. They turned to false gods and nations to save them. They turned to sorcery and spiritualists to find help and rescue. In the end, they received nothing but gloom.

In the face of judgment, Isaiah points the way to Bethlehem and the first Advent truth: The promise of light must come from outside us and despite us. This is what many Protestant reformers described in speaking of salvation as *extra nos*, something that comes from outside ourselves. And if we're honest, it is not the sort of truth we like to hear, as it boldly counters the story we prefer to tell about ourselves. Our preferred story is often revealed in the figures our society most reveres: our celebrities. In 1985, more than forty famous musical artists, headlined by Lionel Richie and Michael Jackson, collaborated to raise money and awareness for USA for Africa's poverty relief. The world's great entertainers—Stevie Wonder, Ray Charles, Tina Turner, Bruce Springsteen, Bob Dylan, Paul Simon, and others—gathered and sang a song for the occasion called "We Are the World."[3] Take note of some of the lyrics and the story they tell:

> *We are the ones who make a brighter day. . . .*
> *We're saving our own lives.*

Relief efforts are admirable, of course. But these musical voices sing a different tune than the prophetic voice we hear in Isaiah. In making a genuine difference, the song conveys the human myth that we *are* the difference. We pull together our best efforts and we save ourselves. This is the human folly that Isaiah warns against, for we cannot and do not light up the darkness. Commendable as relief is, there are no cheap answers in the dark. We cannot make a brighter day despite our best efforts.

Through Isaiah, God declares that the light does not arrive through human initiative; it arrives through an invasion. Isaiah 9:2 makes it plain: "The people who walked in darkness have seen a great light; those who dwelt in a land of deep darkness, on them has light shone." The final verb about light is passive. In other words, God saves, and we receive—rather than create, contribute, or earn—the light of his rescuing grace.

Here is the great turn in our Isaiah passage: The people and the land that are trapped in spiritual and political darkness, staring death and extinction in the face, will see light. Light will shine on them. And not only on them but also on "all nations" through them. Read again Isaiah's vision:

This is what Isaiah son of Amoz saw concerning Judah and Jerusalem:

In the last days

> the mountain of the LORD's temple will be established
>> as the highest of the mountains;
> it will be exalted above the hills,
>> and all nations will stream to it.

Many peoples will come and say,

> "Come, let us go up to the mountain of the LORD,
>> to the temple of the God of Jacob.
> He will teach us his ways,
>> so that we may walk in his paths."
> The law will go out from Zion,
>> the word of the LORD from Jerusalem.
> He will judge between the nations
>> and will settle disputes for many peoples.
> They will beat their swords into plowshares
>> and their spears into pruning hooks.
> Nation will not take up sword against nation,
>> nor will they train for war anymore.

Come, descendants of Jacob,
  let us walk in the light of the LORD. (2:1–5, NIV)

This is the great thrill of Christian hope. However, Isaiah's word presents a different sort of challenge—not of human darkness but of God's promise. It is a divine dream, wonderful and deeply aligned with pure human desire. But given all the darkness around us, this dream feels like a cruel joke. Army tanks turned to lawn mowers? Nations unlearning war? All peoples moving like a river in reverse, up to the holy hill of the triune God? *Give us a break,* we think silently in our souls.

Yet the pattern of Advent faith is not only to be acquainted with the dark but also to live in longing for—and in step with—this divine dream and promise. To put it another way, we must realize that "the night is far gone; the day is at hand" (Romans 13:12). We inch closer to the judgment that brings peace to the world. This is why the great vision of the end of all things in Isaiah 2 comes in the context of judgment but is centered on a merciful invitation: "O house of Jacob, come, let us walk in the light of the LORD" (verse 5). Here's Isaiah's Advent message: Let this great promise of God, this divine dream, have its full effect on us here and now. Let us walk in the light even though our sins are many and the days are dark as night.

Advent Attire: Casting Off Darkness and Putting on Light

How exactly are we to walk forward in light? Listen again to the apostle Paul: "Cast off the works of darkness and put on the armor of light" (Romans 13:12). Advent is therefore a time of serious business and weighty preparation. Open yourself before the Lord through these Advent questions:

- What works of darkness do I need to unlearn?
- Where do I need to put on Jesus's words, Jesus's way, Jesus's life?
- Where does Jesus want to come into my life and heart with his light and grace?

No one can answer these deep questions for you. Keep company with God and his grace by engaging with these questions as gentle guides throughout Advent. If we listen closely to the apostle Paul, we'll learn some of the works of darkness we can no longer be at peace with. If the day of the Lord means the end of hostility and idolatry, then casting off the works of darkness means seeking to uproot these deadly seeds from the soil of our souls.

Ancient Christians reflected at length on the deadly sins of pride, envy, anger, greed, lust, gluttony, and sloth. They spoke of these vices in sobering terms: "Keep a special watch for the one that unfailingly attacks you, whether you stand, walk, sit, get up, pray or sleep."[4] Will you turn from unforgiveness? Will you make an end of bitterness? Will you pull the plug on jealousy? This week, don't let your holiday party look be the only attire that receives your deep consideration. Give prayerful thought to the works of vice you need to put off and the virtues of Christ you need to be clothed in.

To put on Jesus is to put on the great "light of the world" (John 8:12). When you repent and believe, you have put him on. When you walk in his teaching, when you come to his table to receive communion, and when you believe the promise, you put him on. When you anticipate his return, you put him on. Call out, even feebly, to the Light of the world and he will shine on you. Because the great Light has come once and is returning, the darkness in the world—and the darkness lurking in our hearts—will yield. Even today, even now, the great

Light arrives daily on you. As the darkness in you is increasingly banished, the radiance of his light on you, in you, and through you can shine (Matthew 5:16).

Remember how Isaiah spoke of a mountain and a hill to which the nations would flow? Jesus is the one at the holy hill of God who said, "When I am lifted up, I will draw all humanity to me" (see John 12:32). Jesus's cross is the hill from which God's saving light goes out to the nations, fulfilling Isaiah's Advent truth that rescue comes from God, not us. Jesus's return is the place of judgment that brings peace. Thus, casting off vice is incomplete without putting on the One who is the light that saves from darkness. The Light has shone, shines still, and will soon blaze in full glory.

FOR REFLECTION AND DISCUSSION

1. What do you hope to experience or be encouraged by as you journey through Advent? Take a moment to prayerfully write down your thoughts, and revisit them through this season.

2. How does the truth that Advent begins "in the dark" encourage us to be honest with God and ourselves about the state of our lives and the world?

3. Spend some time praying and reflecting on this week's themed prayer. How might this prayer help you step into the beginning of Advent with fresh attentiveness to the Lord and his love and will for you?

Second Week

The Tree of Life

Isaiah 11:1–10
Psalm 72:1–15
Romans 15:1–13
Matthew 3:1–12

There shall come forth a shoot from the
stump of Jesse, and a branch from his roots
shall bear fruit.

—Isaiah 11:1

Blessed Lord, who caused all Holy Scriptures to be written for our learning: Grant us so to hear them, read, mark, learn, and inwardly digest them, that by patience and the comfort of your holy Word we may embrace and ever hold fast the blessed hope of everlasting life, which you have given us in our Savior Jesus Christ; who lives and reigns with you and the Holy Spirit, one God, for ever and ever. Amen.[1]

The Bible is filled with references to trees and plants. Genesis begins in a garden with the tree of life and the tree of the knowledge of good and evil (2:9). The book of Revelation ends in a garden city, with the "tree of life" whose "leaves . . . were for the healing of the nations" (22:2). In the story of the Bible, particularly in the Old Testament, trees and humans are deeply connected.[2] Jesus operates from this tree-centric tradition when he teaches that people, like trees, are known by their fruit, either good or bad (Luke 6:43–45). Throughout Scripture, sin, sanctification, and salvation are described in the language of trees.

Scripture's usage of tree imagery helps us understand the despair and hope in Isaiah 11's discussion of the "stump of Jesse." Who's Jesse? He is the father of David, God's chosen king, whose line of kingship is supposed to forever bless Israel and the world (2 Samuel 7). If any familial line of Israel needs to prosper, it is this one. However, instead of standing tall in strength, the line is decaying because of the people's sin and God's subsequent judgment. The line of kings to lead God's people has been cut down to a stump.

These are the hopeless conditions in which God works most powerfully. Out of a decaying stump will come a small green sprig, a single shoot of life and hope. The wonder of God's saving promise is that out of judgment springs life, out of darkness shines light, out of Jesse's stump grows the tree whose leaves bring healing to the nations.[3] Yet this is where our hearts are stretched to the breaking point. That a stump will sprout into the fully grown Tree of Life—which ushers in the perfect peace that Isaiah previews—is a wondrous promise. But it is a promise that seems to move at a snail's pace.

The Slowness of God

Advent is the time to think about the slowness of God. You've probably thought about God's holiness and goodness, but have you adequately meditated on his slowness? In this season we dare to vocalize the cry of our hearts that usually remains unspoken, stuffed into silence by religious etiquette: "Why so slow, Lord?"

Among other responses to this question, one essential answer is that God is slow because God is love. Japanese theologian Kosuke Koyama writes, "Love has its speed. . . . It is a spiritual speed. It is a different kind of speed from the technological speed to which we are accustomed."[4] Koyama observes that Jesus operates at the slow speed of love. God's promises seem slow because he is expanding the borders of his family; he is so active in giving mercy to the ungodly that he wants to take his time, bringing more and more people into Christ's saving embrace.

Is this just warm, fuzzy preacher talk? Not at all. Listen to God's words through the apostle Peter:

> Do not overlook this one fact, beloved, that with the Lord one day is as a thousand years, and a thousand years as one day. The Lord is not slow to fulfill his promise as some count slowness, but is patient toward you, not wishing that any should perish, but that all should reach repentance. But the day of the Lord will come like a thief, and then the heavens will pass away with a roar, and the heavenly bodies will be burned up and dissolved, and the earth and the works that are done on it will be exposed. (2 Peter 3:8–10)

In the saving promise of God, slowness and suddenness collide. What else would we expect from the God who was willing to metaphorically sprout from a dying stump and to literally gestate, wait, and grow in a woman's womb?

The Slow, Sudden, Surprising Promise of God

God's saving promise is slow, sudden, and surprising. A man preaching a wild message of repentance does not seem a likely first ingredient in the recipe of whole-creation peace that our Isaiah 11 reading describes. But that's precisely what John the Baptist represents. Nearly seven centuries after Isaiah's prophetic promise, John the Baptist confirms the sprout from Jesse's line is on the way: "He who is coming after me is mightier than I, whose sandals I am not worthy to carry. He will baptize you with the Holy Spirit and fire" (Matthew 3:11).

According to John the Baptist, the arrival of God's promise in Jesus means it's time for preparation: Don't be caught flat-footed. Get ready to receive God's promise, and live accordingly. It's one thing to get ready for a party or a crucial work presentation. But how does one get ready for the judgment and rescue of the world? John tells us to prepare by turning around our whole thinking. In other words, repent. Repentance is turning from our dead-end ways, acknowledging our profound moral and spiritual lack, and finding that in Jesus God's mercy is deeper than we could ever hope. This is the work of Advent.

How to Stay Watchful and Ready for the Redemption of the World

Don't let the slowness of God's promise leave you unprepared. Saint Augustine, an African church father in the fourth and fifth centuries, encourages us to keep on when he writes that what "is soon in the sight of God, is late to our 'longing.'"[5] Disciples of Jesus must develop the muscle of hopeful watchfulness, for the kingdom of God emerges slowly and suddenly. Could this be why Jesus speaks of the kingdom in the language of a seed that slowly grows into a tree in which birds of the air find refuge (Luke 13:18–19)? The kingdom of God moves at its own pace, a tempo of slowness that surprises and then reshapes us.

You might have looked at the stump of Jesse and asked, "Isaiah, how can this thing heal the world?" You may have looked at teenage Mary and said, "No way from your body will come God in the flesh." God's saving work unfolds at its own pace and through means that we easily overlook—a stump, a teenage womb, a Roman cross. In due time, the full peace of God's reign comes through the righteousness of God.

Dull teaching in church has programmed some of us to snooze upon hearing the word *righteousness* because of overuse and underexplanation. When you hear *righteousness* in this Advent context, think of God's justice-working, salvation-bringing power. It is an attribute that achieves what it describes. This means God's righteous rule is not ushered in by human progress. There is no application or takeaway in Isaiah 11 apart from what Paul makes clear in our Romans passage: "Whatever was written in former days was written for our instruction, that through endurance and through the encouragement of the Scriptures we might have hope" (15:4). Like the birds that make their nests and flourish in the tree that is the kingdom, we participate in this coming rule of God as recipients, not initiators.

Our Tree of Life

How do we receive this kingdom and restoration with God? Only through the branch of Jesse. Jesus is the branch that sprouts, grows, and goes to the Roman tree—the cross. He is the tree cut down and judged for us, the saving "signal" to the nations (Isaiah 11:10; John 12:32). Then in what was surely the longest, slowest three days the world has ever known, in the surprising power of God, Jesus was lifted up in victory. Alone we are cut down in judgment; with him we are raised and bloom into new life. Every single tree you see is a reminder, a sign of the promise. Jesus is the tree of life—the savior and healer of the world by the slow, surprising, and saving power of God.

FOR REFLECTION AND DISCUSSION

1. What does it mean that God's promises are slow, sudden, and surprising?
2. How can these realities reshape how you wait on the Lord? How might these realities reshape how you journey through this season of Advent?
3. Where do you long to see God's righteousness break into your life? Into this world? How can you pray over and live out of this longing and trust in his promise?

Third Week

The Judge Is at the Door

Isaiah 35

Psalm 146

James 5:7–20

Matthew 11:2–19

Establish your hearts, for the coming
of the Lord is at hand.

—James 5:8

O Lord Jesus Christ, you sent your messengers the prophets to preach repentance and prepare the way for our salvation: Grant that the ministers and stewards of your mysteries may likewise make ready your way, by turning the hearts of the disobedient toward the wisdom of the just, that at your second coming to judge the world, we may be found a people acceptable in your sight; for with the Father and the Holy Spirit you live and reign, one God, now and forever. Amen.[1]

Fear or Comfort?

Non-Christians, and even some Christians, often struggle with the idea of judgment. Yet James demonstrates the reality of a future judgment that supplies strength to the scores of people who daily struggle to survive under the weight of in-justice.

Where does this idea come from in our readings? An old Bible study tip says, "When you see a 'therefore,' ask what it's there for." The use of *therefore* in James 5:7 directs us up into the intense terrain of verses 1–6 and their serious rebuke of the rich who are exploiting the poor. James threatens the unrigh-teous by warning them of God's judgment. Listen to this line: "You have lived on the earth in luxury and in self-indulgence. You have fattened your hearts in a day of slaughter" (verse 5). Then in verse 8, James comforts the suffering and weak by reminding them of God's judgment: "You also, be patient. Establish your hearts, for the coming of the Lord is at hand."

Do you hear it? The Judge at the door is cause for either fear or comfort, depending on the shape of your life and your relationship to the Judge. What is crucial to see here is that the Lord is at hand, returning to judge the living and the dead, and we must be formed by that future. But this formation is a delicate task. Anytime judgment and formation come to-gether, things can quickly become unhinged. I was reminded of this while reading about someone malformed by the future judgment:

> In the years right after I became a Christian as a teen-ager, I thought of the "end of the world" strictly in terms of the future and how things will conclude. I

looked for the soon return of Christ—and would have been shocked to be still living in the twenty-first century. When I was in college in the mid-1970s, I quite seriously contemplated dropping out. Why should I work at preparing for the future when the future wasn't going to come?

In those days, I basically welcomed the development of nuclear weapons, the conflicts in the Middle East. . . . I welcomed wars and rumors of wars. These all meant that the second coming was at hand. The "end of the world" was coming soon, and in that I rejoiced.

At some point, though, I realized with a start that I welcomed, actually, incredible human suffering and the destruction of nature, unprecedented death and bloodshed. I welcomed, in a word, extreme *evil*.[2]

This is futuristic malformation. We are not to make peace with or embrace evil as proof that Jesus is on the way. Rather, the people of God resist and overcome evil through love and endurance because Jesus is on the way. The comfort of Jesus's return is that evil will be judged and banished forever and that God will be with us and we will be with him. Here and now, God desires to rightly form us by the future coming of the Lord. This future formation deals not with predictions about the end of history but with the real grit and grind of living, the "so what?" of the everyday human struggle.

Three times James hits the note of patience, one for each reference in the passage to the Lord's coming. Patience, it's worth noting, can be perverted from virtue to vice when it is preached to keep the suffering in a holding pattern and to halt justice from flowing. Under such perverse circumstances, patience is actually a vice and impatience a virtue. What sort of patience is God placing before us through James? It is not the same sort that white liberals demanded of Dr. Martin Luther King, Jr., claiming equal rights for Black Americans would come someday, slowly, if only the movement would be calm, polite, and, yes, patient. Neither God nor James is a friend of patience as a vice. The virtue of which James speaks is the patience to keep walking with God despite forces of suffering that desire to crush you, trials that overwhelm you, and fear that overtakes you.

If we combine James's call to patience with the call to establish, or strengthen, our hearts, then we see that this patience is the *strength to endure*. It is a patience that says, "Keep going. Jesus is coming. Don't give in to violent retribution or personal despair, for Jesus will judge."

Friends, this is very good news. This is character formation for the weak and the wobbly. How so? The basis of this patience arrives from outside us. It is not a call to be patient because we are virtuous. It is a different brand of patience, sourced and powered by the future.

What is painful for you today? Keep going with God's help, for Jesus is returning soon to restore all things. Where do you feel weak right now? You are in the perfect position to be made strong by the knowledge that Jesus is at the door. Be steady. Be patient. Keep going because the One who redeemed you is near.

Living by the Future

How much of our present living is based on the future reality that the Judge stands at the door, soon to enter? There is no living without reference to the future. It is a matter not of whether we will live by the future but of what future we will live by. What future will form us?

Often, whether inside or outside the church, we default to living by the future of either possibility or futility. Some live in the present believing the future to be an open sandbox of possibility, with dreams, hope, and ideas galore. Others who have been around for a few decades live in the present through the future reference of potential futility: The end is closer, our lists of unachieved dreams grow without a care for our egos, and the question "What should I do with my last decades?" assaults our minds with furious consistency. Both future references are insufficient, and God wants to rid us of these errors.

Open possibility is not a basis for living, because life is vapor (James 4:14) and nothing is guaranteed. Futility is not a basis for living, because the shortage of time does not diminish the value of our lives; neither do the dumpster-fire conditions of the world demand that we cease living with hope. Old, young, and in-between are all granted the thrill of purpose when they live life in reference not simply to possibility or futility but to this certainty: Jesus Christ—the One Who Was and Is to Come—is standing at the door.

Years ago, I read *So You've Been Publicly Shamed* from British journalist Jon Ronson. The book describes the diverse and frightening ways people have rushed to judge and ostracize others, ranging from corporal punishment in colonial days to online shaming in the present. God teaches us that even this is a matter of the future. If there is no true Judge to come, then someone needs to immediately rise up and fill the void. When you don't believe in the nearness of the Judge, you're likely to give everyone a gavel now and let the loudest voices hammer it out. The problem is, who of us is qualified to judge impartially? Do you have the searching insight to parse the deeds, inner motives, and character of your neighbor? Can you even detail the motives and underpinnings of your own failures and successes, your sins and struggles? Only God, who searches each heart and "judges the secrets of men by Christ Jesus" can judge justly (Romans 2:16). The news of Jesus as the judge at the door is deeply sobering and mysteriously comforting.

Let the future of the Lord put its full formative imprint on you.

> God is forming you for endurance: Keep going,
> for Jesus is near.

> God is forming you to put off judgmentalism:
> Put down your gavel; do not even judge
> yourself (1 Corinthians 4:3). Let God judge
> you and everyone else—in his timing.

> God is forming you for joy: When Jesus comes,
> the whole creation will leap for joy.

> God is forming you through repentance: The
> Judge who stands at the door is first the Judge
> who hung on the cross. By his wounds, we
> are forgiven and healed.

Until he returns to set every wrong right, we live not by passive endurance but by patient endurance.

FOR REFLECTION AND DISCUSSION

1. In the James passage included in this week's reading, the Lord's arrival (advent) as judge is good news to the oppressed. How does this reshape your understanding of Advent and the nature of God's justice and judgment?

2. Advent is the season where we remember afresh

that Christ will return as savior and judge. Where
do you need to seek change in your actions or attitudes based on the fact that the Judge is at the door?

3. Revelation 3:20 speaks of Jesus at the door, knock-
ing, seeking fellowship with us. How might you respond to the advent of Jesus in your life—not only
in his final return but also in his nearness now?

Fourth Week

The Holy Family's Faith

Isaiah 7:10–17
Psalm 24
Romans 1:1–7
Matthew 1:18–25

She will bear a son, and you shall call his name
Jesus, for he will save his people from their sins.

—Matthew 1:21

Stir up your power, O Lord, and with great might come
among us; and as we are sorely hindered by our sins
from running the race that is set before us, let your
bountiful grace and mercy speedily help and deliver us;
through Jesus Christ our Lord, to whom, with you and
the Holy Spirit, be honor and glory, now and for ever.
Amen.[1]

Have you ever you thanked God for revealing the living Word—Jesus Christ—through the written word of not one but four gospels? Advent draws our attention to the gift God has lavished on humanity as recorded in Matthew, Mark, Luke, and John. As Advent inches us closer to Christmastide, our attention turns to the dramatic nature of Jesus's first advent in Bethlehem, which is described with arresting detail through the birth narratives in Matthew and Luke. When it comes to Jesus's birth, these two gospels are remarkable in showcasing the glorious truth about Jesus from different angles. Luke attends closely to Mary's jarring experience of the Annunciation, the divine news of the Christ child foretold. Matthew spotlights Joseph's fateful decision to embrace Mary after she's shown to be mysteriously pregnant. Taken together, both gospels show how God has come among us with great might and how his servants embody faithfulness shaped by his arrival.

What Mary Knew

"Mary, Did You Know?," by songwriter Mark Lowry, is a lightning rod for strong opinions. Beloved by some and belittled by others, the song is a December staple. It asks a series of questions about Mary, the mother of Jesus, and her knowledge of the unfolding story of Christ's birth and ministry. "What did Mary know?" is an interesting inquiry—a question of sanctified curiosity—but one we can't totally get to the bottom of. Luke shows us something better than sanctified curiosity by detailing Mary's deep faith:

> The angel said to her, "Do not be afraid, Mary, for you have found favor with God. And behold, you will conceive in your womb and bear a son, and you shall

call his name Jesus. He will be great and will be called
the Son of the Most High. And the Lord God will
give to him the throne of his father David, and he will
reign over the house of Jacob forever, and of his kingdom there will be no end."

And Mary said to the angel, "How will this be,
since I am a virgin?"

And the angel answered her, "The Holy Spirit will
come upon you, and the power of the Most High will
overshadow you; therefore the child to be born will be
called holy—the Son of God." . . .

And Mary said, "Behold, I am the servant of the
Lord; let it be to me according to your word." (Luke
1:30–35, 38)

What did Mary know? Mary knew a great deal. She knew
the Scriptures. She knew her city, Nazareth, was a poor,
frowned-on place. Mary knew that in her culture, marriage
was rightly seen as God-made and sacred. She knew that because she was pledged to Joseph in marriage, bearing a son
prior to their wedding would create a stain of deep, irreparable
shame. Were such a scandalous situation to happen to her, she
knew that she would be set aside, judged, tried, and maybe
stoned. Mary also assumed that such a scandal would never
happen to her because she was a faithful, devoted member of
the people of God. All this she knew—until an angel came to
disrupt everything.

Now Mary knows that to say yes is to have the dreams of
her life swept away. She knows that months before her wedding, her belly will be showing through her tunic, so the town
will be talking and Joseph most certainly will be divorcing. It
will be just her and the promised child: poor, alone, clinging
to this word from God. She knows that this news from the

angel will be a leap into the unknown. All this Mary knows, and still she says, "Let it be to me according to your word."

Faith as Courageous Surrender

Faith is giving God our yes through courageous surrender. This is what we learn from Mary's example. This is a crucial lesson because it's easy to reduce faith to mental agreement. Under this view, faith is about as thrilling as accepting the terms and conditions of an app upgrade; it is dry assent to facts divorced from the drama of real life. It's easy to think of faith as a set of beliefs we agree to that makes our life better, not an active belief that shapes how we live. It is easy, especially in affluent contexts, to make faith cheap and comfy. Yet Mary and Joseph's journey to Bethlehem for the birth of Jesus is anything but comfy. Faith is surrender. Faith is risk.

When we trust in the plan and promises of God, we leap by surrender into the unknown. Ruth Haley Barton puts it well: "Many of us harbor a subtle belief (or at least a hope!) that we can say yes to the walk of faith and it won't require much of us. That we can follow God's will and never have to appear foolish. That we can take the risk of following God and still have our security."[2] Where might you need to surrender in faith to the word of God, to the will of God, all in light of the advent of God?

From Mary, we learn that faith is the courage to surrender to God and his promise despite the requirement of risk. How do we become those who take all our dreams and hopes, our very selves—body and soul, life and years—and lift them up to God, saying, "Let it be to me according to your word and will"? Where do we get the strength to surrender?

Luke clues us in. Before Mary says, "Let it be to me" (verse 38), she is "greatly troubled" (verse 29). In between these two statements stands the path to a faith that surrenders to the Lord. The angel's message, which precedes Mary's response, is drenched in the language of God's covenantal promises. Mary hears from the angel that this child will be given "the throne of his father David" and that the Christ will come by the Spirit as the Most High "overshadow[s]" her (verses 32, 35). These references point to God's mighty faithfulness to his people, a long track record that has now scooped up Mary into the plot-line of God's redemptive story. The same faithfulness shown to King David would now engulf her and be fulfilled in her child. In the same way that the Lord's glory overshadowed and filled the tabernacle, the Most High would overshadow her being to conceive the incarnate Word.

Mary's faith was not blind. It was hope fulfilled through a new era of God's faithful promises. What did Mary know? As a devoted Israelite, she knew her God. She knew God to be merciful from the first pages of Scripture: When Adam and Eve did not obey, God still gave the promise of salvation through a woman's seed (Genesis 3:15). Mary knew that this God, her God, protected his people and his daughters—Ruth, Rahab, Esther, Hagar—in the past. Because Mary knew her God, she could leap into the surrender that is faith with these world-changing words: "I am the servant of the Lord; let it be to me."

Far from being blind, faith is a leap into the unknown, clinging to the God who is known.

Faith as Active Obedience

Where Luke attends to Mary, Matthew focuses on Joseph. If Mary shows us faith as courageous surrender, Joseph shows us faith as active obedience. Before this story was understood by the church as a miracle, it was felt by Joseph as a nightmare. Pressure can make diamonds or burst pipes. But Joseph proves to be a merciful and righteous man. Rather than shame Mary, he seeks a quiet divorce, likely presuming her to have committed adultery. Thus, Joseph won't make a scene; he plans to do what is allowed by the Law so that she can continue with respect, even at a cost to his honor. But then amid his heartbreak, an angel appears in a dream and tells him not to be afraid to take Mary as his wife.

He hears the word of the Lord and does it—at a cost. Can you imagine the neighborhood gossip that followed Mary and Joseph? Under the shadow of Christ's first coming, Mary and Joseph both embody the surrender and courage of Advent faith. Through their faithful example, we enroll in the school of Advent faith, learning that the coming of the Lord means the birth of a new logic. Faith in the Lord's arrival frees us from seeking validation from anyone or anything but the Lord.

The True Exemplar of Faithfulness

As Jesus grew into manhood, Mary and Joseph watched and waited in faith. In their hearts, they must have pondered questions like, "Will our son do and be all that the Lord said?" While we learn faith from Mary and Joseph, it is ultimately their son Jesus who gives us the truest and greatest union of faith as surrender and obedience. Jesus surrendered in joy to the Father's will. He was born to live, to suffer, to die, to rise, and soon to return. He "surrendered," in a sense, his divine rights to share our humanity (Philippians 2:5–11).

Like his earthly father, Jesus did not simply surrender; he put sweat and work into active obedience. He lived righteously and died sacrificially. These things did not come easily for Jesus simply because of his divine nature. Each act of obedience required true strength of soul. The faithfulness of Jesus is what we are given to know—not as a song of speculation but as the truth of history that saves. In him, we can surrender and obey the Lord who first surrendered and obeyed for us: "She will bear a son, and you shall call his name Jesus, for he will save his people from their sins" (Matthew 1:21).

FOR REFLECTION AND DISCUSSION

1. How does Mary's story in Luke's gospel reveal something about the nature of faith?
2. How does Joseph's story in Matthew's gospel reveal something about the nature of faith?
3. How are Mary's and Joseph's displays of faith distinct? How are they related? What might they teach us about the nature of faith in response to God's promises?

CHRISTMASTIDE

The Great Exchange

Christmas is the enfleshment of God, the
humiliation of the Most High and divine participation in all that is painful, ugly, frustrating, and
limited. Divinity takes on humanity, to restore
the image of God implanted at creation but sul-
lied by sin. Here is the great exchange Christmas
ponders, that God became like us that we might
become like God. God accepted death that the
world might accept life. The Creator assumed
temporality to redeem creation from futility.

—LAURENCE HULL STOOKEY, *Calendar: Christ's
Time for the Church*

D oes Christmas really need an introduction? From pho-
tos with Santa Claus to the joy of ripping open gifts as
youngsters to church services with choirs and glim-
mering candles, a simple utterance of the word *Christmas* floods
our minds with memories and images both sweet and difficult,
both cultural and personal. These images can feel contradic-
tory. Is Christmas about ugly-sweater parties with friends or
co-workers, stressful road trips to see family, or quiet moments
of prayer by candlelight—or a jarring mix of all three and more?

The range and clutter of pictures that this holiday evokes suggest we need a reintroduction to Christmas. Let's meet it again—not as a torrent of activities but as a coherent, wondrous season in the story of salvation.

An introduction to Christmas begins with an adjustment of length. For many, it has been relegated to a single day. But if we meet Christmas as understood within the church year, we find that Christmastide is not one day but twelve days. Just as the victory of Christ's resurrection at Easter demands a whole season of rejoicing, so too the wonder of the Word made flesh requires a season of celebration and feasting. A reintroduction to Christmas means a fresh embrace of it as a *season* in the church's life. Ashley Tumlin Wallace commented, "In the world in which we live, we are given no time to prepare for the birth of our Lord and Savior and then no time to celebrate it once we get there."[1] In Advent, the church year gifts us time for preparation, and in Christmastide, we journey into the season of celebration over Christ's birth, the glad tidings for all creation.

Christmastide Spirituality

At the heart of Christmas stands the mystery of the Incarnation. That the eternal God willingly condescended to become true man in Jesus to defeat sin and evil is the source of the world's hope, the starting line of our salvation, and the cause of our rejoicing. Additionally, it is the reality of a wondrous, mysterious interchange.

Christians often think of Christ's cross as the place of spiritual exchange since Christ takes our sins on himself and we receive his righteousness (2 Corinthians 5:21). But the Incarnation also inaugurated a great exchange that makes possible the redemption of the cross. C. S. Lewis speaks of this in a powerful way: "The Son of God became a man to enable men to become sons of God."[2] This means that Jesus became human to restore and lift humanity into the family of God with all the resulting benefits.

Yet another exchange at work through the Incarnation is that we share in God's nature, becoming more like Christ. Athanasius, a fourth-century African church father, wrote of this aspect, boldly stating, "The Son of God became man so that we might become God."[3] This means the eternal Son of God truly united himself to human nature in becoming a real, enfleshed human being. And in doing so, Jesus—the eternally preexisting, eternally begotten, uncreated Son of God—has made a way for us to share in God's divine nature (2 Peter 1:4). In other words, we can become Christlike because Christ became man to redeem the brokenness of humanity.

If your mind feels stretched, it is because to speak of the Incarnation is to dance with mystery and paradox at the same time. It is a mystery that stretches our minds and hearts beyond what we can conceive. Reflecting on Jesus's incarnation, theologian T. F. Torrance writes:

> This is a mystery that is not conceivable in ordinary human thought—it is a miracle. And if [believers] know something of this miracle they will know that even in their knowing of it is a very wonderful thing, that it is an act of God. They know the mystery by faith, in the power of the Spirit, but not by themselves alone. It is a gift of God.[4]

At Christmas, we receive, by the Spirit, the gift of pondering the manifold mystery of the Word made flesh.

While the Incarnation is the truth at the heart of Christmas, the chief spiritual discipline of this season is celebration.

"If Advent is a season of waiting," writes author Bobby Gross, "Christmas is a season of wonder."[5] We might add, if Advent is centered on longing, Christmas is centered on rejoicing. The holiest response to God becoming human for our salvation is to rejoice in praise and thanksgiving. To let out a song of praise among the people of God, to feast in thanksgiving over a delightful meal, to raise a glass in gratitude with family and friends—all this is a living testimony that darkness has been swallowed up by light in the birth of our Savior.

Oddly enough, it takes discipline to celebrate in this way. Since we are so accustomed to Christmas as a single day, we're quite ready to return to life as normal once the calendar flips to December 26. More than that, celebration is harder than lounging. Celebration exercises the heart's thanksgiving muscles, which atrophy without the soul's savoring of the Incarnation's mystery. At a heart level, the work of celebration at Christmas begins with worship and immersion in the mystery of the Word made flesh. The first step is to inhabit the wonder and glory of the Christmas story according to Scripture. Place yourself there at the manger with Joseph and Mary. Imagine yourself standing with the shepherds as the angels appear. Ponder these things in your heart as you open the Scriptures. Let meditative reading birth wonder.

The discipline of celebration can then take the necessary and important forms that work best with the contours of your life stage. Keep the twelve days of Christmas in the way that best helps you and others rejoice in Christ. Practice gift giving in the way that best stirs your heart to rejoice in the gift of life eternal. While the rest of the world moves on from Christmas in a day, linger in the church's time, stay awhile in the story of the gospel, and rejoice that unto us a child is born.

Christmas Practices

What spiritual practices mark discipleship to Jesus in the season of Christmas? Here are a few suggestions for you to practice individually or communally.

Embrace Christmas as a season. Let your soul linger in the good news of Christ's birth by not rushing past Christmas. Here are some practical, embodied ways to linger and luxuriate in the gospel story during Christmastide:

- Keep your Christmas tree and decorations up until the season ends on January 6, the beginning of Epiphany.

- Determine beforehand how you want to celebrate the twelve days of Christmas and the various feast days at home or with others.

- Use resources like Danielle Hitchen's *Sacred Seasons* for meals and activities that align with and accentuate the celebratory joy of Christmastide.

- Keep some of your gifts and gift giving for the twelve days to embrace the whole of the season.

- Continue to light a candle each evening to symbolize the coming of Light into darkness.

Go to church. Worshipping on Christmas Eve and, if able, on Christmas Day is a gift that brings us into the communal joy of Christ with us. Take advantage of what your local church is doing, and savor worship with the body of Christ.

Practice celebration and hospitality. Christmastide gives you lots of time to host a Christmas party. This is also a great opportunity to reach out to neighbors and share a meal together.

Sing Christmas carols and hymns. Now's the time to press play on your favorite Christmas music—hymns, carols, and renditions from all genres. This is the season to make a joyful noise to the Lord.

Meditate on the Incarnation. Take a passage like John 1:1–18 or the birth narratives of Luke and Matthew, and engage with it slowly. Consider the humility of Jesus in becoming like us. Carve out moments of quiet for reflection.

Christmas Feast Days

Each season has notable feast days in which the church is called into a deeper experience of the life of Christ together.

Christmas Eve (December 24): There's debate on whether Christmas Eve is rightly understood as part of Advent or Christmas. Part of the tension comes from an early church practice of a midnight mass on Christmas Eve in addition to one on Christmas morning.

Christmas Day (December 25): Also known as the Nativity of Our Lord, this is the day we rejoice that God truly is Immanuel—God with us. Delight in all God's gifts, namely the gift of Christ for our salvation.

Feast of Saint Stephen (December 26): It's shocking that immediately after Christmas Day the church honors the first Christian martyr, Stephen. While Stephen is a bright example of Spirit-filled faith (Acts 6:5), the timing of his martyrdom's commemoration reminds us that like Christ and his journey from the crib to the cross, Christ's disciples must in their own way take up their crosses as well. Consider reading Acts 6–7 to commemorate this day.

Feast of Saint John (December 27): This day celebrates John the Evangelist, the beloved disciple of Jesus and author of the fourth gospel, 1–3 John, and Revelation, according to tradition. John's life and ministry encourage us to believe in the gospel of Jesus (John 3:16) and abide in the love of God (1 John 2:24). Consider reading 1 John on this feast day.

Feast of the Holy Innocents (December 28): This day memorializes the infant Hebrew boys who were murdered because of Herod's wrathful fear of the Christ child (Matthew 2:1–18). The early church viewed these children as martyrs, and in remembering them, we recognize the darkness in our world against the most vulnerable. This is a day to pray for and bless the weak and vulnerable among us, especially children.

Feast of the Holy Name (January 1): Sometimes called the Feast of the Circumcision of Jesus, this occurs on the eighth day of Christmas to remember that on the eighth day after his birth, Jesus was named and circumcised at the synagogue in accordance with Jewish law (Luke 2:21). The names given to the Christ child—Jesus ("the Lord saves") and Immanuel ("God with us")—remind us that our hope is found in him alone. Since this feast also falls on New Year's Day, when many in Western culture make self-improvement resolutions, the church year offers us the chance to root the upcoming year in the truth of who Jesus is.

Reading Christmas Texts and Devotions

As you read the following Scripture texts and devotions, you'll meditate on the wonder of the Incarnation. There is a devotional for Christmas—which can be used on Christmas Eve or Day—as well as a devotional for Christmastide, the stretch of days after Christmas Day. Our gospel passages will place us into the story of Christ's birth first from Luke's detailed perspective and then from John's rich theological and poetic vantage point. While the chief response to the Incarnation is worship and wonder, our readings show that we must also prepare room to receive Christ. This means we must recognize and reject false hopes so we can fully receive the Word made flesh with faith and joy.

Christmas Eve

The Manger Speaks

Isaiah 9:1–7
Psalm 96
Titus 2:11–14
Luke 2:1–14

This will be a sign for you: you will find
a baby wrapped in swaddling cloths and
lying in a manger.

—Luke 2:12

O God, you have caused this holy night to shine with
the brightness of the true Light: Grant that we, who
have known the mystery of that Light on earth, may
also enjoy him perfectly in heaven; where with you and
the Holy Spirit he lives and reigns, one God, in glory
everlasting. Amen.[1]

Luke's account includes many spectacular elements of Jesus's birth. Angels appear to lowly shepherds. Then, these holy angels declare the staggering news of the Incarnation. Next, a chorus of heavenly voices breaks out in praise. But one small detail is especially spectacular because it's such a shock: Jesus is born and laid in a manger.

The manger speaks a profound message. Its importance is clear since Luke goes out of his way to mention it three times, its only occurrences in all of the New Testament:

> She [Mary] gave birth to her firstborn son and wrapped him in swaddling cloths and laid him in a manger, because there was no place for them in the inn. (Luke 2:7)

> This will be a sign for you: you will find a baby wrapped in swaddling cloths and lying in a manger. (verse 12)

> They went with haste and found Mary and Joseph, and the baby lying in a manger. (verse 16)

God speaks a life-giving, soul-strengthening word through the manger that we need to hear in the deepest part of our being.

The Humility of the Manger

What does the manger speak? The manger speaks the message of humility. God has become small for us. How often do people inside and outside the church think God is powerful but distant, strong but mostly standoffish? The birth—and birthplace—of Jesus corrects these soul-shriveling misconceptions.

In Jesus, God embraced the frailty and vulnerability of becoming a child. And as if that were not enough, he was not born in a five-star palace. He was born and laid in a manger, a trough where donkeys and horses fed and slobbered.[2]

There's a petting zoo not far from my home. When they approach the animals rollicking about in the muddy pens, my young children shriek with excitement—until they get close. Then they shrink back in disgust. Because farm animals stink. The manger where the Christ child lay would likely have been of a similar condition. Quiet your mind and imagine Mary standing at the stone manger, scooping out the feed and slop with her bare hands, replacing it with soft hay, and laying God in the flesh to sleep.

Isn't it shocking that the Son of God entered the world in not the best conditions but the lowest? Some people today possess not only smartphones but even smart cribs, equipped with rocking motions, sleep-tracking analytics, built-in monitors, and sound machines. I can't imagine anyone I know putting their child, grandchild, nephew, or niece in a stone-cold hay-bed manger by choice. But for our sake, this is where God laid his infant head.

The Manger That Satisfies

The manger speaks of the humility of God, but there's something deeper at work too. Look again at Luke 2:12, where the angel tells the shepherds that a swaddled baby in a manger "will be a sign for you." What exactly is the sign the angel is pointing out? Finding a baby in swaddling clothes is about as normal as a sunny day in Southern California in July. The sign is the manger. The Savior of the world in a manger? Now, that's something to write home about. And it's the manger that speaks of what Christ came to offer us.

Remember what a manger is. The English term comes from the Old French word *mangier* and the Latin word *manducare,* both of which mean "to eat."[3] As a place where animals feed, a manger is essentially a source of life. The shepherds would have recognized the symbolism since they may have loaded mangers with food for their sheep each morning.[4] Of all the places where Christ could be born and rest his infant body, he chose the manger to proclaim this message: "I am the bread of life; whoever comes to me shall not hunger" (John 6:35). Jesus offers himself as the bread for our souls; he gives his body to sustain our lives. The Savior rests in the manger—where animals feed—because Jesus came to satisfy the hunger in every human heart that nothing else can satisfy.

Humanity's Hunger Pains

Our hearts hunger to know we matter. Our hearts grumble with hunger pains to know that we are loved, that we can be forgiven of our sins and wrongs, that the worst things about us are not the truest. Our hearts hunger to know there's hope beyond what we see—to feast on something other than tears and sorrow (Psalm 42:3).

Ironically, at this time of year, there is a real temptation to satisfy this hunger at all the wrong mangers. The manger of more is especially alluring. It preaches that the answer to our hearts' hunger is to consume, acquire, and conquer. Here, we gorge our souls and lives with *more:* more money, more trips, more stuff, more achievements. Or we gorge ourselves with more and *better:* a better house, a better job, better friends, a better body, or even dreams of a (better) spouse. Yet this manger turns out to be a poisonous well of deceit. The more we get in quantity or supposed quality, the hungrier we become for the bread this world cannot offer. There's even an enlightened version of the manger of more where we try to satisfy the ache in our hearts with more peace, more quiet, and more calm—with more of *less*. But the quieter and less cluttered our homes and souls get, the more we sense that the deep hunger inside remains, lurking under a well-kept surface.

Whatever your favored false manger is, the cold truth needs embracing: Never have humans experienced such abundance yet been so empty. A few decades ago, psychologist David G. Myers released a book called *The American Paradox: Spiritual Hunger in an Age of Plenty*. The title says it all. Why do each of us feel a rumble of disappointment in our gut about five days after we open all our Christmas gifts? Gifts are good, but the deepest longings of our hearts are meant to be filled by God.

The Bread for a Weary World

"What does not satisfy when we find it," Christian author C. S. Lewis writes, "was not the thing we were desiring."[5] The yearning behind every other longing can be filled only in the One who humbled himself to become a child and to rest in the manger. Admit that you've feasted at false mangers, but don't get too discouraged. It's good that you're hungry. It's good that your heart is famished for something too rich to satisfy. God's got you halfway to the right manger. Don't be discouraged, but do understand more deeply what God has come to do. Turn away from the bread that doesn't satisfy. Do not trust in the manger of more—trust in the humble manger and the God who redeems and who made you for himself.

Jesus gave his life for the world, moving from the manger to the cross to the empty tomb. We can draw endless hope from the truth that the manger speaks of Christ's power to save and satisfy. Christian writer and activist Dorothy Day pointed

out one beautiful hope drawn from the setting of Jesus's birth:
"I'm so glad that Jesus was born in a stable. Because my soul is
so much like a stable. It is poor and in unsatisfactory condition. . . . Yet I believe that if Jesus can be born in a stable,
maybe he can also be born in me."[6]

Christmas is the time to be glad with Dorothy Day, with
the shepherds, with all believers across the ages. Christ makes
his home in lowly places and in lowly people and lifts them up
to eternal life. Today, let us come clean and recognize our
hunger, all our longings that cannot be satisfied by the work of
our hands, the purchasing power of our wallets, or the social
cause we think will make everything all right. Today, we rejoice that by faith in the Savior, our souls and lives can be
filled—not by fanciful externals but by the hope and love that
come from God to us.

FOR REFLECTION AND DISCUSSION

1. How have you thought about the significance of
   Jesus's birth in the manger/stable? What new or old
   insights are you pondering in light of our reading?
2. Where are you experiencing hunger and longing
   in your life? How does Christ and his manger speak
   to that longing?
3. In what ways might you be looking for satisfaction
   or fulfillment apart from Christ? Are there false
   mangers you are tempted to turn toward?

Christmastide

For Us and for Our Salvation

Isaiah 52:7–12

Psalm 98

Hebrews 1:1–12

John 1:1–18

The Word became flesh and dwelt among us.

—John 1:14

Almighty God, you have given your only-begotten Son to take our nature upon him, and to be born [this day] of a pure virgin: Grant that we, who have been born again and made your children by adoption and grace, may daily be renewed by your Holy Spirit; through Jesus Christ our Lord, to whom with you and the same Spirit be honor and glory, now and for ever. Amen.[1]

"If I feel physically as if the top of my head were taken off," the poet Emily Dickinson once said, "I know that is poetry."[2] By

Dickinson's definition, John 1 is poetry, wondrous truth that melts the head and the heart. On Christmas Day, we stand at the threshold of the greatest wonder of the world: the enfleshing of God. In Christian theology, we call this truth the Incarnation. John 1:14 declares, "The Word became flesh and dwelt among us" and places us on the edge of a great mystery that the preexistent, eternal Word of God became truly human, a squirming, sneezing, needy baby. What do we do with such a breathtaking reality?

Can analogies help our hearts grapple with what is beyond the limits of the mind?

Can you imagine a chef who so loves the recipe she is creating that she actually becomes a dish of sweet candied yams? Or a gardener who so loves her flowers that she becomes a rosebush?[3] Can you imagine a man who loves dogs so much that to save them, he leaves all his beloved human capacities and cultures behind to become one?[4]

While these analogies get us thinking, none really captures the act of the eternal God joining himself to creaturely humanity. Getting a handle on this wonder of the Word made flesh is a bit like trying to scale a great mountain. What is the best approach to such a towering truth? One possible path is to ask *how* and venture out on ancient theological terrain, moving step by step through the church's oldest creeds and councils. Instead of setting off on this trail, place in your mind the question of *why*. To ask why the Word became flesh is to ascend on a path that leads to the very heart of God.

Among Us for Us

Why did the eternal God in Christ become a true, living, enfleshed person? The Nicene Creed, a fourth-century Christian declaration of faith that millions of believers confess each

Sunday, tells us the answer: "For us and for our salvation he came down from heaven, was incarnate from the Holy Spirit and the Virgin Mary, and was made man."[5] The Word became flesh and dwelt among us *for* us.

John clues us in to this "for us" aspect of Jesus's incarnation when he says in John 1:4–5, "In him was life, and the life was the light of men. The light shines in the darkness, and the darkness has not overcome it." The Word is life and light. Our world, where we live, is darkness and death. Thus, the Incarnation is a for-us movement of God into the realm of darkness to resurrect us back to life. Divinity moves into humanity to set us free from the darkness that is destroying us. In other words, the Incarnation is a rescue mission launched by the mystery of God made small and flesh in the Christ child.

No one needs to spend more than a moment or two scanning the news headlines to recognize that humanity is under darkness and seemingly spiraling further into decay. A few Christmases ago, I came across a post from a film critic that powerfully brought this point home:

> Last night, in the middle of a big family dinner with my mom and my wife's parents, my 11-year-old daughter suddenly started sobbing uncontrollably. When asked what was wrong, she howled, "Everyone's going to die, someday!"[6]

How's that for a Christmas dinner icebreaker? How would you respond if you were seated at that table, a slice of corn-bread in your hand, as the whole room went quiet aside from this preteen's sobs?

One common response would be to say, "Yes, death is natural; it's the circle of life. But what really matters is that we enjoy the time we have with each other." While this may be the best answer we can muster apart from Christ, it is bankrupt. It is no answer at all.

The Word Who Rescues

That eleven-year-old's tears emerged from a heart that was honest enough to express the tragic reality of our existence. They proclaimed a wise reality check: The best moments of this life are tainted by the long and looming shadow of death. Early church father Athanasius explains what Scripture teaches about humanity's fall into sin and death: "The race of humans was perishing. . . . The work [humankind] made by God was being obliterated."[7] "The wages of sin is death" (Romans 6:23), and humanity has been working overtime. That sin and death are having a field day among humanity is, in God's view "monstrous" and "unfitting."[8] The young girl's tears—and what they point to, death itself—are why the Word became flesh. God will not stand by while we, his handiwork, plunge ourselves into death and ruin.

To capture the for-us rescue of the Incarnation, Athanasius uses the example of a city. Creation, he says, is like a glorious city founded by a great king. But the city is then attacked by a vicious band of robbers because of the carelessness of the city's inhabitants. At the bleakest moment, suddenly and surprisingly, something strange happens. Rather than watch from a distance, the king throws *himself* into the fray, avenging and rescuing his citizens and saving the city from destruction.[9] This is the wonder of the Word becoming flesh.

The Word became flesh and dwelt among us for us. The Word became flesh to put our enemy underfoot and to trample over death. Life conquers death by taking human flesh and resurrecting—not as a spirit but as flesh forever. The Word became flesh to liberate you and me into life eternal. This is the great gift of Christmas from the heart of God, carried from heaven, set in the manger, offered to all.

For us and for our sakes, he came down. Tears of grief over death's unrelenting assault will give way to tears of victorious joy because the Word was made flesh for us. Therefore, we rejoice in the words of the great hymn:

Born that man no more may die,
Born to raise the sons of earth,
Born to give them second birth.[10]

FOR REFLECTION AND DISCUSSION

1. Why do analogies fall short in contemplating the wonder of the Incarnation? In what way are they helpful, though limited, exercises?
2. In what sense is Jesus's incarnation a movement of rescue?
3. What stirs in your heart when you think about the Incarnation as God's action against sin and death?

EPIPHANY

The Light That the Darkness Cannot Overcome

The season of Epiphany is designed to show
that there is no road to the glory of God
through human seeking; it cannot be summoned by
human endeavor. It cannot be repeated too often:
it comes as pure gift.

—FLEMING RUTLEDGE, *Epiphany*

Fire. That's what my elementary-aged children think of in reference to the church calendar—wild, dancing flames. For them, the Epiphany feast day tradition of burning Christmas trees in a massive bonfire, savoring king cake, and singing about the manifestation of the Savior to his nation's rivals encapsulates the joy of Christmas, and that's almost purely off the strength of the fire. The frightening yet captivating tower of flames unleashed from multiple trees piled high fills the night in a blaze of light.

During Advent, the church awaits the light to break into the darkness. In Christmastide, we rejoice that the light has come. During Epiphany (also called Epiphanytide), we focus on the light manifested to the world. These seasons make up the Cycle of Light, and this progression declares God's powerful love to the world. It is too small a thing for the light of Christ to shine in one place, among one people; the light must blaze brightly before all peoples, leading us to the fullness of life with God.

Epiphany Spirituality

Epiphany comes from the Greek word *epiphaneia*, which means "appearance" or "manifestation."[1] As we've seen, each season of the church year has a cluster of interconnected themes for our spirituality as disciples. Epiphany's central theme is the glorious manifestation of Jesus as the Son of God and savior of the world. This manifestation occurs as we receive and reflect Christ's light as pure gift. The radiant glory of Christ calls us into the story of Christ. The light has come to us and will shine, in word and deed, through us (Matthew 5:16).

An effective witness must experience that of which they testify. My children became passionate megaphones for the awesomeness of our Epiphany bonfire after they beheld the fire lighting up the thick dark night in streaks of red-flamed glory. In the same way, Epiphany is about beholding and experiencing and then proclaiming the glory of God in Jesus Christ.

Defining God's glory is a complex task; words fall short in the face of such a stunning reality. To help, Scripture gestures toward the weight and wonder of God's glory through images such as light (2 Corinthians 4:6) and fire (Exodus 24:17). Both are substances that captivate but must be mediated and approached with great care. God's glory encompasses the radiant beauty of his manifold perfections. The human heart can comprehend only a sliver, a fragment, of his fullness, yet it is life altering all the same. In this sense, God's glory is the shining revelation of his triune sublimity graciously broadcast for us to behold and marvel at. It is displayed not just in the beauty of creation (Psalm 19:1–2) but most powerfully in the person of Jesus Christ, who is "the radiance of the glory of God" (Hebrews 1:3) and "the light of the world" (John 8:12).

Epiphany is all about the glory of God in Jesus made public before the sin-stricken world, which rejects his glorious rule. Rather than abandon this world, God reveals himself to it, drawing us into the story of Jesus that we who behold him might then proclaim him so others might behold him and be restored. For this reason, the season focuses on the star shining before the wise men (Matthew 2:1–12), the baptism of Jesus and the voice from heaven (Matthew 3), and the calling of the disciples (John 1). These encounters prove that God is in the business of revealing himself to the whole world. Epiphany calls us deeper into this glorious divine mission.

Christian theologian Lesslie Newbigin observed that "mission begins with a kind of explosion of joy."[2] This is an apt description of Epiphany. Like the wise men who saw the radiant star of Christ that drew them into praise and worship, we follow the same script. Isn't it wonderful that God loves the world? Isn't it remarkable that there is more mercy and light in him than sin and brokenness in us? Isn't it almost too good to be true that God has come among us in Jesus to save, heal, redeem, and remake all things—even us? What begins in a spark of wonder and praise over God revealed in Jesus soon spreads like a flame as the glory of Christ lights up this dark world.

Epiphany Practices

What practices mark worship and discipleship during Epiphany? Several could be named, but these three form a helpful starting place for individuals and communities.

Abide in Jesus daily. Jesus did not mince words. He said clearly, "Apart from me you can do nothing" (John 15:5). To abide in Jesus is to rest and re-center our lives in him through daily faith and allegiance. Abiding is crucial to the whole of discipleship and therefore to Epiphany spirituality. Robert Webber puts it well: "Unless you are in union with Christ in your soul, you cannot manifest Christ in your life."[3]

How do we abide in Jesus? We abide objectively by faith in his saving work. Remember that through the double bond of faith and the Holy Spirit, you are united to Jesus. He lives in you, and you live in him. You can say with the apostle Paul, "The life I now live in the flesh I live by faith in the Son of God, who loved me and gave himself for me" (Galatians 2:20).

Abide in Jesus subjectively by rehearsing and believing this good news each day. Rehearse the truth of the gospel as soon as you roll out of bed. Preach the good news to yourself daily.

Chalk the door. Chalking the door to one's home is an ancient Christian practice. This act is done in prayer outside, using chalk to write the following above one's front door:

[the first two digits of the year] + C + M + B + [the last two digits of the year]

The letters *C, M,* and *B* stand for *Christus mansionem benedicat,* meaning "May Christ bless this house." The plus signs represent Christ's cross, and the numbers indicate the year. Done on the feast of Epiphany, this practice is a way of asking that Christ and his blessings would dwell in both your heart and your home for your sake and for any who need refuge. Hopefully, your pastor will perform this blessing for you, or you may do so with friends or family.

Practice hospitality. The practice of hospitality expands our hearts. Through it, seminary professor Christine Pohl observes, "we resist being a people concerned only for ourselves. Instead, we receive the call of Jesus to look to the interest of others by opening our hearts and homes, making room for others as God has made room for us."[4] Hospitality is the act of expansive welcome in Jesus's name.

Epiphany Feast Days

Each season has notable feast days in which the church is called into a deeper experience of the story of salvation.

Epiphany (January 6): On this day, in Western churches, we celebrate Christ in his appearance to the Magi, a sign that Christ came as the light not only of Israel but also of, to, and for the world. (The Eastern church focuses their Epiphany celebrations on the Lord's baptism.) Traditions include making king cake, lighting a bonfire with Christmas trees, and engaging in general joyous merriment.

The Baptism of Our Lord (first Sunday after Epiphany): The first Sunday after Epiphany is set aside to honor the baptism of Jesus. This feast celebrates that at Jesus's baptism, he was publicly revealed in Trinitarian fashion as the Son of God and the Savior of the world (Matthew 3:13–17).

Candlemas (February 2): This feast celebrates the presentation of the infant Jesus in the temple by his parents, Mary and Joseph. At the temple, Simeon and Anna behold Jesus and confess and rejoice that he is indeed the long-promised Savior of Israel and the world (Luke 2:22–38). This feast is also known as the Presentation of our Lord.

Feast of Saint Valentine (February 14): While most are familiar with the commercialized Valentine's Day, not as many are aware of the Christian origins of Saint Valentine. While the precise history is unclear, some maintain that Valentine served God as a priest during an era of persecution under Roman emperor Claudius II. A faithful preacher of the gospel and shepherd to the poor, Valentine purportedly continued to marry couples after the emperor banned marriages to force men to fight in the Roman army.[5] This day offers believers the chance to consider and live out the theological virtue of love (1 Corinthians 13:1–8).

World Mission Sunday (second-to-last Sunday of Epiphany). This day calls the church to unite and focus on its mission to preach, love, and serve all people and all nations in Christ's name.

Transfiguration Sunday (final Sunday of Epiphany). Epiphany, a season of light and revelation, is aptly closed by the transfiguration of Jesus in glory before his disciples. The transfiguration features prominently in all three Synoptic Gospels and captures well this season in which we seek to behold the light of Christ by faith.

Reading Epiphany Texts and Devotions

As you read the following Scripture texts and devotions, you'll encounter a thematic through line of revelation and mission. This emphasis reflects the dual nature of Epiphany, as the light of Christ shines not only on us by grace but also through us. Because Jesus is the invisible God revealed, this season centers on him powerfully, with an emphasis on gospel passages. Because Epiphany is also about mission, you'll read about the challenges of bringing the light of Christ to others. What is the way of mission with Jesus in the shadow of colonialism and amid cultural confusion? These are the Epiphany themes we'll explore.

First Week—The Baptism of Our Lord

He Enters the Waters

Isaiah 42:1–9

Psalm 89:20–29

Acts 10:34–38

Matthew 3:13–17

Then Jesus came from Galilee to the Jordan to
John, to be baptized by him. John would have
prevented him, saying, "I need to be baptized by
you, and do you come to me?"

—Matthew 3:13–14

Eternal Father, at the baptism of Jesus you revealed
him to be your Son, and your Holy Spirit descended
upon him like a dove: Grant that we, who are born
again by water and the Spirit, may be faithful as your
adopted children; through Jesus Christ our Lord, who
lives and reigns with you and the Holy Spirit, one God,
now and for ever. Amen.[1]

The entry point into understanding Jesus's baptism is a wild prophetic preacher: John the Baptist. Let's set the scene. John's ministry is booming. Crowds are flocking to him for baptism. He is not preaching a "seeker-friendly" message. His blood is boiling with spiritual boldness. Visualize the moment: John is standing at the Jordan River before a long line of people, of all shapes and ages, waiting to be baptized. Off in the distance, another crowd of spectators is thinking about it but unsure, all while John belts out his message:

> I baptize you with water for repentance, but he who is coming after me is mightier than I, whose sandals I am not worthy to carry. He will baptize you with the Holy Spirit and fire. His winnowing fork is in his hand, and he will clear his threshing floor and gather his wheat into the barn, but the chaff he will burn with unquenchable fire. (Matthew 3:11–12)

The line of people shuffles closer, faces covered with that sacred mix of fear and joy, some even crying tears of repentance. Then John spots none other than Jesus.

No doubt John was shaken and surprised. With a bit of sanctified imagination, we might envisage the conversation between John the forerunner and Jesus the Savior. Perhaps John quipped, "Jesus, you came all the way from Galilee to the Jordan? You must be here like a manager checking on the business. I am indeed telling everyone the true message. I'm telling them that I am doing the water baptism for repentance, but the One to come—you—will bring the Spirit-fire baptism of salvation."

What did John think when Jesus looked him dead in the eye and in essence said, "You don't understand. I'm here to be baptized by *you* like all of *them*"?

Whatever the actual discussion was, verse 14 tells us that John tried to prevent Jesus from receiving baptism. He was bothered by Jesus's desire to be baptized. But why?

The Scandal of Divine Humility

Imagine being seated at a five-star restaurant. Out of nowhere, the chef comes and sits at your table, hands you the apron, and says, pointing toward the kitchen, "Everything you need is back there. I would love if you would cook for me, please." You would likely put a gentle hand on that chef's shoulder and say kindly, "Your plan will not work out well for either of us. You really don't know how this restaurant thing works." Most of us would be deeply confused, maybe even distressed, by this proposed role exchange.

John the Baptist experienced a similar but more confusing reversal. In the verses preceding our reading, John had just said that Jesus was mightier than he and that John was not worthy to even untie Jesus's sandals. Yet Jesus came to John and asked to be baptized—the whole proposal reeked of blasphemy. Do you see how this baptism was an epiphany at the Jordan? John understood the seriousness of God's holiness, but he was not prepared for this revelation of God's humility. Are we?

Christ Is Lower Still

Jesus's baptism reveals to us that although he is not a sinner, he wants to be among sinners, quite literally. He journeys to the Jordan. He stands in line. For most people, in that moment he is indistinguishable from the sinful crowd. He has taken their lot as his lot. He has taken our burden as his own.

The baptism of Jesus reveals God's humble identification with sinners and his sacrificial reversal of our situation. This reversal is what John struggled to get over. Jesus carried sins into that water, just as he carried sins on himself when he died on the cross. However, the sins Jesus took to the water—like the ones he took to the cross—were not his but ours. Jesus's baptism of repentance was the preparation, but it links to the cross as a definite act of salvation. This is the theological truth revealed at his baptism.

In the playfulness of God, Jesus's baptism proclaims the truth of Christ both theologically and topologically. That is, even the physical place where Jesus was baptized preaches truth. Place matters in the Bible. Jesus came to John at the Jordan River, which is one of the lowest bodies of water on the planet. Here in Earth's true low place, God incarnate showed his human face to sinners—not with fire and brimstone but with his own baptism for repentance.

Jesus's baptism reveals it. The gospel reveals it. The physicality of the Jordan reveals it: Jesus meets us in our lowest state and brings us back to life, back to God, by carrying our burdens on his psyche, his soul, and his body. Behold the saving humility of God revealed in the baptism of Jesus.

Divine Humility, Divine Delight

We must admit John's reluctance to baptize Jesus made solid theological sense. How could a sinful prophet baptize the Holy One of God? Father Simeon, a Trappist monk, formerly known as Erasmo Leiva-Merikakis captures this paradox powerfully: "The human hand held out in a gesture of forgiveness

over the all-pure and holy Head would surely incur horren-
dous blasphemy. Would it not wither on the spot? But what if
the Master himself should request it?"[2]

Indeed, in Matthew 3:15, Jesus requested baptism as part
of the divine plan to "fulfill all righteousness." This humility of
God had been part of the plan from the beginning. One of the
great images of Christ comes in Isaiah 42:3, which says, "A
bruised reed he will not break, and a faintly burning wick he
will not quench." What Isaiah 42 declares is fulfilled in Christ's
baptism. Isaiah foretells the tenderness of the Savior toward his
wayward people. If you know Christ's humble tenderness, you
can endure nearly anything. No more wondering whether
Jesus is done with you because you keep failing. How can we
know this tenderness to be true? The baptism of Jesus. You
can try to get Jesus to be harsh with you in your sin and weakness, but he never will. Our God is too holy and humble. He
entered the waters for us.

This is why you can remix the old church rhyme and say,
"Jesus loves me, this I know, for his baptism tells me so." A
well-known Methodist hymn highlights what Jesus came to
do at the Jordan River: "He came to share repentance with all
who mourn their sins, to speak the vital sentence with which
good news begins."[3] What does Jesus speak? "John, I'm here
to be baptized like them."

What does the Father think of all this? Christ's great act of
humility for sinful humanity brings deep delight to God the
Father. Jesus the Son undergoes a sinner's baptism, which John
thinks may be blasphemy, but then the heavens open and God
applauds. The Spirit descends. The Father speaks: "This is my
beloved Son, with whom I am well pleased" (Matthew 3:17).
The Trinity is revealed in beauty and unity. And God is revealed
to be unmistakably thrilled that the mission to rescue humanity
is reaching its apex as Jesus wades into the waters of baptism.

If Christ was humble enough to carry our sins into the water for repentance, we must know that in humility, he was pleased to give his life for our sins on the cross. His heart for sinners is revealed from eternity to the Jordan, to the cross, and to this very moment for all to behold and receive.

FOR REFLECTION AND DISCUSSION

1. What role has the baptism of Jesus played in your faith and spiritual formation?
2. What do you make of John's reaction to Jesus's desire for baptism? In what sense is John right? In what sense is he wrong? What does this suggest about the grace and humility of Jesus?
3. What does Jesus's baptism say about his heart toward you?

Second Week

The Fourfold Epiphany

Exodus 12:21–28

Psalm 40:1–11

1 Corinthians 1:1–9

John 1:29–42

The next day he saw Jesus coming toward him,
and said, "Behold, the Lamb of God, who takes
away the sin of the world!"

—John 1:29

Almighty God, whose Son our Savior Jesus Christ is
the light of the world: Grant that your people, illumined
by your Word and Sacraments, may shine with the radiance of Christ's glory, that he may be known, worshiped,
and obeyed to the ends of the earth; through Jesus
Christ our Lord, who with you and the Holy Spirit lives
and reigns, one God, now and for ever. Amen.[1]

Epiphany is the season of manifestation, the appearing of Jesus to the world as the one savior, the one light, the one way to life with God. John the Baptist again features prominently in the manifestation of Jesus to the world. In contrast to last week, here we find John understanding more clearly who Jesus is. John gazes on Jesus and proclaims, "Behold, the Lamb of God, who takes away the sin of the world!" (John 1:29). This statement is itself an epiphany, a fourfold revelation:

1. It reveals God has a lamb.
2. It reveals the world has sin.
3. It reveals there is one way for sin to be taken away.
4. It reveals that this sin-bearing Lamb is doing something so thrilling that we must behold him, believe in him, marvel over him.

To modern ears, the language of the lamb might seem odd. But to John and his disciples, rooted as they were in the worship life of Israel, the language was readily understood. Our Exodus passage, describing the Passover, is the world they knew by heart. Whereas present-day Americans might identify the word *lamb* with "wool sweater," first-century Israelites would associate it with "blood atonement."

The phrase *Lamb of God* is a holy vocation twice applied to Jesus. And while John's application of it to Jesus likely confused his disciples a bit, some of them soon became Jesus's disciples (John 1:35–42). The fourfold epiphany was seen, the message was at least partially understood, and they began to follow Jesus the lamb. Fast-forward to our day, and this message to behold the Lamb of God who takes away the sins of the world gets lost in translation, even at times inside the church.

Crooked Knowledge

Sin can be taught and understood in manner that's warped and unbiblical. In college, I once met with a Christian mentor to discuss spiritual growth. Offhandedly, I said, "I'm just a lowly sinner; I'm not worth anything."

He stopped me and said, "I think you need some better theology."

He was right. There is a vast difference between sin as brokenness and sin as worthlessness. Christianity teaches not only that all have *sinned* before God and others but also that all have *value* before God and others—and that the former reality does not extinguish the latter.

The John 1:29 epiphany of Jesus as our saving sacrifice means we must come to terms with the conditions that require the sacrifice in the first place. We cannot deeply understand the gift of the Lamb unless we understand something of the problem of sin.

There are a thousand ways to get sin wrong. Fatal errors usually happen by bouncing to various extremes like children on a playground seesaw. One extreme thinks of sin only through a wide lens. In this view, sin means that something is wrong in society and its systems but not that anything is broken in us (or at least in the one holding this view) personally. Sin is external, social, but rarely internal, individual, and personal. An error that swings in the opposite direction thinks of sin too narrowly, claiming that it is only in people but never in the world's systems. This view of sin zooms in only on individuals.

The multitude of ways to wrongly conceive of sin prove how lethal sin is. Sin makes us "crooked even in the knowledge of [our] crookedness," as Swiss theologian Karl Barth said.[2] The most dangerous way to get sin wrong is to consider it as only horizontal, never vertical. That is, we err in a deadly way when our theory of sin or why things are wrong focuses on people and never centers on God. Our knowledge of our crookedness—of sin—will remain crooked unless we begin to understand the end for which we were made and the One who crafted us by hand.

A Frame for Living

Every person lives by four theories that hold together like a frame. This framework, which some call a worldview or a social imagination, becomes the reference for how we see, think, and live. It is built on these premises:

1. *Purpose.* What is the purpose or meaning of life?
2. *Brokenness.* Something is wrong in the world, and it is [fill in the blank].
3. *The world.* The combination of purpose and brokenness create our sense of what this world is.
4. *A solution.* What's the fix for what ails us? What's the remedy that enables us to reach our purpose?

Australian pastor and author Mark Sayers offers great insights on these fundamental questions, presenting important theories at work in our world.[3] One example he uses is hedonism, which is the general outlook that life is primarily about the pursuit of pleasure. Considered within the above frame, hedonism says the following:

1. The *purpose* of life is to simply eat, drink, and be merry.
2. What's *broken* in the world is that people prevent others from seeking fulfillment via pleasure and self-expression.

3. The *world* is essentially a fun house, so enjoy yourself as
   you see fit.
4. The *solution* to what ails the world is more pleasure and
   fewer rules; if it hurts no one, just do it.

When made explicit, such frameworks remind us people are always searching for the solution to the deep problem that is called sin. Even when we misread, misname, or undersell it, religious and irreligious people still know something is warped in ourselves and in the world.

The fourfold epiphany of John 1:29 offers us a way into the true frame of the world—the way in which what's broken can truly be mended. To deeply grasp this gift of grace, we must reckon rightly with what's gone wrong. We must reckon with sin.

Coming to Terms with Sin

What then is sin? What is this reality that Jesus takes away? How would you answer these crucial questions?

Scripture uses different words—*sin, transgression, iniquity*—that we can sum up in this way: Sin is corruption, violation, and rebellion (Romans 6:19). It stains the conscience and accrues a debt against the holiness of God. Sin cannot be domesticated or presented politely. It is a power over us and the wrong done by us (3:9–10). Sin is rebellion against God's good way; it is the human bent to live without reference to the One who gives us life (1:21–22). Sin is the foul accumulation of the thoughts, words, and deeds we commit that transgress God's way and the good thoughts, words, and deeds that we leave undone. Sin is the condition in your bones that leads you to do those things you wish you wouldn't and hinders you from doing the good you wish you would (7:15–18). Sin is the dethroning of God and the exaltation of self that separates us from God, our selves, others, and creation (Genesis 3:1–7). Sin is our essential illness.

Behold the Lamb

No human, apart from Jesus, can escape sin. The apostle Paul says, "None is righteous, no, not one" (Romans 3:10). Christianity teaches that human goodness cannot and does not atone for sin. You cannot balance the scales through acts of goodness. Instead of people running to God to present acts that atone, it is God who runs to us.

In John 1:29, the gospel is revealed not only in words but also in imagery. Ask yourself this: How does a lamb conquer? Lambs are not fighting types. A lamb conquers only by surrender, by self-giving love.

Where is your sin—past, present, and future? It is blotted out. It is expunged. It is removed. What are you? You are cleansed. You are cleared. You are forgiven. You are made new. By what power and authority? The Lamb of God. For what purpose? That you would be restored in conscience, soul, and purpose to the Trinitarian God who made you to live in the knowledge that you are united to and beloved by him. In this stunning self-giving, it is God in Jesus who overcomes the debt and power of sin and heals the divide between Creator and creature.

This is expiation not according to human wisdom but according to the love of God. It is the thrill of the gospel, revealed in Jesus. While humanity gropes around in the dark, the gospel declaration is revealed to all who will listen: "Behold, the Lamb of God, who takes away the sin of the world!"

It is Christ the Lamb who marches to the cross to save us from the jaws of death and the clutches of sin. Jesus is the

epiphany—the manifestation—of the one true expiation. He
is the one true remedy for the world's sin, which is present in
the world's systems and structures and dark inner corners of
our own hearts.

We must practice at least two life-giving things in light of
this fourfold gospel epiphany. First, don't become so sophisti-
cated in your view of yourself that you forget you have sin that
needs cleansing. Second, don't get so down on yourself that
you forget God's Lamb has atoned for you. Behold Jesus, the
Lamb who was slain but still lives ever for us (Revelation 5:6–9).

FOR REFLECTION AND DISCUSSION

1. What's the difference between sin as worthlessness
   and sin as brokenness? What conception or definition of sin has shaped you the most?
2. Consider the four theories that provide a frame
   for living. What answers does Christianity offer
   to each? What range of answers are offered in the
   broader Christian faith?
3. How does the imagery of Jesus as the Lamb of God
   convey the good news?

Third Week

A New Way to Fish

Amos 3:1–11
Psalm 139:1–18
1 Corinthians 1:10–17
Matthew 4:12–22

"Follow me," [Jesus] told them, "and I will make
you fish for people." Immediately they left their
nets and followed him.

—Matthew 4:19–20, CSB

Give us grace, O Lord, to answer readily the call of
our Savior Jesus Christ and proclaim to all people the
Good News of his salvation, that we and the whole
world may perceive the glory of his marvelous works;
who lives and reigns with you and the Holy Spirit, one
God, for ever and ever. Amen.[1]

"Follow me . . . and I will make you fish for people." That is Jesus's recruitment pitch. And it works—Peter, Andrew, James, and John follow him. What does this call to fish for people mean? And what makes it so irresistible? The answers to these questions cast fresh light on the season of Epiphany. Inside the recruitment call Jesus gives to his first disciples rings a call that still speaks today. "Come, follow me," Jesus says to us, "and I'll transform you into people who live for the sake of others."

Lower Status for a Higher Calling

We've considered the revelation of God's humility in Jesus's baptism and the revelation of sin and its solution in Jesus as the Lamb of God. Now in his calling the disciples, we face the revelation of Jesus as the one who invites people to apprentice under him, thereby disrupting their lives and molding them for a greater purpose. It's easy to domesticate this passage by thinking the disciples' decision to follow Jesus is a simple choice. It isn't. These early disciples are branded as fools. James and John leave their dad, Zebedee, behind in the boat to follow Jesus. The family business may now go belly-up. Their wallets suffer, their families suffer, their plans suffer—yet they answer Jesus's call despite the cost.

These first respondents move to a lower status in pursuit of a higher calling. Their fishermen's pension is over, but they have proximity to the Savior. The calling of these disciples demonstrates that God invites us into a life that is about more than making ends meet: The Lord makes us participants and partners in the work of his kingdom. That's what it means, in part, to be fishers of people. It's something Jesus makes us into and something we join through partnership with God.

Fishing in a New Way

Jesus teaches these first disciples to "fish for people." When we hear this phrase in church, we think immediately of evangelism, or helping nonbelievers hear the good news about Jesus. But the phrase has a deeper context. Biblically speaking, fishing for people was not something humans did. It was an activity reserved for God or a nation God raised up. And it was something you did not want done to you. Several instances in the Bible illustrate this point, but consider Amos 4:2, just a few verses past our Old Testament reading:

> The Lord GOD has sworn by his holiness
>   that, behold, the days are coming upon you,
> when they shall take you away with hooks,
>   even the last of you with fishhooks.

The Old Testament understanding of fishing for people is full of gloom and points to being caught in judgment.[2] As Jesus's ministry unfolds, we witness that he's engaged in a different type of fishing. People are not being caught in judgment and carried away into exile. They are now being caught into the kingdom for a homecoming to the divine.

In Jesus's day, Galilee was a hotbed for religious revolutionary types. Perhaps these first disciples thought Jesus was bringing fiery judgment to the Romans, who were oppressing their people and under whose torturous technology—the cross—Jesus himself would die. Could this misunderstanding about fishing be why those disciples were slow to grasp so much of what Jesus taught and did?

Luke 9:52–55 tells a strange story of Jesus and the disciples that illustrates the confusion. When Jesus and his disciples are not received by a village of Samaritans, the disciples' response is literally fire and brimstone. James and John look at Jesus and ask, "Lord, do you want us to tell fire to come down from heaven and consume them?" In response, Jesus "turned and rebuked them." In other words, "No, not that type of fishing." Disciples of Jesus catch people with the message of salvation, not the fires of judgment.

Proximity and Transformation: Becoming Fishers of People

All this pushes us into the real question: How does Jesus turn his followers into fishers of people? How does Jesus "make" these disciples fit for the task when their hearts and their minds are, like ours, prone to shrink to the size of their misconceptions? How can Jesus take you and me and make us partners in God's kingdom work in the world?

Several years ago, bestselling author Malcolm Gladwell popularized the "10,000-hour rule."[3] This theory suggests that a fundamental factor to achieving greatness in a particular field or skill—think Stephen Curry as a basketball shooter or Bill Gates as a computer programmer—is ten thousand hours of elite, intensive training. When Jesus says, "Follow me," he offers the first disciples—and us—something greater than this. Ten thousand training hours are a pathway to intensity and constancy, but Jesus's promise of "Follow me" is the pathway to intimacy with him. Jesus is offering you not ten thousand hours of trying to teach yourself but more like a lifetime of hours with the One who knows the human heart inside and out, with the world's one lover and savior, who shines forth the beauty of full humanity and the glory of full divinity. Insofar as we are close to him, he transforms us. This is the wonder of grace.

Through intimacy and proximity with Jesus, the student

becomes like the teacher. Savor the depth of Jesus's gracious recruitment pitch: "Follow me, and I will *make* you fish for people." Follow and be made by Jesus himself. For three years the disciples are gradually shaped into fishers of people. They are transformed by Jesus's words—and a continual proximity to him, day by day. Jesus's pedagogical approach and curriculum have not changed much. His textbook is the same edition: He wants to shape us by his presence and words.

In God's grace, we possess the treasured fourfold gospel—Matthew, Mark, Luke, and John. It has been granted to us to meet Jesus in his Word. And it would be wise of us to apprentice at his feet by giving priority to the Gospels in our Bible reading, personally and communally. In many liturgical traditions, Sunday worship always includes readings from the Old Testament, the New Testament, and a gospel. The living voice of the Savior shapes us through his Word read and proclaimed and applied to his people by his Spirit.

When Fishing for People Goes Wrong

There's almost nothing worse than Christians so zealous to fish for people that they make it more difficult for people to enter the kingdom. Pastor and author Rich Villodas shares of his earnest but admittedly aggressive attempts to share the gospel early in his faith. At work, Villodas set a Bible verse in large font as the screen saver for his office computer. After being reprimanded by his boss, he then wore shirts with Scripture verses on them since he knew his boss wouldn't tell him to take his shirt off. Villodas admits these efforts didn't produce "healthy conversations about faith."[4] Indeed, zeal without knowledge produces a great deal of Christian cringe. This leaves non-Christians thinking the gospel is kitschy.

Misguided zeal is not the only way fishing for people can

go wrong. Again, Jesus gives a simple but stunning invitation and promise: "Follow me . . . and I will make you fish for people." However, sometimes we amputate Jesus's command, shortening it to only "Follow me." Other times, we remove its beating heart—"Follow me; stay close to me"—and try to reach people and change society in our own wisdom and strength. The amputation error ("Follow me," full stop) is all piety with no mission. The other error ("*I* will be a fisher of people") is all activity with no engine. Neither is what Jesus asks, yet how many of us bounce back and forth between the extremes?

From Self to Others

Jesus offers us a better way. His invitation of being with God leads not to doing *for* God but doing *with* God. To fish for people is to live in a way that helps influence them toward Jesus in word and action. It is his light through us. This call is a gift, but it has a cost. Remember what we said earlier: In answering yes to Jesus's call to discipleship, his first respondents moved to a lower status in pursuit of a higher calling. To be fishers of people, we must leave something behind on the shore; we must turn our back on our desire to think only for self, for us, for in-house concerns.

Jesus reverses the hold of sin on our hearts. Sin convinces us to live only for self, but Christ frees us to fully live for God and for others. Saint Augustine, one of the early African church fathers, taught that sin curved us in on ourselves. But look what Jesus does to people: He says, "Follow me; leave behind all your stuff. Enjoy me, and I'll help you bring God's grace and blessing to other people." He realigns us from self to others. Where we are curved in on ourselves, Jesus straightens us out to live for the sake of the world.

How, then, do we fish for people? Especially in an age

where many see Christianity as not only unbelievable but also harmful? The key is remembering that a major part of evangelism is simply being a compelling and caring person—someone people want to turn to when questions begin to spark in their hearts or things in their lives begin to crumble.

Who came to Jesus? Sinners on their last hope. People whose loved ones were dying. People whose consciences were shredding them from the inside out. Do you desire to fish for people with Jesus? Stay close to him, and get close to your neighbors. Jesus will make you his ambassador. Intimacy with Jesus creates influence for Jesus.

FOR REFLECTION AND DISCUSSION

1. When you reflect on Jesus calling you into his grace and into his mission to be a fisher of people, what do you feel in your heart and think in your mind?
2. What distortions or fears keep you from partnering with Jesus in the work of discipleship and mission?
3. Who in your life is far from God but close to you? Spend some time praying about this person, God's love for them, and how you might partner with God in their journey toward faith.

Fourth Week

Come and See

1 Samuel 3:1–20
Psalm 63:1–9
1 Corinthians 6:9–20
John 1:43–51

Nathanael said to him, "Can anything good
come out of Nazareth?" Philip said to him,
"Come and see."

—John 1:46

O God, you know that we are set in the midst of many grave dangers, and because of the frailty of our nature we cannot always stand upright: Grant that your strength and protection may support us in all dangers and carry us through every temptation; through Jesus Christ our Lord, who lives and reigns with you and the Holy Spirit, one God, for ever and ever. Amen.[1]

In 1942, a group of scientists gathered at the University of Chicago and achieved something incredible and horrible: a sustained nuclear reaction. Nicknamed the Chicago Pile-1, the world's first nuclear reactor launched "the rise of both nuclear energy and nuclear weapons." The key to this development was a chain reaction, which involved "arranging uranium in just the right positions" to make its neutrons hit other atoms and cause them to split, throwing off their neutrons and splitting more atoms.[2] In later experiments, this would be used to trigger explosions.

Both the Chicago Pile-1 and John 1 are about chain reactions. But one can be unto death while the other is unto life. Missiologist Lesslie Newbigin used similar imagery to describe the church's mission:

> Mission begins with a kind of explosion of joy. The news that the rejected and crucified Jesus is alive is something that cannot possibly be suppressed. It must be told. Who could be silent about such a fact? The mission of the Church in the pages of the New Testament is more like the fallout from a vast explosion, a radioactive fallout which is not lethal but life-giving.[3]

An Invitation

John 1 is our invitation to the gospel chain reaction that spreads Christ to the world by bringing him initially to our friends. Having been found by Jesus, Philip immediately knows the first friend he must tell, so he rushes with excitement to Nathanael. Yet Nathanael's point of view is different. Nathanael is like a brick wall of skepticism. "How can the Savior of Israel and the world be found in Nazareth?" he scoffs.

We can't blame him. Because Nathanael is smart, he thinks the origins of Jesus are an automatic disqualification. Nazareth is too poor, small, and insignificant. If God raised up the Savior, would he really live in a backwoods region never once mentioned in the Old Testament? Later in John, the Pharisees doubt Jesus's identity for this exact reason (7:52). Nathanael is a true-blue skeptic when it comes to Jesus. We all have friends or children like this. Some of us may lean this way ourselves.

What would happen if we shifted this gospel encounter into a more contemporary scenario? It might go something like this:

Nate works eighty hours a week, getting promotion after promotion. But then he admits to his friend Philip, "I kinda just feel numb inside."

Philip replies, "I know it sounds odd, but the only thing that keeps me from feeling dead inside is Jesus."

Nate gives him a look and says, "Christianity? Please. There's nothing good there."

Philip responds, "Come to church and see for yourself."

Many people today may be asking, "What good can come from Christianity besides racism, misogyny, homophobia, and power plays?" What's the right reply? There's a place for good conversation and debate. Read a bit of good history and you'll quickly find that while Christians are far from perfect, most of our society's beliefs about human dignity, care for the poor, and equality come from Christianity.[4] Even so, information only goes so far. The best reply to a skeptic world, our skeptical friends, and even our skeptical hearts is an invitation to come and see: to encounter Jesus through his people and through hearing how Jesus is truth, goodness, and beauty.

The gospel chain reaction is fueled by joy, as Newbigin notes, but its on switch is invitation. A faithful follower of

Jesus doesn't need to know all the answers to all the questions. Mission is both easier and harder than that. To be part of the gospel's life-giving chain reaction, you simply need to know Jesus and know people who don't know Jesus. Then, think daily on all Jesus has done for you and find a chance to speak and live in a way that says, "Come and see."

The panels of the Isenheim Altarpiece were painted by Matthias Grünewald in the sixteenth century and are on display at the Unterlinden Museum in France. In the painting's center panel, Jesus hangs on the cross. Off to the side stands John the Baptist with a long, bony finger pointing at Jesus's broken body as if to say, "I'm not the focus. Look at Jesus." In John 1, Philip is the raised finger pointing to Jesus, the main character. Philip is in a supporting role, and Nathanael is the one transformed. What greater glory on earth exists than to be the raised finger used by Christ?

Maybe this feels too oversimplified. Perhaps you're thinking, *"Come and see" is fine in areas where the residue of cultural Christianity is still thick. But this strategy is irrelevant at worst and naïve at best where I live. People here have deep objections to the faith.* Let me offer this word: The power of invitation is tied to the One to whom we point. The extent to which we believe "come and see" is powerful is proportional to the power we ascribe to Jesus to save. If we think Jesus is a semi-capable savior, we will think invitation is semi-powerful. "Come and see" ignites the gospel chain reaction because Jesus is powerfully able and joyfully eager to lead people to himself. Get people to Jesus; he'll do the rest. Notice how Philip recedes from the narrative once he says, "Come and see." It is Jesus who does the transforming. He is the engine of the gospel chain reaction.

Grace Changes Everything

What's this "come and see" encounter with Jesus like? Jesus and Nathanael trade affectionate, clever barbs. Then Jesus delivers a gracious mic drop that sends Nathanael's heart ping-ponging through his rib cage: "Before Philip called you, when you were under the fig tree, I saw you" (John 1:48). Nathanael's brick wall of skepticism crumbles. He is gloriously undone.

What's so special about this comment? Clearly it is more than an accurate prediction, because Nathanael's response is to worship Jesus. If Jesus were only predicting a fact like a magician, Nathanael would simply say, "Encore, please!" Instead, he worships Jesus as the Messiah. A mysterious thing happens between Jesus and Nathanael here that is perhaps too tender for John to explain. Could it be that the shady fig tree— occasionally referenced in rabbinic literature as a place of prayer and meditation—is where Nathanael was sitting, praying, and pouring out his heart to God?[5] The prophet Elijah and the prophet Jonah both are recorded in Scripture under trees and plants at their lowest points (1 Kings 19:4–5; Jonah 4:6). Could it be that Jesus is really conveying to Nathanael, "I know the deepest parts of you. I see you. And I'm here to save you"? Whatever the case, Nathanael knows Christ has seen him fully. Once Nathanael is invited to Jesus and gets near him, Jesus's grace melts Nathanael's skepticism.

Jesus is doing the same work today. Brick walls of skepticism are crumbling. Contrary to what many say, people are more open to the grace and truth of Jesus, and this has been happening for quite some time. Did you know that after the 9/11 attacks in the United States, church attendance in

Australia—a country on the other side of the world—increased for a short time? Why? As pastor and author Mark Sayers writes, it was "because the Western secularist bubble of radical individualism and hyperconsumerism was pierced. Briefly, the mythology that it is possible to live a life without God or greater meaning for many people was rattled."[6] Today, bubbles are bursting everywhere. More quickly than you think, the belief that "nothing good can come out of Christianity" can become "I've come to see that Jesus makes sense of everything."

Jesus's Word to Us

Jesus turns from his encounter with Nathanael to address everyone—including us. In effect, Jesus is saying the "come and see" movement, the gospel chain reaction, will permeate the whole world because the heavens are open. Jesus is the place where heaven comes to earth, the location where life with God is available. Referencing the Old Testament story of Jacob seeing the ladder leading up to heaven (Genesis 28:12–13), Jesus makes clear that he is the way to heaven and life with God now and eternally.

Do you believe this? The heavens are open because Jesus descended and ascended for us. In Jesus, the hope of heaven is touching earth and people are being found. Be found by him, raise the "come and see" finger, and join the chain reaction unto life and the joy of his life-giving mission.

FOR REFLECTION AND DISCUSSION

1. What's your relationship and history with evangelism and invitation? Are there wounds you need to

process with other believers to more fully engage in God's mission?

2. In what way is joy the key, humanly speaking, to our mission and witness?

3. What might it look like for you to live in a "come and see" way?

Curing the Colonial Heart

Isaiah 49:1–7
Psalm 67
Acts 1:1–8
Matthew 9:35–38

Then he said to his disciples, "The harvest is
plentiful, but the laborers are few; therefore pray
earnestly to the Lord of the harvest to send out
laborers into his harvest."

—Matthew 9:37–38

Almighty God, through the outpouring of the Holy
Spirit, you revealed the way of eternal life to every race
and nation: Pour out this gift anew, that by the preaching of the Gospel your salvation may reach to the ends
of the earth; through Jesus Christ our Lord, who lives
and reigns with you, in the unity of the Holy Spirit, one
God, for ever and ever. Amen.[1]

The first president of Kenya observed that early missionaries
came to his land with the Bible. Then, "they taught us to pray
with our eyes closed. When we opened our eyes, they had the
land and we had the Bible."[2] This represents the dark side of
mission or evangelism. That the Christian gospel—the message of God's redeeming love for humanity—has often been
mixed with imperialism and colonialism is a serious tragedy
and a legitimate barrier to faith. Of course, Christianity was
vibrant in Africa well before European colonists arrived.[3] But
the hard history still stands. Imperialist faith—what can be
called the colonial heart—often saw missions as a way to spread
Christ with a heavy mix of racial and cultural superiority.
Thus, since they deemed the natives to be lesser, godless, and
incompetent, colonists felt they were doing the natives a real
favor in taking the land, in God's name. The colonial heart
lived by both faith and lies.

We must confront these sober truths head-on. If we don't,
we will struggle to obey Jesus's call to mission because we will
be haunted by the sense that evangelism is at some level a corrupt power play. Without a strong counter vision of mission,
the perversions in the past will give us a subconscious, fearful
pause about engaging in evangelism and mission in the present. Matthew 9 reminds us that these past failures, though
historical, are far from biblical. Mission is not a matter of co-
ercion or arrogance. It is a matter of compassion, as Jesus himself demonstrates.

If you know what the term *compassion* means, you'll know
this isn't paternalistic. *Com-* means "with," and *passion* refers to
pain or suffering. Thus, *compassion* is akin to "suffering with
another."[4] Jesus heals and preaches the gospel out of solidarity
with the people he sees who are afflicted. Jesus sees the crowds

in pain, and his heart goes out to them. Mission is not a grab for power; it is an act of compassion.

The needs of the people Jesus was among were undeniably clear. They were sick, diseased, and starving. Depending on your context, this description may not be your daily reality. Perhaps many of the people you will see this week are not in that position. Externally, everything appears to be fine, or even more than fine, with them. This reminds me a bit of our house search when my family first moved to Virginia. One house that seemed well kept and promising was a ranch-style home in a vibrant neighborhood. Then we walked in the door—only to be assaulted by the smell of cigarette smoke and to find the whole interior gutted. Things appeared great on the outside, but a state of emergency existed just behind the front door. Similarly, there are people who appear to be great, based on their externals, but on the inside they're depressed, afraid, lonely, and barely making it out of bed each day.

Harassed and Helpful in the Modern Age

In Matthew 9, the weighty language of "harassed and helpless" carries the idea of "cast down and beat down" or "distressed and dispirited." This sort of helplessness is often marked by physical realities, which is why mission includes deeds of mercy. But it's also marked by internal realities, which is why mission includes the work of proclamation.

Jesus said the truth sets us free (John 8:32), so naturally, lies enslave and corrupt. In a sense, even the physical realities of being harassed and oppressed come from lies. Consider world hunger. In 2022, the United Nations World Food Program estimated it would take $7 billion to end world famine. If that seems like a lot, in 2021, Americans alone spent $11 billion in one day—Cyber Monday. The program's communications team doesn't pull punches: "We know what it takes to end world hunger, and we know what it costs. We simply need the collective will to make it happen."[5] The tragedy of world hunger continues through the lies of scarcity and greed that say, "The abundance I have is not enough, so I won't give; I will hoard."

Another pervasive falsehood that leaves us and those around us cast down and beat down is "the fundamental lie of modernity: that we are our own."[6] Author Alan Noble calls this "the Unbearable weight of Manufacturing Personal Meaning." Having to generate your own meaning and value is terrible, exhausting news. When humans must define our ultimate meaning and value, we default to our income, productivity, youthfulness, looks, or authenticity. Left to ourselves, we rest the weight of our lives on the most alluring yet precarious objects we can find.

Lies are killing us, but as Jesus gazes on the ancient and modern weak and weary, his heart bursts with mercy. Matthew's editorial comment is that the people are "like sheep without a shepherd" (9:36). Yet Jesus uses different imagery to teach his disciples to embody his compassionate heart for the people and mission. He declares that on the one hand, the harvest is huge but on the other hand, there are barely any workers (verse 37). So, he says, pray that the Lord of the harvest will send workers into his harvest. What's happening here? Jesus is extending his compassion so that the mercy in his heart flows into his disciples, multiplying his salvation to many.

Compassion for the Harvest

What follows in Matthew 10 is Jesus's commission of his twelve disciples to heal and preach in his name. They become the workers they prayed for. Prayer transforms them into little

Christs, ambassadors of Jesus, God making his saving grace known through them. It's important to recognize that when Jesus sends them into the harvest, he gives them this instruction for the preaching: "Go nowhere among the Gentiles and enter no town of the Samaritans, but go rather to the lost sheep of the house of Israel" (verses 5–6).

Why preach to Israel before the rest of the world, as Jesus later tells them (Matthew 28:19–20)? This is crucial, for it tells those of us who are outside Israelite heritage that before we are workers in the harvest, we are those who are harvested. God has compassion not only on his people, Israel, but on us too. If you know you are not just the worker but also the harvested, judgmentalism dies and you live on mission in gratitude, not arrogance. Why? The grace you proclaim, the mercy you extend, is what God first gave to you. How do Christians avoid colonialism, arrogance, and domination in Jesus's name? Remember, the gospel came to us but did not start with us.

We are the Lord's harvest. Which means Jesus's prayer of compassion for harvest workers has been and is being answered. Every faithful church in your town is proof. Every minor and major character in your spiritual journey proves that the harvest is plenty big and that through Christ the workers are laboring. Today the harvest is especially plentiful as the Christian church explodes in the Global South.[7] Odds are, if you are a Christian in the world today, you are a woman from western Africa, China, or Latin America.[8] The heart of Christ triumphs over the colonial heart.

In the West, projections declare a continued staggering decline in the number of people who identify as Christians[9] and a steady, significant population of "nones"—those with no religious affiliation at all. How are we to proceed as the church? The church scandals that have rocked American churches the last few decades make hope for the harvest seem implausible. Even now, you may be thinking, *I understand all the objections my neighbor has to Christianity. Christianity is not just the last choice for them; it's not even on the menu of possibility.* While it is wise to be alert to the colonial heart, there is an equal and opposite need to stand guard against the cynical heart, which says Christianity is all but done for.

At this moment, we walk as the church in history has always walked—by faith in our Lord's promise. Believe Jesus's heart, where his infinite compassion flows through every artery. Believe Jesus's all-seeing diagnosis: The problem is not the magnitude of the harvest but the need for more workers. Let us pray to the owner of the harvest, God, asking him to do his thing. Will you make the daring choice? Will you push aside the colonial heart and the cynical heart, trusting only in the heart of Christ?

Christ can reach any human heart because all of us are made to yearn for the belonging he alone offers. Asking whether the harvest is still plentiful is like asking whether a living human heart still pumps blood. The harvest is plentiful because we are made for God and God desires that none would perish (Ezekiel 18:23; 1 Timothy 2:3–4; 2 Peter 3:9). And the Lord who desires none to perish has come near in Jesus and made his heart known, funneling his compassion to every part of his body so that we who have tasted his grace would bring others in love to the same feast.

FOR REFLECTION AND DISCUSSION

1. From your perspective and experience, how are people today "harassed and helpless"? In what ways are religious leaders at fault? In what way are lies the culprit?

2. Based on our reading, how does Jesus relate to you when you are beat down?

3. To what degree do you really think the harvest is plentiful, as Jesus stated? Why? Is your answer shaped by cynicism, realism, or faith?

The Transfiguration

1 Kings 19:9–18
Psalm 27
2 Peter 1:13–21
Mark 9:2–9

He was transfigured before them, and his clothes
became radiant, intensely white, as no one on
earth could bleach them.

—Mark 9:2–3

O God, who before the passion of your only-begotten
Son revealed his glory upon the holy mountain: Grant
that we, beholding by faith the light of his countenance,
may be strengthened to bear our cross, and be changed
into his likeness from glory to glory; through Jesus
Christ our Lord, who lives and reigns with you and the
Holy Spirit, one God, for ever and ever. Amen.[1]

Epiphany is bookended by the voice of God the Father. The season that began in Mark 1 in the waters of Jesus's baptism ends in Mark 9 in the light of Jesus's transfiguration. All three Synoptic Gospels (Matthew, Mark, and Luke) capture the moment of transfiguration in detail. The transfiguration is vital for their presentation of Jesus and what it means to follow him. Tragically, however, it rarely figures into our understanding of Jesus and discipleship.

Grasping the Transfiguration

It is happening so fast. One second, the disciples are with their teacher. The next moment, Jesus is transfigured in a blaze of glory, and two of the mightiest prophets from the Old Testament, Moses and Elijah, appear among them. And then the prophets begin, according to Mark's account, to chat with Jesus while the three disciples pick up their jaws from the floor in shock and terror.

What exactly is going on here? The transfiguration of Jesus is a theophany, a revelation of God in his godliness to human persons. The disciples are well acquainted with Jesus the man. But now, on this mountain, the divinity of Jesus bursts forth through his humanity.

Venture into these deep waters with holy curiosity. What would it be like to behold this? Mark doesn't provide many details, but what he does say is central. This is a moment full of light.

Mark 9:3 says Jesus's "clothes became radiant, intensely white, as no one on earth could bleach them." Matthew 17:2 says, "His face shone like the sun, and his clothes became white as light." It would be a serious mistake to think that Jesus simply glowed or that a flood of light came on him from above, like a spotlight from heaven. Rather the transfiguration is the bursting forth of Christ's glory. Thomas Aquinas, the medieval theologian, wrote: "At his Transfiguration, Christ showed his disciples the splendor of his beauty."[2] The Matthew passage's suggestive comparisons "shone *like* the sun" and "white *as* light" show that this transfiguration light is uncreated. Do you hear it? Sunlight—the greatest source of visible light—is a simple human reference point for the radiance that shone from Jesus. This light that flows from Jesus is self-existent, the light of the glory and life of God.

This is the Light of the world, of which all other lights—sun, stars, supernovas—are obscure, created copies. It makes sense, doesn't it? Jesus is no object that reflects light; the light flows out of him. In the transfiguration, it's as if his divine nature is burning forth through his humanity so all on this mountain can marvel.

Why, at this moment among these disciples, does Jesus reveal his glory? This theophany happens at a turning point in Jesus's life and ministry. If we flip back one chapter to Mark 8, the turning point becomes clear. The disciples and the crowds have been wondering who Jesus really is. Then the aha moment finally arrives for the disciples. It is Peter—the group's spokesman—who shows spiritual understanding that Jesus is not simply a teacher but the Son of God, one with God (verse 29). Jesus affirms Peter's confession while revealing with new depth his forthcoming sacrificial activity.

Verse 31 describes the pivotal moment: "He began to teach them that the Son of Man must suffer many things and be rejected by the elders and the chief priests and the scribes and be killed, and after three days rise again." Peter—again representative of the whole group—can't stomach that Jesus would suffer a shameful criminal death, so a power struggle starts: "Peter took [Jesus] aside and began to rebuke him. But turning and seeing his disciples, he rebuked Peter and said, 'Get behind me, Satan! For you are not setting your mind on the things of God, but on the things of man'" (verses 32–33). Jesus reveals that the way of sacrifice is both for the Lord and for his disciples (verse 34).

All this is the immediate backdrop to the transfiguration. Why, then, does Jesus reveal his glory to Peter, James, and John? It seems he shows them the end of the road so they might not be discouraged when they arrive at his cross and have to carry their own as his followers. Jesus, the light, essentially says to the disciples, "Trust me." If they listen to the Light and heed the glory before them, then no matter what threats await them or what trouble they witness, they can say the words of Psalm 27:1 with full-throated confidence: "The LORD is my light and my salvation; whom shall I fear?"

The saving light shown to them then is shown to us now in the message about Jesus. The gospel of his sacrificial death, luminous resurrection, and impending return reveals the beauty of his light and glory. Why? For the same reason his glory shone on the mountain—to comfort us so that we won't faint from carrying our crosses in following him. Whatever trial you face, whatever pain you endure in worshipping and aligning your life to Jesus's kingdom, is more than worth it in the end. The light of his glory makes trials feel as light as feathers once we come into the full weight of Jesus's shining beauty (2 Corinthians 4:17).

How to Listen to Light

In the greatest *Duh!* statement of the New Testament, Peter blurts out, "It is good that we are here" (Mark 9:5), essentially saying that beholding the beauty of God is indeed a good thing. Have you ever caught a glimpse in your mind's eye or the inner chambers of your heart of the beauty and power of God's glorious character? It's a joy to savor and crave. But in a way, Peter's tent-erecting suggestion flattens the glory into thirds: 33.3 to Jesus, 33.3 to Elijah, 33.3 to Moses. Jerome, an early church father, comments, "He [Peter] certainly did not realize what he was saying when he was conferring honor upon the servants equally with the Lord."[3] Isn't it easy to let good things from God take our eyes off the great thing from God—Christ himself? If I had a dollar for every time Christians get caught up in the best new Bible study technique or Christian bestseller, forgetting to focus only on the One who died and rose again, I'd be rich enough to move up several tax brackets. To save Peter in his confusion and fear, to save us from taking our eyes off the Lord of light, the voice of God booms in interrupting love:

> A cloud overshadowed them, and a voice came out
> of the cloud, "This is my beloved Son; listen to him."
> And suddenly, looking around, they no longer saw
> anyone with them but Jesus only. (verses 7–8)

God speaks the same words as he had at Jesus's baptism—"This is my beloved Son" (Matthew 3:17). But now the voice interrupts human confusion with the instructions that lead us from death to life: *Listen to Jesus.*

Listen to Jesus. Look at Jesus. You don't need to think about God's servants; you need to marvel at God's Son. Within the context of Mark 8 and 9, this means that the executive team of disciples—Peter, James, and John—need to listen to what Jesus has just told them about his cross and their crosses. God's saving word to the world is revealed in this word: Listen to the Light of the world, who said, "I give my life as a ransom for many." (See Mark 10:45.) Listen to the Light who swallowed up death in his death and breaks the penalty of sin and power of evil.

To listen to the Light is to take Jesus at his word about his identity and work, his cross and resurrection. Many versions of Jesus are presented to us on the ideological shelves. There is a progressive vision of Jesus who is all revolution and no atonement. One theologian described this Jesus by saying, "A God without wrath brought men without sin into a kingdom without judgment through the ministrations of a Christ without a cross."[4] There is also a conversative vision of Jesus who is all atonement but no compassion toward sinners, unless they are of the "respectable" variety. Each of us is liable, like Peter, to co-opt the light. Will you put away ideological thoughts? Will you listen to the Light?

What happens when we listen to the Light? When we look to Jesus only, the human face of God, God shines his saving light on us. This is the true light that gives life to the dead: "God, who said, 'Let light shine out of darkness,' has shone in our hearts to give the light of the knowledge of the glory of God in the face of Jesus Christ" (2 Corinthians 4:6).

FOR REFLECTION AND DISCUSSION

1. How have you understood the transfiguration? What new insights are you considering in light of our readings?
2. How does the context of Mark help us understand the importance of the transfiguration for the disciples? How can reflecting on the glory of Jesus help you in your current challenges and life situation?

3. Do you agree that there are various versions of Jesus presented to people? How can we best take Jesus at his word? What does this passage from Mark show as central to any faithful conception of Jesus's identity and ministry?

LENT

A Bright Sadness

As we make the first step into the "bright
sadness" of Lent, we see—far, far away—the
destination. It is the joy of Easter, it is the
entrance into the glory of the Kingdom. And
it is this vision, the foretaste of Easter, that makes
Lent's sadness bright and our lenten effort a
"spiritual spring."

—ALEXANDER SCHMEMANN, *Great Lent*

In early 2023, the morning TV show *Today* invited Hollywood actor and believer Mark Wahlberg onto the broadcast as a guest. Surprisingly, Wahlberg was invited not to promote an upcoming film but to speak about his Lenten prayer practice. As Wahlberg sat on-air, with ashes in the shape of the cross on his forehead in step with the Ash Wednesday tradition, the bottom third of the TV screen read, "Mark Wahlberg's 40-Day Challenge."[1] Although Wahlberg attempted to describe Lenten spirituality, the show's producers chose to recast Lent as the personal challenge of a famous individual.

This gaffe demonstrates how easily Lent becomes rebranded as a personal journey, a self-guided voyage toward personal growth or self-improvement. Calling such an endeavor "Lent" is like calling a mug full of oil "coffee." The outward appearance is similar enough—there's a mug with dark liquid in it—but the real substance is far from authentic. We may not go so far as to rebrand Lent as our personal challenge. Yet in our fixation on individuality, customization, flexibility, and self-centeredness, we are no less prone to rebrand Lent into our image, into something that centers on ourselves to the neglect of the true nature of this season of the church year.

Lenten Spirituality

To get Lent right, we need a strong grasp of what Lent is. Each season of the church year draws us into the life of Jesus and calls us to follow him by accenting a particular aspect of the Christian story. In Lent, we return to the heart of our spiritual life with God through repentance and renewal and begin to journey toward the Cross and the Resurrection.

Lent has been called "a time to repent," "a bright sadness," and even "spring cleaning for the soul." It is a forty-day period of repentance, fasting, and prayer in readiness for the great feast of the Resurrection. The season began in the early days of the church as a time of preparation for those seeking to be baptized at the Easter Vigil. The forty days represent our Lord's time of fasting in the wilderness (Matthew 4:2). Ash Wednesday marks the beginning of the Lenten season, which continues into Holy Week. Lent is less of an individual undertaking a journey and more of the church following the footsteps of her Lord. Rather than becoming a spectacle of self-improvement, Lent is a call "to abstain from adoring at the shrine of the self" and to draw near to God.[2] Somber joy is the tenor of Lent. We come to grips with sin in a fresh way—but always with an eye toward the truth that "there is more mercy in Christ than sin in [and around] us."[3]

The New Testament speaks powerfully of Christian virtue in the language of putting on and putting off (Colossians 3). Lenten spirituality operates similarly. The call of Lent is an intensity of spiritual focus, putting off the vices and even the good things that keep us from focusing on Christ while simultaneously putting on the virtues and habits that cause us to walk in good works. This is why even non-Christians know that Lent involves "giving up" certain things. God's people put off lesser goods to savor the greatest good: God, who himself is goodness.

Though many nonliturgical churches have begun to participate, there are devout Christians who remain skeptical or unfamiliar with Lent. Sometimes skepticism of Lent comes from a fear of legalism—the belief that our devotion to God is what secures our standing before him. To others, Lent seems like a heartless imposition of discipline for no real purpose. I want to offer four reasons why observing Lent is a gift believers ought to embrace:

1. **Renewal.** Lent offers us an intentional return to the heart of our faith: our brokenness and sin and the greater grace of God in Jesus Christ applied to our hearts by the Holy Spirit.
2. **Preparation.** We need more than a Good Friday service to prepare for the joy of the Resurrection that comes on Easter Sunday and in Eastertide. Without some level of intentional preparation, Easter will "sneak up" on us. By following the story of Jesus through Lent, we enter into Easter more alert with anticipation for its celebration because we've attempted to walk out the whole journey

of Christ's story, not simply the final climax. Lent allows us to enter the story of our salvation, movement by movement.

3. **Participation.** In Lent, we slowly and intentionally journey as God's people, with Jesus, toward the Cross and Resurrection.

4. **Sanctification.** In Lent, we put off the sin and sluggishness that hinder us, and empowered by grace, we give ourselves to more intensive spiritual practices that form us.

Since Lent is a season of getting real about our sin and weakness, it's expected that your attempts to keep a holy and intentional Lent will at some level fail. The goal is to keep not a perfect Lent but a holy one—a Lent in which we ask God for the grace to draw near to him, while trusting he will enable us to do what we cannot. In the process of stumbling through Lent, we find that Christ is always near, sympathizing with our weakness, remolding our desires, and conforming us not to our idealized selves but into his own likeness.

Lenten Practices

What are the particular practices that mark worship and discipleship in Lent? Several could be named, but these three form a helpful starting place for individuals and communities.

Maintain a fast. When Jesus spoke of fasting, he used the language of "when," not "if" (Matthew 6:16–18). In other words, fasting is an expectation, not extra credit, when it comes to the life of a disciple. The common neglect of this discipline makes Lent a vital season for believers. Fasting is the choice to abstain from food to feast on God, enter a time of heightened prayer, or express mourning and repentance. Lenten practice includes partial or whole fasts.

- **Partial fasts.** These involve cutting out part of one's diet, like alcohol, meat, caffeine, sugar, or desserts. In doing so, we curb our cravings, depend on God, and trust Jesus will meet us in our hunger—and hunger-induced irritation.

- **Whole fasts.** These fasts involve abstaining from entire meals for a brief time, either a few hours, a whole day, or multiple days. In a whole fast, one continues to drink water and juice. Be sure to consider your medical needs before doing a whole fast. If a whole fast is new to you, a good practice is to abstain from breakfast or lunch one day a week during Lent.

- **Digital (or other non-food-related) fasts.** While fasting is primarily in relation to food, it is also spiritually beneficial to abstain from other things to attend to God. Digital fasts, in which we fully or partially abstain from social media, streaming services, or entertainment, are increasingly important for disciples in our screen-centric culture.

It is common to fast at the beginning of Lent (Ash Wednesday), throughout the duration of Lent (Wednesdays and/or Fridays), and on Good Friday at the end of Lent leading up to Easter Sunday. The best practice is to participate in a fast with your church or with a group of believers. Since Lent is the journey of God's people with Jesus, resist the urge to exclusively personalize or customize your fasts. In other words, make sure part of your fasting is in some way communal. This not only helps you keep going when things get hard but also illustrates that deep truth that our faith is communal.

Remember that each Sunday is a "mini-Easter" in which we celebrate the risen Christ, so there is no fasting on Sundays, only feasting in Jesus's name. This respite helps us maintain our Lenten disciplines and prepares us for the joy of Easter.

Engage in more prayer. In prayer, we draw near to God and he draws near to us. We listen, confess, praise, petition, and unburden our hearts before our heavenly Father, who knows our frames and our needs. Consider how you can increase your communion with God through prayer in this season. Fasting naturally combines with prayer, so look to use the time you would have been prepping or eating a meal—or on a screen—to engage in prayer.

Consider praying daily this Lenten Prayer from Saint Ephrem:

O Lord and Master of my life, take from me the spirit of sloth, despair, lust of power, and idle talk.

But give rather the spirit of chastity, humility, patience, and love to Thy servant.

Yea, O Lord and King, grant me to see my own transgressions, and not to judge my brother, for blessed art Thou, unto ages of ages. Amen.[4]

Do acts of service and almsgiving. Almsgiving—giving to the needy—is a fast from excess. We sacrifice financially so that we learn to live by God alone. Put positively, almsgiving is an act of love for God and others. Like fasting, almsgiving is not an effort to earn something from God. It inclines us toward his gracious transformation by the Holy Spirit. How can you put aside money and items in this season to be generous to those in need around you?

Notable Days in the Church Year During Lent

As with each season, Lent has notable days in which the church is called into a deeper experience of the life of Christ together.

Ash Wednesday (the Wednesday before the first Sunday in Lent): The forty days of Lent begin with Ash Wednesday. In the Bible, ashes are a sign of human mortality and repentance (Job 30:19; Matthew 11:21). On Ash Wednesday, liturgical churches generally offer services in which leaders impose ashes on the forehead of each congregant in the shape of the cross as an act of repentance and faith. The emphasis on Ash Wednesday is the seriousness of sin and the mercy of God. This reflection on death and life and sin and grace is a proper launching point into the Lenten journey. If your church does not have an Ash Wednesday service, you can attend one at any local Anglican, Lutheran, or Roman Catholic church without having to be a member or change traditions.

Saint Patrick's Day (March 17): Saint Patrick was a great missionary and bishop among the Irish people, who once abducted and enslaved him. This is a day to read Patrick's story and celebrate the gospel's advance in the Lord through the Lord's faithful servants.

The Annunciation (March 25): This feast commemorates the appearance of the angel Gabriel to the Virgin Mary, announcing that Mary would first miraculously conceive then

give birth to Christ, the Son of God (Luke 1:26–38). This
feast is marked nine months prior to Christmas. When March
25 falls during Holy Week or the first week of Easter, this feast
is moved to the Monday after the second Sunday of Easter.

Laetare Sunday (fourth Sunday in Lent): Just as there is a
Sunday of rejoicing in the somber season of Advent (Gaudete
Sunday), so too in Lent. Both *laetare* and *gaudete* are Latin
terms for "rejoice."[5] This Sunday encourages us to remain
steadfast as the end of Lent approaches. Pink candles are a
common way to mark this day.

Reading Lenten Texts and Devotions

As you read the following Scripture texts and devotions, you'll
contemplate temptation, the dynamics of the spiritual journey,
and existential desire. The season kicks off with a special Ash
Wednesday devotional to be read on that date. This will launch
you into the Lenten season. Working from Genesis as well as
the gospel of John, these Lenten reflections will guide you
into the deep realities of the spiritual life: our human need and
the mercy of God. Throughout this season, keep your eyes set
on Jesus as we journey toward the joy of Easter by first travers-
ing the difficult but life-giving terrain of Lent.

Our True Selves

Isaiah 58:1–12

Psalm 103:8–14

2 Corinthians 5:20–6:10

Matthew 6:1–6, 16–21

He knows our frame;

he remembers that we are dust.

—Psalm 103:14

Almighty and everlasting God, you hate nothing you have made, and you forgive the sins of all who are penitent: Create and make in us new and contrite hearts, that we, worthily lamenting our sins and acknowledging our wretchedness, may obtain of you, the God of all mercy, perfect remission and forgiveness; through Jesus Christ our Lord, who lives and reigns with you and the Holy Spirit, one God, for ever and ever. Amen.[1]

We have never supplied God with new information. From every angle with comprehensive sight, the Lord knows us fully. And on Ash Wednesday, God calls us to put away our false selves and practice true self-knowledge before his searching light. Today we remember our frames. Today we confess our sins. Today—despite all our posturing and all our products—we remember that we are dust.

True knowledge of self will lead to true knowledge of God, and true knowledge of God will lead to true knowledge of self.[2] Ash Wednesday offers us both, through confession, silence, and the acknowledgement of our sin and mortality. All of these are represented in a common practice on this day in many churches: the imposition of ashes on our foreheads.

Even if you do not partake of this Christian practice, reflection on this act is valuable and instructive. The ashes bring us to true knowledge of self by placing us under the microscope of God's exacting judgment. Ashes in biblical times were a symbol of sorrow and sin and a living reminder that death, the wages of sin, is waiting for each of us. On Ash Wednesday, this is the truth we stare in the face through the very marking of our foreheads. This act makes tangible the truth that we cannot escape the touch of death because we have not been free from sin. We are marked. We are judged. Despite our attempts to be good and do good, before God we are found lacking.

Instead of running from this knowledge of self and God, Christians throughout the world make it visible. The dust touches your face and, from your skin, preaches a sermon:

> I acknowledge my faults,
>> and my sin is ever before me.
>> Against you only have I sinned, and done this evil in
>> your sight,

so that you are justified in your sentence, and blame-
less in your judgment.[3]

Is this public marking a violation of Jesus's teaching in
Matthew 6 to not make our piety a sign of public religious
bragging? It could be. But if you ask God to help you know
his holiness and help you mourn your sin, this act is not per-
formance. It is repentance. It is an outward sign of an inward
prayer: *Jesus, Son of God, have mercy on me, a sinner.* In this way,
the imposition of the ashes is a bridge that guides us into the
whole of Lent because in confession, we draw near to God—
not through posturing but with honesty before his holiness.

What if you've not done the imposition of ashes? What if
the practice is not available where you worship? You are at no
significant disadvantage, because the truth and repentance to
which the ashes point are available by grace to all. No ashes?
Then do the deeper work. Confess your sins to God. Put off
your false self, and throw yourself on the mercy of almighty
God.

The Shape of the Cross

On Ash Wednesday, it's not simply that dust streaks our foreheads. We are marked by ashes in the shape of the cross. Psalm
103 reveals that God knows your sin and your weakness. And
in his holy mercy, he meets you not with the judgment you
deserve but with the compassion he alone can extend. The
psalmist proclaims:

He does not deal with us according to our sins,
     nor repay us according to our iniquities.
For as high as the heavens are above the earth,
     so great is his steadfast love toward those who fear him;

as far as the east is from the west,
>so far does he remove our transgressions from us.
>(verses 10–12)

Our sin marks us. But in confessing our sins and good deeds that we think make us better than others, turning from both, and then trusting in Christ alone, we are marked not only by mortality but also by the cross that saves. This gospel truth gives us even more reason to come to God on this day. It is, as the apostle Paul says, God's kindness that leads to our repentance, not our repentance that leads to his kindness (Romans 2:4). God will not cast us off, even though we deserve it. The Lord will meet our dust and death with his cross and eventually his resurrection.

Even if ashes do not touch your forehead on this day, the deep work is to cling to the hope of the Cross to overcome our sin. This is the hope we enter as we journey through Lent. But today, the ashes bring us to true knowledge of self and true knowledge of God. We are found dying and helpless, yet God is found near and merciful.

FOR REFLECTION AND DISCUSSION

1. What is your experience with Ash Wednesday?
2. Ash Wednesday brings us face-to-face with our mortality and salvation. As you think on your mortality, what do you feel? As you think of being fully known and loved by God, what do you feel?
3. Read through Psalms 51 and 103. What do you want to say to the Lord? What do you sense the Lord saying to you?

First Week

The Triple Temptation

Genesis 2:4–9, 15–17, 25; 3:1–7
Psalm 51
Romans 5:12–21
Matthew 4:1–11

Now the serpent was more crafty than any other
beast of the field that the LORD God had made.
He said to the woman, "Did God actually say,
'You shall not eat of any tree in the garden'?"

—Genesis 3:1

Almighty God, whose blessed Son was led by the Spirit
to be tempted by Satan: Come quickly to help us who
are assaulted by many temptations, and, as you know
the weaknesses of each of us, let each one find you
mighty to save; through Jesus Christ your Son our
Lord, who lives and reigns with you and the Holy Spirit, one God, now and for ever. Amen.[1]

In Lent, we return to the fundamental realities of life: human need and divine mercy. It's therefore fitting to begin the season attending to the first book of Scripture, Genesis. Genesis is like a mural of human history—truth in bright color and story—and at its heart is tragedy that enters through temptation.

"I can resist everything except temptation," Oscar Wilde, the Victorian aesthete and writer, has a character say in *Lady Windermere's Fan.*[2] Maybe you can relate. Temptation is not something limited to gambling addicts or serial adulterers. Temptation does not discriminate; its hooks come for us all.

The fundamental temptation arrives in Genesis 3:1 when the serpent says to the first woman and, by extension, the first man: "Did God actually say, 'You shall not eat of any tree in the garden'?" If we attend to our reading passage, we recognize that God has said nothing of the sort (2:16–17). Shouldn't the serpent's prompting be an easy rejection, like swatting an already-dead fly? All the woman must do is say, "No, you've got it all wrong. He said we can eat of any tree except one. Everything is pretty much ours." This, of course, is not what happens. The woman—as well as the man—swallows the bait of temptation and responds this way:

> The woman said to the serpent, "We may eat of the fruit of the trees in the garden, but God said, 'You shall not eat of the fruit of the tree that is in the midst of the garden, neither shall you touch it, lest you die.'" (3:2–3)

The Temptation of the Anti-Word

What is happening here? The serpent wins a hellish victory through the sly suggestion that God is not a good creator but a harsh withholder. Both Satan and his bait to disbelieve God's word and goodness are the "anti-Word."[3] The very framing of the question puts God's goodness on trial. And once this tempting premise is engaged, the verdict is already certain, forming in the minds of the first humans: *If this God isn't that great, then it would be good for us to violate what he said and chart our own path.* The woman swallows the bait, even adding a prohibition God never gave. She enters the debate on faulty ground, emphasizing the one prohibition rather than the great permission that everything God has is ours.

This fundamental temptation of the anti-Word is a living mural that presents itself in every corner of the world, standing before you at every waking moment. Nearly every decision you make is connected to the question of God's goodness or God's withholding. The anti-Word unlocks the door for disaster to break in, but there are three other reasons for humanity's plunge into ruin—a triple temptation that actively threatens us.

Pleasure, Possessions, and Pride

First John 2:16 illumines the extensive nature of temptation, saying, "Everything in the world—the lust of the flesh, the lust of the eyes, and the pride of life—comes not from the Father but from the world" (NIV). Early Christians discovered in this verse the hellish heartbeat of a triple temptation. This verse holds a key that unlocks the dynamics of temptation in Genesis 3:6:

When the woman saw that the tree was good for food,
and that it was a delight to the eyes, and that the tree
was to be desired to make one wise, she took of its
fruit and ate, and she also gave some to her husband
who was with her, and he ate.

"The lust of the flesh" occurred through the temptation of
pleasure when the first woman "saw that the tree was good for
food." "The lust of the eyes" transpired when the woman saw
that the tree was "a delight to the eyes"; early Christians,
working from 1 John 2:16, viewed this as the temptation of
possession. "The pride of life" came into play when she saw
that "the tree was to be desired to make one wise." The triple
temptation, then, is fundamentally about enshrining ourselves
through self-gratification (*pleasure*), self-accumulation (*possessions*), and self-exaltation (*pride*).

Again, Genesis is a living mural history of the human
family—our glory and our fall, primarily through the exaltation of self over against our Creator. Joan Chittister writes,
"Lent is the period in which, learning to abstain from adoring
at the shrine of the self, we come to see beyond the divinity
we have made of ourselves to the divine will for all the world."[4]
As those who share in this family resemblance, each of us must
consider how we have fallen prey to the triple temptation to
displace God and enshrine ourselves and our wants.

Lent itself is easily shifted into a self-improvement project,
a merely religious way to worship at the shrine of self. The
Today show's reframing of Lent as a forty-day challenge named
after a religious celebrity actor is one glaring proof. But so are
our Lenten attempts to make the season highly personalized
rather than communal, rooted in goals of optimizing ourselves
rather than attending to God. Our personal fasts can easily
become a badge of uniqueness or elitism when not, at some

level, shared in community. If my Lenten fasts are exclusive and highly personalized—if I fast only from my favorite show or my niche hobby—there's little that unites me with Christ's body, and soon, Lent becomes "my" thing, another way to express my singular identity. Discussion about Lent with other believers simply becomes a platform to compare notes on all our unique fasts rather than on our shared experience of attending to Christ. In this way, Lenten fasts can become just another way we gorge ourselves on self-centeredness.

In reality, Lent is not about self-improvement or personal uniqueness. Lent is God's gift to us meant to shatter the shrine of self and return us to his throne of grace.

Curbed, but Not Cured

We experience this return and renewal in part through the spiritual practices of the season. Fasting curbs our self-gratification and our obsession with indulgence and pleasure. Almsgiving battles against our obsession with more. Prayer moves us away from pride and toward humility before God. The core practices of Lent are painted in the family mural as weapons of righteousness in the battle scene against the triple temptation. Done in the light of God's grace, they are means God uses to curb our self-worship and to push back on the trifold temptation. Yet while these practices curb, they do not cure.

The "shrine of the self" is implanted inside us through sin. Our Romans 5 passage refers to Genesis 3 to tell us that through Adam, death and sin entered the world and are powers we are subject to. What can overcome sin and death? No practice can. Only a representative who succeeds where we have failed.

In Matthew 4:1–11, Jesus is assaulted by the same anti-

Word and the same triple temptation that plagued the first humans and threatens us. When Satan, first active through the serpent in Genesis 3, entices Jesus to turn stones to bread, the temptation is one of self-gratification: to bow to pleasure over God's will. When Satan tries to lure Jesus into getting all the glory of the world by pledging himself to Satan, the temptation is to bow to possessions and the lust of the eyes. When Satan urges Jesus to cast himself down from the temple's pinnacle and be rescued, the temptation is to flaunt his self-exaltation and bow to the pride of life.

Maybe you're thinking, *Well, of course Jesus overcame these temptations. He's God after all, right?* Yes, but Jesus was truly human. His temptation was as real as ours, only more difficult. Christian author C. S. Lewis illumines the issue: "Only those who try to resist temptation know how strong it is. . . . We never find out the strength of the evil impulse inside us until we try to fight it: and Christ, because He was the only man who never yielded to temptation, is also the only man who knows to the full what temptation means."[5] Jesus knew a harsher temptation than we will ever taste, yet he stood firm.

A deeper appreciation of Jesus's faithfulness emerges when we consider the nature of his third temptation. In Matthew 4:8–10, Jesus is tempted to rule all the world through a simple and secret bowing of the knee—not to God but to Satan. Jesus wasn't asked to become an atheist or to deny God—only to bow to the enemy. To gain all the kingdoms, all possessions, all things without suffering on the cross. Jesus is offered a short-cut to glory, a fast track to lordship over the world. And Jesus refuses, for without a cross, such a deal would result in a humanity without hope. Why? The shrine of self and the penalty of sin would still stand.

Jesus understands that the mural must be fulfilled, the story of humanity must be redeemed, and where we failed under lesser tests, he must stand strong under the great tests that in Adam devoured us whole. Jesus succeeds where we failed, and in his victory, a new portion of the mural of human history is painted.

How do you overcome the anti-Word and the triple temptation? Only through the Overcomer himself. God is not a withholder but a gracious giver. He gives us the world. We plunged this world into ruin, yet he gives us life again through Jesus who walks in our place and overcomes what brought us into devastation. We locked hands and hearts with evil, but in refusing the triple temptation, Christ overcomes it—for us—and marches headlong toward the Cross.

FOR REFLECTION AND DISCUSSION

1. If the fundamental temptation is to see God not as good but as cruel, not as generous but as withholding, where do you most see this temptation in your life? Which biblical passages or insights from this week's devotion can help you see God rightly?

2. Of the triple temptation (pleasure, possessions, and pride), which feels most threatening to you? What spiritual practices can help you curb this temptation?

3. How might these passages help shape your devotional life and your mindset as we embark on the journey of Lent?

Second Week

The Hero's Journey

Genesis 12:1–9

Psalm 33:12–21

Romans 4:1–5, 13–17

John 3:1–16

Now the Lord said to Abram, "Go from your
country and your kindred and your father's
house to the land that I will show you."

—Genesis 12:1

Almighty God, you know that we have no power in
ourselves to help ourselves: Keep us both outwardly in
our bodies and inwardly in our souls, that we may be
defended from all adversities that may happen to the
body, and from all evil thoughts that may assault and
hurt the soul; through Jesus Christ our Lord, who lives
and reigns with you and the Holy Spirit, one God, for
ever and ever. Amen.[1]

God loves to bless the world. Five times in Genesis 12:1–9, God is obsessed with blessing. This is all well and good. Yet the good gets better when we zoom out to consider all that has come before God's blessings. In Genesis 3–11, humanity enacts three catastrophic evils:

- Genesis 3 recounts what theologians call "the Fall." The first humans reject God through their desire to replace him by falling prey to the fundamental temptation that God is cruel and untrustworthy. The fallout of humanity's sin is an exile from God's presence, a fracture of all creation, and the introduction and extension of evil and death into every part of life.

- By the time we reach Genesis 6, humanity has accomplished a tragic achievement. The world is so deeply plunged into sin that humans are described as contemplating wickedness and evil always—to the point "the LORD regretted that he had made man on the earth, and it grieved him to his heart" (verse 6). God then washes the world clean in a flood of judgment and renewal in the story of Noah's ark.

- In Genesis 11, humanity wants to make their name great by controlling God through a tower, called Babel, where he will reside.[2] God comes down not to be controlled but to confuse them and their languages as the due judgment for their sinful arrogance.

There are futility and frustration at every turn. Genesis 11 ends with a list of names and the record of a barren woman (verse 30). It seems like this may be the final cycle of the human story. Things are *that* bad. Instead, God speaks. In Genesis 12:1–4, God declares to a wandering nomad a staggering promise to bless him and, through him, all the families of the earth caught in the fallen cycle of evil. God is revealed not as simply kind but as promise-keeping, obsessed at every turn with upending the never-ending cycle of human evil with divine mercy.

The Journey Out of Self

This blessing centers on a hinge that comes to a person, a man named Abram. The hinge is a one-word call: Go. To receive the promise, Abram (later renamed Abraham) must leave behind the familiar. It's not hard to sense the gravity of this call to go. There is no FaceTime available, nor could Abram expect an eventual family reunion with printed T-shirts. The call to go is the funeral of his past life and the launching of a life into the unknown. Through the Lord's blessing centered on the word "go," Abram is to be born again, and so will the world if we follow his leap into the journey of faith.

God's word of promised blessing calls us out of ourselves and into the true spiritual journey. The problem is that most refuse the call precisely because it launches us into the unknown. The refusal of the call is such a fundamental human challenge that it is ubiquitous in our arts and stories. Movie fans know refusing the call to adventure is part of the deep structure of all films, as far ranging in genre as *Star Wars* and *Legally Blonde*. Whether the protagonist stands on the brink of leaving Tatooine or heading to law school at Harvard, these stories are riffing on the archetypal reality of Abram's call to go.

If we're honest, wouldn't we give Abram a pass if he refused the call precisely because of the risk of the unknown?

"Go to the land I will show you." Few, if any, of us—even in our adventurous moments—look at a map and then decide to drive around with no known destination. It's nonsensical and dangerous. As an ancient patriarch, Abram had many people under his care, and his decisions shaped their livelihoods. What, then, enabled Abram to make the journey? The strength of the promise. He believed God's promise, and it was counted to him as righteousness (Genesis 15:6).

The Inner Journey and the Gospel Call

Abram's trek has both a literal element and a spiritual element. In calling him to go from his home, God leads Abram on a journey that is as much internal and spiritual as it is physical and historical. Some Jewish rabbis find in Abram's call an inner call to "go out to yourself."[3] There may be some wisdom to such an observation. Abram embarks on a journey that is not only traceable on a map but also walked out in his soul.

Abram's excursion is not simply self-guided. He is not an ancient prototype of a successful friend who quits a high-paying job to travel for a year to find themselves. Self-discovery apart from the promise of God is a contradiction in terms. If we seek to find ourselves apart from God's promises, we simply end up lost and knotted up in our own pride or despair.

Abram does not call himself to the journey; it begins with the call of God and has a destination: a place with God, a life with God, and an assurance of being God's blessing to others. The same is true for you. No matter your résumé, income level, checkered history, beleaguered present, or murky future, your life is not aimless if you take up this call.

The voice that said "Go" to Abram is the same voice of the same promise-keeping God who walked among the devastation and glory of real human life, among real, complex humans, and then lifted his voice: "Follow me . . . and I will make you fish for people" (Matthew 4:19, csb). The God who spoke to Abram has spoken his word to us—the gospel word of blessing, that through Abram's seed, Jesus of Nazareth, we have life with God and all the gifts this life entails. Through Abram's seed, we relinquish the shrine of self and become an outpost of blessing. Through Abram's seed, the evil of this world will be undone. That is the glorious destination that awaits all who come to Jesus, all who are caught up into his journey of redemption.

How do we receive this gift? Like Abram, we trust God and his promise and go on this journey of faith (Romans 4:2–3). Life with God results not from our good works but from the favor of God given by grace through faith—our faith to say yes to God's "Go," which is a call to come to Jesus, follow him, and be led by him into eternal life.

Lent is one segment within the broader journey of the Christian life. For forty days, we enter the story of Jesus from his temptation to the Cross. This is the time to ask God for the courage and faith to not refuse his gracious call. It is the time to enter the heroic journey, to walk in the thrill of faith. What's your next step of faith with Jesus? German theologian Joseph Ratzinger (Pope Benedict XVI) once said, "We were not created for an easy life, but for great things, for goodness."[4] To meet God's gospel promise with personal trust—even if it's faint—is the hero's journey because it is the good and royal purpose for which you were made.

The Journey of Abraham's Seed

God's blessing comes to us in Jesus, the seed of Abraham (Galatians 3:14, 29). Like Abraham, Jesus went out from his Father's house, one more glorious than the Old Testament patriarch ever knew. Jesus went out from the company of angels to the land that he made. He went on the hero's journey to free people from the shrine of self. There were turns in Abraham's journey when he came to the land and it was occupied by the Canaanites (Genesis 12:5–8). Jesus came to the land that was occupied by death and Satan, who delights in the fracture of God's good world. Yet Jesus saw the occupied land, understood the stakes, and, with his face set like flint, journeyed on for our sakes.

At the right time, Jesus did not shy away from the march to the cross on which he died. Abraham's journey and Israel's journey are central to the story. But the journey of Jesus that we follow in these days of Lent—from his temptation to his cross to his resurrection from the dead that gives us new life with God—is the one that enables our own.

FOR REFLECTION AND DISCUSSION

1. Reflect on or write out your spiritual journey thus far. What was your "go" moment? Where are you now? What is Christ doing in you?
2. What have you been learning about the adventure of faith with Jesus through the journey of Lent so far?
3. What ideas or comforts hinder you from going deeper with Jesus in the journey of faith?

Third Week

A World of Thirst

Exodus 17:1–7

Psalm 63

Romans 1:16–32

John 4:5–26, 39–42

Jesus answered her, "If you knew the gift of
God, and who it is that is saying to you, 'Give
me a drink,' you would have asked him, and he
would have given you living water."

—John 4:10

Heavenly Father, you have made us for yourself, and
our hearts are restless until they rest in you: Look with
compassion upon the heartfelt desires of your servants,
and purify our disordered affections, that we may behold your eternal glory in the face of Christ Jesus; who
lives and reigns with you and the Holy Spirit, one God,
for ever and ever. Amen.[1]

"If one man were to . . . give form to every feeling, expression to every thought, reality to every dream . . . the world would gain such a fresh impulse of joy. . . . But the bravest man amongst us is afraid of himself. . . . We are punished for our refusals."[2] This is what Lord Henry Wotton, a character in the 1891 novel *The Picture of Dorian Gray*, says to the young, impressionable protagonist. The message is that to repress any desire is wrong but to express all desire is to truly live.

The theme of desire runs through each of our Scripture readings. In Exodus 17, we watch the drama of desire as the people of God journey through the wilderness. Psalm 95 reflects on this wilderness drama. In Romans 1, the apostle Paul offers a piercing reflection on desire and idolatry. Then, in John 4, we see the healing and fulfillment of desire in the presence of Jesus. These passages are not museum artifacts, and you are not a detached reader. God addresses us through his written Word, which is living and active (Hebrews 4:12).

We can't be all that disinterested because at the center of each of our beings is a well of desires that spring into various actions and choices. If you attended church this past week, you were there because of some desire, some thirst. Even your last post on social media was because of desire. Your most recent lie stemmed from desire.

You're also alive at a fascinating time. Ours is in an era where we're defined by our desires. And no one, we are often told, should ever defy desire. The spirit of Lord Henry is thick and alluring. If the old guard wanted all desires repressed, the new guard says pretty much all desires must be expressed. Christianity says both are half-truths and therefore full lies.

All Thirst

Our desires are a sign of thirst. However, we must drink not from wells of our own making but from the well that heals and satisfies. And this is what makes Exodus 17 so fascinating. To fulfill the desire of his people, God brings them to the wilderness. To satisfy their deepest thirst, God brings them to a place with no water. Why? To teach that desire is to be shaped by experience. More specifically, the experience of God's mercy is meant to rewire our desires.

Let's recall Israel's story: They cried to God to be set free from slavery, and God rescued them with signs and wonders (Exodus 7–12). Now they're in the wilderness on the way to the promised land, and they're grumbling for water. God answers in Exodus 15 with the miracle of sweet water. In the next chapter, the people grumble because they yearn for food, and God answers by raining down bread from heaven. They have experienced rescue, and now they are experiencing provision. God rescued a people, and now he is forming their hearts through the wilderness. Instead of yearning for the easy way out when trouble comes, instead of being controlled by their lowest appetites—food, water, sex, comfort—God is forming them to withstand and to trust. He is enlarging their souls by reshaping their desires.

Think of these scriptural words that teach us to thirst for the deeper desires:

Man shall not live by bread alone, but by every word that comes from the mouth of God. (Matthew 4:4)

I consider that our present sufferings are not worth comparing with the glory that will be revealed in us. (Romans 8:18, NIV)

If it is hard for us to say these things with straight faces and honest hearts, it is because our desires for God are too weak. God gives us experiences of thirsting and waiting to reshape and enlarge our desires. He expands the capacities of our souls. Instead of seeing the waiting and disappointment as a healing, stretching work, Israel believed they were abandoned. Exodus 17 is a mirror of our disordered desires. If a good thing or desire is withheld from us, we think, *Where is God?* This is the mistake of living by a "what have you done for me lately" theology. This deadly theology says, "God must come through right now or else we're finding an idol." Which is precisely what Israel will do in the chapters to come. We need more than the wilderness experience to mend our desires because, as Romans 1 teaches us, idolatry has bent them.

Thirsty Souls at Broken Wells

In my early days as a church planter without an office, I would often work at a Panera Bread. While the staff was kind, the music was horrible. The place had only one playlist, so I'd hear the same generic pop songs on repeat. Once while I was digging into Romans 1, I heard these lyrics from the chorus of a popular American Authors song: "Do whatever I want, like I'm born to run."[3] In this case, the playlist was providential. "Do whatever I want" sounds like freedom, but without a virtuous, redeemed, enlarged heart, it is a sign of divine judgment. Romans 1:28 spells this out clearly: "Since they did not see fit to acknowledge God, God gave them up to a debased mind to do what ought not to be done." Idolatry results in unchecked desires. God hands us over to ourselves, and that is a dangerous place to be.

For Paul's original hearers, the proof of the judgment on unchecked desires—specifically sexual immorality and violence—

would be clear from a glance at society's rulers as well as society itself. Paul is writing to a people and place whose emperor took for his sexual pleasure any man or woman he wanted and would kill any family member that might threaten his power. Paul writes of a Gentile world with no bounds and no creed but the spirit of Lord Henry. But then the tables are turned on all of us in Romans 2:1. Note the shift in the language from "they" to "you":

> Therefore you have no excuse, O man, every one of you who judges. For in passing judgment on another you condemn yourself, because you, the judge, practice the very same things.

This web of sinful desire is one in which *all* find themselves trapped. How do we get free from our disordered affections? God in Jesus comes near to heal. You will always thirst until you drink deep from the truth that through Jesus alone, the eternal God crowns you his beloved child and precious possession. The problem is less our desires and more our foolish returns to broken wells. Resolve to go to the One who gives living water.

The Rock and the Cross

A satisfaction is given in and with Jesus that even pain and suffering cannot steal. With Jesus, you are promised to one day never thirst again. Jesus by the grace of his gospel plants a new set of desires that springs up inside you. These desires lead to eternal life—knowing God and knowing that God knows you fully and embraces you completely (John 17:3). How can this happen to small, wayward, thirsty hearts?

The answer is found in a return to Exodus 17. Before water flows from the rock, something wonderfully strange happens. Read verse 6: "Behold, I will stand before you there on the rock at Horeb, and you shall strike the rock, and water shall come out of it, and the people will drink."

Before the rock is struck, the Lord stands before it. This is a picture of the Cross. Jesus gives himself so that the water of eternal life—the fulfillment of all human longing satisfied with God—will flow into the real world, to real people with good or bent desires, shrunken hearts, crooked pasts, and deep idolatry. Water flowed from the rock, just as water and blood flowed from the Savior's pierced side (John 19:34). This is why Romans 1 can boldly say the gospel is the power of God for salvation. We know he can satisfy because he gave himself for us.

FOR REFLECTION AND DISCUSSION

1. What have you learned about your desires through the journey of Lent thus far?
2. How does God often use "wilderness" experiences to shape our desires? How have you experienced this in your life?
3. What do you find yourself thirsty for (praise, acceptance, fame, control, power, etc.)? What does the Lord want you to do with these desires?

Fourth Week

The Gaze of Mercy

Micah 6:1–8
Psalm 37:1–11
1 Corinthians 1:18–31
Matthew 5:1–12

Blessed are the merciful,
for they shall receive mercy.

—Matthew 5:7

Gracious Father, whose blessed Son Jesus Christ came down from heaven to be the true bread which gives life to the world: Evermore give us this bread, that he may live in us, and we in him; who lives and reigns with you and the Holy Spirit, one God, now and for ever. Amen.[1]

The opening words of the Sermon on the Mount are some of the most well known in world history. How are we to hear and understand them? Are they an impossible ideal, something we should aim for but can never live up to? Are they a Lenten discipleship exam, a measuring stick to see how much of a disciple you really are?

The Sermon on the Mount is not an unachievable ideal or an exam to dread; it is the revelation of a world. Jesus's words pull back the curtain to reveal reality—to unveil what's true, who is blessed, and how reality works. It shouldn't surprise us that something much deeper than a test or standard of perfection is happening in Jesus's words. It's Jesus. And he's on a mountain. This reminds us of Moses on Mount Sinai mediating God's revelation to his people (Exodus 19–20). Jesus is in an exalted place speaking exalted words. He speaks a message sorely needed and worthy of our attention: "Blessed are the merciful, for they shall receive mercy."

The Unbreakable Bond of Mercy

Mercy is an expression of love in two brushstrokes: a withholding of punishment—thus including forgiveness—and a supplying of aid to those in need. John Calvin, the sixteenth-century theologian, described the merciful as those "who are not only prepared to endure their own afflictions, but to take a share in the afflictions of others."[2]

To call mercy a challenge is to earn an advanced degree in understatement. We are often masters of suspicion, highly skilled in furtive glances and cold attitudes toward people who seem a tad shady. We are adept at envying those who receive the credit we think we deserve. We are proficient with our mental gavels, offering harsh judgment toward anyone who messes up royally and publicly. We know how to practice hostility toward people we brand morally, culturally, and intellectually backward. But do we know how to be merciful?

Mercy is not a spiritual elective. In Matthew, Jesus's exalted words consistently reveal an unbreakable bond between showing mercy and receiving mercy. The Lord's Prayer, which Jesus teaches on this same hill, reveals the same point of Matthew 5:7 from a fresh angle. Most churches pray the Lord's Prayer every Sunday, yet it's easy to forget the radical nature of what we say when we entreat the Lord:

> Forgive us our debts,
> > as we also have forgiven our debtors. (6:12)

Matthew reveals Jesus is deeply concerned with this merciful way of living. In 6:14–15, Jesus states, "If you forgive others their trespasses, your heavenly Father will also forgive you, but if you do not forgive others their trespasses, neither will your Father forgive your trespasses." Later, Jesus teaches the same point in a parable about an unforgiving servant and a master (18:21–35).

What's all this mean? In Matthew, Jesus reveals that mercy is not optional. Biblical commentator Dale Bruner sums it up well: "Fullness of received mercy exists to be passed on, not stored up."[3] With three emphatic teachings in Matthew—once in the Beatitudes, once in the church's definitive prayer, and once in a parable featured in all four Gospels—Jesus says mercy is essential to the life of faith. Receiving mercy is tied to showing mercy. Have you embraced or overlooked the inseparable bond between these two?

Missing Mercy, Missing God

If we miss the unbreakable bond of mercy, then we miss something deep about the nature of God. Mercy is not optional to a faith-filled life, because it is core to the very nature of God. The movement of mercy begins with God.

Think back to another mountain encounter: God and Moses on Mount Sinai. Moses is being formally and terrifyingly introduced to the Lord. What does the Lord do? He makes the most important thing about him clear to Moses. Exodus 34:6 paints the picture: "The LORD passed before him and proclaimed, 'The LORD, the LORD, a God merciful and gracious, slow to anger, and abounding in steadfast love and faithfulness.'"

Knowing God means knowing the One who is mercy. The way to mercy is a continual felt understanding of who God is. Lent is the season to be reintroduced to God, who makes himself known to us in his glory and mercy.

The Meaning of Mercy: The Gaze and the Gut

Imagine sitting at a coffee shop or on the stoop of a busy street and people watching, judging each person on their looks, style, and appearance. Imagine seeing a man with tattered clothes that expose his midsection as he staggers along, trailed by a putrid stench. You know what it would be like to judge this man. Yet mercy would see him not with judgment but with compassion.

God's grace gazes on us in our guilt and responds with an undeserved forgiveness. And God's mercy gazes on us in our hurt or distress and supplies compassion and help regardless of our merits. Understanding God as merciful makes us merciful, for we understand ourselves as those who need and receive mercy from his divine heart. Your deep need and personal history are met with his tender mercy.

Mercy consists of the gaze and the gut. Consider the words of 1 John 3:17 in the regal King James Version: "Whoso hath this world's good, and seeth his brother have need, and shutteth up his bowels of compassion from him, how dwelleth the love of God in him?" Mercy is a matter of how we view those in distress and how we feel about and respond to them in their hardship.

No one understood that mercy is a matter of one's gaze and one's gut better than Jesus, the image of the invisible and merciful God. Jesus's sight and inner being were molded in mercy. Matthew 9:36 says, "When he saw the crowds, he had compassion for them." On another occasion, "he saw a great crowd, and he had compassion on them and healed their sick" (14:14).

When humanity was trapped in sin, the triune God saw and willed in his eternal heart to seek us. Compassion means sharing in the suffering of another. That's mercy of the highest degree. If this is who God is for us, then who are we to withhold mercy from anyone? God's mercy molds us to live mercifully.

The Rival to Mercy

Rather than tender mercy, we often operate in hidden cruelty. Try to live out mercy and you'll find something in you wars against it, stifling and replacing the virtue with cheap and destructive alternatives. When you see bad things happen to bad people, what do your gaze and gut say? When we see someone stressed with a broken-down car on the side of the road, sometimes the first impulse of our gazes and guts is to be glad it isn't us. Eventually, we may extend kindness. But still, our first internal instinct is often not mercy's compassion but cruelty's coldness.

For centuries, Christians have identified envy as mercy's fiercest enemy. Mercy is a heavenly virtue, while envy is a hellish vice. Mercy is sadness at someone's misfortune; envy is sadness at someone's success—or happiness at someone's misery.[4] Envy comes in silently through a fixation on us. Mercy, however, grows in the soul through a fixed gaze on the mercy of God and the need of one's neighbors.

Things are complicated in our time as we have access to endless stories of misery around the world. To cope with the onslaught, we develop selective mercy. Thinking we have only a set portion of compassion, we budget out our mercy, spending it on certain people and situations. Often, selective mercy becomes performative mercy. *I'll care here, I'll give here, and I'll cry here so everyone knows that I'm doing what Jesus says and that I'm not like those mean Christians over there*, each of us may think to ourselves.

In your envy, in your secret cruelty, in your sin—the exalted Christ comes not in words but in the flesh to atone and renew. The mercy of God has come to us. On one hill, Jesus teaches us mercy. But on Calvary's hill, he enacts mercy so that we would receive it. God's mercy molds us to live mercifully by destroying the hold of vices that keep us from mercy. You already have his mercy. Now see with his eyes. Feel with his gut. This is neither your impossible ideal nor your discipleship exam. This is your biography. By mercy, Jesus is remaking us to show forth his mercy to the praise of his glorious grace.

FOR REFLECTION AND DISCUSSION

1. How would you define mercy? Can you think of a time when you experienced or extended it?
2. Why is receiving mercy connected to extending mercy? How does this connection draw us to contemplate Christ?
3. How might God be calling you to receive his mercy? Are there particular relationships in which God is calling you toward receiving or extending mercy?

Fifth Week

The Lord's Tears

Ezekiel 37:1–14
Psalm 130
Romans 6:15–23
John 11:18–44

Jesus wept.

—John 11:35

Almighty God, you alone can bring into order the unruly wills and affections of sinners: Grant your people grace to love what you command and desire what you promise; that, among the swift and varied changes of this world, our hearts may surely there be fixed where true joys are to be found; through Jesus Christ our Lord, who lives and reigns with you and the Holy Spirit, one God, now and for ever. Amen.[1]

The shortest verse in the Bible—"Jesus wept"—can be confusing. This whole tragic situation over which he weeps could have been prevented. Martha and Mary get word to Jesus that their brother, Lazarus, is in really bad shape (John 11:3). Jesus receives the news but comes across as unconcerned:

> When Jesus heard it he said, "This illness does not lead to death. It is for the glory of God, so that the Son of God may be glorified through it."
>   Now Jesus loved Martha and her sister and Lazarus. So, when he heard that Lazarus was ill, he stayed two days longer in the place where he was. (verses 4–6)

Why does Jesus wait? And why does he weep when his delay seems to be the source of the tragedy? What's with the waiting? What's with the weeping?

Waiting and Weeping

Jesus waiting to arrive is strange because we consider speed to be a sign of care. The more something matters, the sooner it should be attended to. No one says, "My love language is a late arrival." No bride or groom shows up late to their wedding as a demonstration of their unflagging devotion.

It's also strange because it is a sign of tremendous vulnerability from the human face of God. No matter how we try to untangle ourselves from the lies that crying signals weakness or that men should not cry, it's a phenomenon when the powerful weep. We saw this unassailable evidence with an internet meme. During his 2009 Basketball Hall of Fame induction speech, Michael Jordan, the global basketball legend, began to cry. The photo of that moment became the Crying Jordan

meme. One of the greatest athletes of all time, with an estimated net worth of $3.5 billion, stood at the podium with
reddened eyes and streaks of tears winding down his cheeks.
Why did this photo become so popular? One former media
theory professor is quoted as saying, "It's the ultimate alpha
[male] in a vulnerable position."[2] In another sense, such vulnerability from a persona so powerful and revered is a target
for both ridicule and admiration.

There is, then, a surprising revelation about God in the
waiting and weeping in John 11 that we must not glide past
but slowly contemplate. Why the waiting? Jesus can wait because he is fully tapped into the work the Father has given him
to do. When you are so singularly minded, so controlled by a
vision, that you can't help but see everything else in relation to
it, you have "tunnel vision." Jesus possessed the most compassionate and holy tunnel vision known to humankind, though
he described it in culinary terms: "My food is to do the will
of him who sent me and to accomplish his work" (John 4:34).

So, when the sisters' message, saying the one he loves so
much is flatlining, Jesus, controlled by the work of salvation,
sees the full picture. He views Lazarus's illness through his
larger work of making the glory of God public. So, he waits.
Then he weeps. Then he resurrects.

Waiting and Weeping from Our Perspective

Doesn't it seem harder to be in Mary's and Martha's shoes?
Think for a minute from the sisters' point of view. They know
Jesus could have gotten to town in two days instead of four
days, and they cannot make sense of the delay. If Jesus is able—
and he is—why the no-show? Why the waiting? Certainly,
you or someone dear to you can relate. Perhaps you've come
to God expressing both faith and need. Perhaps you've prayed

diligently, asking God not for riches or for fame but for his will in your life according to his Word. Maybe you've prayed fervently for his will in the life of your kids or your friends. And then nothing.

One of the great lessons of waiting in this moving encounter is that sometimes God delays in order to demonstrate. At times, God will delay his action to do something greater— not at this time but in due time. Disciples must seek to become comfortable with the discomfort of waiting, like Mary and Martha did. If we live in allegiance to Jesus, love him, and are loved by him, we have to enroll in the same classes as Mary, Martha, and Lazarus. We must grow accustomed to the waiting. Because sometimes, in his omniscience and his omni-but-mysterious kindness, God waits to work in power.

Tokens in the Waiting

The delay doesn't negate his goodness. In fact, God supplies tokens of his goodness in the waiting. Jesus gives his word to comfort Martha: "I am the resurrection and the life . . . and everyone who lives and believes in me shall never die" (John 11:25–26).

That Jesus rose from the dead means you can face any delay, any unanswered prayer, any trauma, or any loss because at the end of the age, what awaits you is a joy and glory to which no pain can compare. It's a glory that will rewind every regret, heal every wound, and right every wrong. It is the glory of seeing God in the face of Jesus Christ. Hold to the word Jesus offers all of us in our waiting: "I am the resurrection and the life."

Still, I know it can be hard to do this. Most American funerals are marked by composed decorum. In many other cultures, it's the opposite. The loud wailing and weeping over

Lazarus are signals of love. A rich family like Mary's and Martha's would have hired professional wailing women and flute players in a procession of mourning. When Mary rushes to meet him, Jesus is "deeply moved in his spirit and greatly troubled" (verse 33), and then he weeps. Why does Jesus weep if he is the one who caused the waiting? Why does he cry if in his divine nature he knows what he plans to do? Jesus weeps because of the size of his heart and scope of his love. What do the Judeans say in verse 36? "See how he loved him!" There are layers to every tear that rolled down the Savior's cheeks. Yes, Jesus was weeping for his close friend. Yet he was also crying for us and all who are placed under the hold of death.

As Jesus gets close to our great enemy, his heart is pierced with anger and sadness at what death has done to us because of sin's hold. Let his tears interpret your own. We can see his tears and marvel, "See how he loves us." Trust him in the waiting because we have the record of his weeping and we know that resurrection awaits.

FOR REFLECTION AND DISCUSSION

1. How have you understood Jesus's tears over Lazarus's death? What strikes you most as you consider this encounter?
2. How do Jesus's tears challenge our cultural notions of strength, leadership, and power?
3. What delays in your life have led you to question God's goodness and love? What hope can you draw from Jesus's engagement with Mary, Martha, and Lazarus?

HOLY WEEK

The Journey to Redemption

True and humble king, hailed by the crowd
as Messiah: grant us the faith to know you
and love you, that we may be found
beside you on the way of the cross, which is
the path of glory. Amen.[1]

H oly Week, the week between Palm Sunday and Easter
Sunday, draws us into the mystery of the gospel. It
concludes Lent and leads us into the most significant
and sacred days in world history. At the start of Holy Week,
the gospel narratives portray Jesus's last earthly days, which are
full of parables and teaching about his identity, the kingdom,
the hypocrisy of the religious leaders, and, of course, his impending death. Typically, specific church services are not held
to memorialize the events early in Holy Week.

However, Holy Week then reaches its apex in its last three
days: Maundy Thursday, Good Friday, and Saturday's Easter
Vigil, which leads into Easter Sunday. Christians throughout
history have called these the Great Three Days, or the Triduum.
These are the days set aside to remember Jesus's suffering,
death, burial, and glorious resurrection, and they include the
most crucial services of the church year. As we step into Holy

Week, we enter again into the meaning of our salvation and God's saving love for us and this fallen world.

Palm Sunday commemorates Jesus's triumphal entry into Jerusalem as Lord and King and his entrance into the final days of his earthly life. This vital moment in salvation history fulfills scriptural prophecy (Zechariah 9:9) and reveals Christ as King. In many liturgical churches, the Palm Sunday service includes a special procession (entrance) in which the whole congregation enters the church together, often holding palm branches, as a reenactment of Jesus's entry into Jerusalem. The Scripture readings for Palm Sunday preview the major movements of Holy Week.

Holy Monday and **Holy Tuesday** are closely linked as the days in which Jesus cleansed the temple, cursed the fig tree as a visual parable, and taught in vivid terms about the impending arrival of his kingdom. Working from a harmonized reading of the Gospels, most believe Monday centers on Jesus's cleansing of the temple while Tuesday centers on his teaching controversies. In this way, both days are filled with Jesus's stark and confrontational actions and teaching in the temple area, his rebuke of its religious leaders, and his staggering claims to divine identity and authority (Matthew 21:23–23:39).

Spy Wednesday reveals how the plan to kill Jesus kicked into high gear (Matthew 26:3–5; Mark 14:1–2; Luke 22:1–2). Judas, through Satan's devices, conspired to betray Jesus. This betrayal, in league with the religious leaders, is where this day takes its name, as Judas "sought an opportunity to betray" Jesus (Matthew 26:16).

On **Maundy Thursday,** we remember that Jesus instituted the Lord's Supper, served his disciples in the time of his great distress, and commanded us to love one another. (*Maundy* comes from the Latin term *mandatum,* meaning "commandment.")[2] The service may include foot washing and ends with the stripping of the communion table and a reading of Psalm 22. The stripping of the table represents the stripping of Jesus's garments in preparation for his death on the cross. As the table is emptied and we hear Psalm 22, we meditate on Jesus's suffering—his betrayal, his arrest, and ultimately his crucifixion.

Good Friday is a continuation of Maundy Thursday but now with our gaze fixed on the death of our Savior. There is a tension in our reflection on the Cross. We experience both sorrow, for "it was [our] sin that held Him there"[3] as we often sing, and a somber joy, for we know his death was itself a death blow to the whole of sin, our sin, and death itself. In this service, the use of black cloths on the communion table embodies the somber note as we mourn our sin and reflect on our Lord's rejection and suffering.

Holy Saturday, also known as Silent Saturday, testifies that Jesus died and was buried. Various denominations observe this day differently, emphasizing and reflecting on Jesus's descent to the dead, Joseph's burial of his body, and the disciples' resultant despair and confusion. Holy Saturday reminds us that God works even in the silence and that with Christ death is overcome by life.

Experiencing Holy Week

As you read the following Scripture texts and devotions, you'll notice a shift to daily devotionals. This will enable you to contemplate Christ through the week leading up to Maundy Thursday, Good Friday, and finally Easter Sunday. The most pivotal days of this week—Maundy Thursday and Good Friday—feature longer devotionals to immerse you in these crucial realities and to aid you, particularly if your church does not offer services on those days. Ask the Lord to lead and shape you as we enter Holy Week and journey into the very heart of the gospel story.

God's Mighty Acts

Isaiah 52:13–53:12
Psalm 22
Philippians 2:5–11
Luke 23:1–49

All his acquaintances and the women who had
followed him from Galilee stood at a distance
watching these things.

—Luke 23:49

As we stand on the edge of Holy Week, we acknowledge that in our own way, we too are right there, watching the last days of Jesus at a distance. Whether they acknowledge it or not, all people, throughout history, are caught up in the story of God. Holy Week wakes us from our slumber and carries us to the height of God's work in the world, the final earthly days of Jesus of Nazareth. Scripture carries us across time and space in even more than our five senses, for it is living and active (Hebrews 4:12). It has the power to collapse time and show us that what happened then is what defines reality even now.

Our Scripture readings form a biblical panorama, drawing us into the true story and sacred work of Christ and helping us, as the liturgy for Palm Sunday says, to "enter with joy upon the contemplation of those mighty acts."[1] God places before us mighty acts from the views of Isaiah the prophet, David the psalmist, Paul the apostle, and Luke the historian.

A Panorama of Redemption

Isaiah 53 shows us that Jesus is the suffering servant, the man of sorrows—even though on Palm Sunday he is the man of applause. As Psalm 22 moves us from the third to the first person, we hear Christ's words as he suffers for our sakes and our forgiveness, crying out, "My God, my God, why have you forsaken me?" (verse 1). In Philippians 2, the apostle Paul writes from prison, speaking of the wonder of Jesus's incarnation, humiliation, and exaltation. In Luke 22, Luke places us in the final days of our Lord from the garden to the cross to the empty tomb.

Together these readings envelop the whole of Holy Week and plunge us into the weight and wonder of God's mighty acts to rescue and renew the world. As one writer puts it, we now begin "a weeklong pilgrimage into a personal experience with Christ rejected, crucified, buried, and risen."[2] Jesus is calling you to take this pilgrimage—to set your mind on these mighty acts and to be defined by him by being defined by them.

In Luke 19:28–40, Jesus at long last takes the turn to enter the city of all cities (Jerusalem, the home of the temple) during the week of all weeks (the Passover celebration). Commentators describe Jerusalem at this time as a beehive, buzzing with rumors of revolution and tension. Roman soldiers roam the streets in staggering numbers. And Jesus's entry into the city is like whacking that beehive with a stick.[3] For this Palm Sunday entrance, he isn't traveling by foot; he is proceeding into the city on a donkey. Jesus is making a mighty statement. Centuries before Christ, Zechariah the prophet spoke of a royal procession: "Shout aloud, O daughter of Jerusalem! Behold, your king is coming to you; righteous and having salvation is he, humble and mounted on a donkey, on a colt, the foal of a donkey" (9:9). Jesus is laying claim to that crown.

And what do the disciples and crowds do? The word spreads in hushed tones and loud shouts: "Jesus from Nazareth is a few miles that way, and he's coming on a colt." Our closest American comparison is the buzz and shouts and noise of a championship parade. The people have received their king. Yet we know that the crowds will soon turn to reject him. From the east comes the march of Christ the Lord, the true and humble king. It's the trot not of warhorses but a single donkey. There are no swords in sight, only palm branches. There's no sound of a battle drum, just the shouts of praise, "Blessed is the King who comes in the name of the Lord!" (Luke 19:38). One procession inspires fear; the other would make even the stones worship.

Reflecting on Palm Sunday, African American minister Howard Thurman pondered, "I wonder what was moving through the mind of the Master as he jogged along on the back of that faithful donkey."[4] We don't know what is running through Jesus's mind, but we do have a sense about the disposition of his heart. Jesus has, Luke tells us, set his face toward Jerusalem (9:51). This echoes Isaiah, who said the suffering servant set his face like flint toward his goal (50:7).

Do you know what this means? Jesus takes this procession into conflict and death with purpose. Jesus determines to lay down his life for our salvation. He has "humbled himself by becoming obedient to the point of death, even death on a cross" (Philippians 2:8). In concert with the Father and Spirit, Jesus resolves to enter the cosmic conflict and subdue sin and death by offering himself to our fate. We cannot read his mind, but as he rides that donkey on the journey to the cross, we can know his heart. Marvel at the courage and love of our Lord.

Perched on his donkey, riding in to save us, Jesus knows who we really are: curved in on ourselves, fickle, performative, weak, sinful. Still, he determines to ride on for our sakes. To such might and mercy, all we can do is marvel and proclaim, "Blessed is the King who comes in the name of the Lord!"

Truth to Ponder: Jesus courageously marched toward the cross for our sakes, fully knowing our needs and weaknesses yet loving us to the end.

O Lord, you who were cheered and jeered by the very same crowd, have mercy, I pray, on my own duplicitous ways: confessing one sin openly, while hiding another; blessing God out of one side of my mouth, while cursing my neighbor out of the other; smiling in public but raging in private; lauding justice but denying it in practice; loving God and money equally much; and all other sins besides. Grant me the grace of integrity, of being one thing through and through, no matter what the cost. In the name of the One who loves us to the end. Amen.[5]

Holy Monday

The Temple and the World

Mark 11:15–19

He was teaching them and saying to them,
"Is it not written, 'My house shall be called a
house of prayer for all the nations'? But you
have made it a den of robbers."

—Mark 11:17

On the heels of Palm Sunday, Jesus entered the temple courts and caused a righteous ruckus. Too often we identify with Jesus in this story, thinking that based on his example, we, too, need to be righteously angered at the impurities and corruption in our communities of worship. No doubt there's truth to this impulse. But in this temple episode, the issue of anger is secondary to the primary issue: authority for the sake of the world.

Who has the right to enter your house and begin rearranging furniture and throwing out items on the curb? Only the owner. Jesus's actions demonstrate a breathtaking authority that includes righteous anger. The Lord is angry because the Lord is in charge. His actions prove his authority as the Lord of the temple and Savior of the world. The temple is meant to be a house of prayer and worship for the whole world but has tragically become a "den of robbers." N. T. Wright makes the point that in Jesus's era, the Greek word translated as "robbers" here was a term used "for the revolutionaries, those we today would call the ultra-orthodox, plotting and ready to use violence to bring about their nationalist dreams."[1] This means Jesus is cleansing the temple because its purpose has been perverted not only by virtue of greed and unjust economics (Matthew 21:12) but also through ungodly exclusion.

The temple was "to symbolize God's dwelling with Israel for the sake of the world," but now it was narrowing in on itself in nationalistic fervor.[2] Jesus will not stand for such defilement and exploitation; he uses his authority not to exploit but to redeem. And in a few days' time, the temple of his body will be broken to cleanse creatures and all creation. No longer will death's corruption reign, for the Lord will vanquish our final foe. On this day, we ask the Lord to cleanse the impurity of our worship, our churches, and our hearts and, by his authority, to make us what we were made to be: wholly his, for the sake of the world.

Truth to Ponder: For our sake and for the sake of the world, Jesus stewards his authority to cleanse, restore, and redeem.

> Almighty God, whose most dear Son went not up to joy but first he suffered pain, and entered not into glory before he was crucified: Mercifully grant that we, walking in the way of the Cross, may find it none other than the way of life and peace; through Jesus Christ our Lord, who lives and reigns with you and the Holy Spirit, one God, for ever and ever. Amen.[3]

Holy Tuesday

The Cursed Tree

Mark 11:12–14, 20–23

As they passed by in the morning, they saw the
fig tree withered away to its roots. And Peter
remembered and said to him, "Rabbi, look! The
fig tree that you cursed has withered."

—Mark 11:20–21

The cursing of the fig tree from our Scripture reading seems
so bizarre and fickle. What did that tree ever do to Jesus? From
Mark's account, the cursing likely occurred on Holy Monday,
but the lesson about this came "in the morning" the next day
(Mark 11:20). What are we to learn from this episode considered "one of the most difficult stories in the Gospels"?[1]

Mark clues us in by inserting the temple cleaning into this
fig tree episode (verses 15–19). The fig tree cursing is sym-
bolic of the impurity and fruitlessness of the Israelites' religious
system. The lack of life and fruit is evident in that the Lord's

arrival is met with controversy and ultimately crucifixion—
and from the fact that the temple has become "a den of robbers" (verse 17) as we saw yesterday. The temple was to be the
meeting place between God and Israel and, through Israel, to
extend God's saving light and blessing to the whole world. Yet
it had been corrupted. The temple in Jesus's day appeared pure
and vibrant externally while being warped and fruitless internally.

What in our day—or in our lives—appears to be aligned
with God's Word and ways but is in fact warped and lifeless? If
we lack the eyes to see rightly, impurity appears clean and
empty religiosity can seem whole and holy. Both Jesus's encounter with the temple and the fig tree teaching moment call
us to consider a hard question: In what ways are we found
impure or fruitless? Where are we externally polished but internally lifeless? Jesus taught clearly that we have spiritual life
and bear spiritual fruit only insofar as we abide in him (John
15). But this week reminds us that we can abide in him only
by his grace. Our spirits may be willing, but our flesh is weak.
Thanks be to God, Jesus does not curse us but becomes a curse
for our sake on the cross.

Truth to Ponder: God sees past appearances and offers life to
the lifeless.

> O Lord our God, whose blessed Son gave his back to
> be whipped and did not hide his face from shame and
> spitting: Give us grace to accept joyfully the sufferings
> of the present time, confident of the glory that shall be
> revealed; through Jesus Christ our Lord, who lives and
> reigns with you and the Holy Spirit, one God, for ever
> and ever. Amen.[2]

Spying Hearts

Matthew 26:1–16

Then one of the twelve, whose name was Judas
Iscariot, went to the chief priests and said,
"What will you give me if I deliver him over to
you?" And they paid him thirty pieces of silver.

—Matthew 26:14–15

Seventeenth-century Christian philosopher and scientist Blaise
Pascal claimed human nature could be distilled to two realities
that all persons share: greatness and vileness.[1] On Spy Wednesday, the human capacity for vileness is on full display. Judas
exchanges the greatness of apostleship to Jesus for a chunk of
change. Spiritually speaking, this tragic exchange mirrors our
willingness to trade proximity with God to prostrate ourselves
before idols: money, power, autonomy, comfort.

Our familiarity with Judas's betrayal leads us to overlook
how deeply this moment must have pierced the hearts of Jesus

and his disciples. How many meals had Jesus, Judas, and the other disciples eaten together? How many times in their three years together had they shared in back-slapping laughter? How many times had they wept together on seeing healing after healing? The vileness of Judas's betrayal not only transgressed God's law but also surely cut Jesus to the heart.

"What are you willing to give me if I deliver him over to you?" Judas asks the chief priests. In our vileness, we, too, make our creator and redeemer a means to an end. Judas's betrayal on Spy Wednesday demands we look in the mirror to assess our allegiance to Jesus. The contrast between the woman's costly devotion to Jesus (Matthew 26:7) and Judas's betrayal for money could not be more stark or challenging. What is our "asking price" to deny or downplay Jesus? Power, pleasure, popularity, money, comfort? And how much? As Judas turns, silver in hand, to spy out a chance to betray Jesus, we also must spy; we must search out our own bents toward betrayal. The realization that we all have a "price" yet Jesus loves us still is a grace too deep for words—but a grace proved in the holy events of the days to come.

Truth to Ponder: Jesus knows fully your capacity for betrayal and sin yet chooses to go to the cross for your sake.

> Assist us mercifully with your grace, Lord God of our salvation, that we may enter with joy upon the meditation of those mighty acts by which you have promised us life and immortality; through Jesus Christ our Lord, who lives and reigns with you and the Holy Spirit, one God, for ever and ever. Amen.[2]

Maundy Thursday

The Last Supper

John 13:1–15

Now before the Feast of the Passover,
when Jesus knew that his hour had come to depart
out of this world to the Father, having loved
his own who were in the world, he loved them
to the end.

—John 13:1

Maundy Thursday is the unveiling of the heart of Jesus. The meaning of the meal (which points to the Passover), the list of guests (which includes those who would soon betray and abandon him), and the act of washing feet (an act reserved only for slaves) all harmonize in one voice to declare, "Behold, the Lamb of God, who takes away the sins of the world." Leading into the three great days to come, God, in his grace, holds this out for you to contemplate: Jesus loves the world by laying aside and taking up.

Jesus lays aside his garments and takes the servant's towel to bless his betrayer, his denier, and his weak-willed friends. But the garment and the towel tell a deeper story. They preach the gospel symbolically. Jesus laid aside his divine rights like an outer garment, and he took up human flesh much like he put on the slave's towel (Philippians 2:4–11). On this night, the One who took the form of a servant by becoming human, putting on flesh, takes on the wardrobe of a lowly slave, putting on a towel to stoop and to wash, to serve and to die. Just as he left the supper table to wash and serve, he left heaven to suffer and save. Behold Jesus, who lays aside his glory to take up our humanity to serve, to love, to wash us by his blood sacrifice to which his final meal points. He is near to you as the one who serves. He is the Lamb of God prefigured in the Passover.

It is no surprise, then, that Jesus says to Peter and to us: "If I do not wash you, you have no share with me" (John 13:8). If self-giving service is the heart of Jesus for us, then to reject his service is to be cut off from him. Peter begins with human wisdom. You can imagine him shaking his head, saying, "Those non-enlightened disciples might let you touch their nasty feet, but I won't! I know how low I am and how great you are!" This is right and wrong all at the same time. Peter's comment represents the human conscience snatching the steering wheel away from Jesus the Lord of glory. Beware how our own pride, agendas, and conscience keep us from receiving the grace of Jesus.

Once Peter gets over himself and his eyes are opened to the true stakes, he responds with true spiritual wisdom: "Lord, not my feet only but also my hands and my head!" (verse 9). Peter wisely thirsts for grace upon grace. He craves mercy from head to toe; he wants Christ, the whole Christ, and nothing but the Christ. This is what you and I need.

We do not need more self-help tips, more life hacks for efficiency, or a call to fix the problems of life by ourselves. We need transformation and mercy from head to toe—every part of us—and we are reminded on this night that what we need Jesus is exceedingly and forever willing to give. Dale Bruner says the lesson from this encounter is simple: "Let us let ourselves be loved by the Lord."[1]

As we enter these Great Three Days, Jesus asks us, "Do you understand what I have done?" We are loved and served by him. This Maundy Thursday act is a picture of the gospel and an example of the new commandment that Jesus gives on this same night: "A new commandment I give to you, that you love one another: just as I have loved you, you also are to love one another" (verse 34).

Jesus teaches us that his act places a call on us. By his service, we are cleansed. And we are now enlisted to serve. This is a charge to walk with Jesus on the path of humility. There is no person too far gone for Christ's guest list, so there is no person we can write off our serve list. Who has betrayed you? Love and serve them. Who has denied you? Love and serve them. Who has abandoned you? Love and serve them. Whom has your city forsaken? Love and serve them.

To be served by Jesus is to then serve in Jesus's name. We are to serve one another—not just once a year with a foot-washing service but in things that are mundane and major, as a way of life patterned after Jesus our Savior.

This act and this commandment reveal a holy order. Before we lift a hand to serve Christ, he is the one who serves us. The meal, the guest list, and Christ's action place the spotlight on his movement to the cross where he will lay aside his life. On this night, we remember that before we are those who serve, we are first and always those who are served and loved by him to the very end, even to the point of death on a cross.

Truth to Ponder: Jesus displays his heart of service toward this world and toward you in his willingness to stoop and wash feet, which points toward the sacrifice of his life for our sin.

> Almighty Father, whose most dear Son, on the night before he suffered, instituted the Sacrament of his Body and Blood: Mercifully grant that we may receive it in thankful remembrance of Jesus Christ our Savior, who in these holy mysteries gives us a pledge of eternal life; and who lives and reigns with you and the Holy Spirit, one God, for ever and ever. Amen.[2]

Good Friday

The Twisted Truth

Matthew 27:27–31

When they had mocked him, they stripped him
of the robe and put his own clothes on him and
led him away to crucify him.

—Matthew 27:31

On this day, everything seems twisted. The crowds shout "Crucify!" about the Lord who came to rescue. The robbers crucified alongside Jesus mock the very person they ought to petition for mercy. Everything about Jesus's final hours seems convoluted. Why, then, do we call this day good? One can call this day and these events good only by trusting Jesus in his choice to give himself over to the Roman battalion and then to the Roman cross. While this was his choice, he was not the only one making choices. The religious leaders plotted. The Romans conspired. The people shouted. Satan schemed. But

God was working too. The good of this day is a somber good: Look at what horrors God has suffered for us.

As we consider every angle of Matthew's narrative, we look at every character:

- the people crying "Crucify"
- Pilate knowing the truth but being afraid to embrace Jesus
- the Roman soldiers mocking Jesus and nailing him to the cross

We look on them and encounter fragments of ourselves; we encounter the worst of us. Something is revealed about us on this day: that even as God moves toward humanity in mercy by becoming human, we'd rather kill him than be healed. The hold of sin—human independence from God—is so strong among us that when God comes near, we use our greatest force and bring out earth's battalion not to embrace him but to mock him, not to worship him on a throne but to kill him on a cross.

Will you consider the cross for a moment? It is arguably the symbol most known in the world. Matthew does not need to describe the realities of crucifixion to his original readers, who know its terrors by heart. So, he speaks with great restraint: "When they had crucified him, they divided his garments among them by casting lots" (27:35). Yet for us, the cross can too easily become domesticated. The crosses on our necks, on our flesh, on stickers on the backs of our car bumpers obscure its original dread. Remember that crucifixion was purposefully a slow, public, shameful death—a death by which the human body was exposed to the gawking eyes of the crowd, to the harsh nature of the elements, to the invasive approach of birds and insects, all as a statement that the ragged body on the cross was unfit for membership among the human race, unfit for this earth, unfit to ever be spoken of again.

The cross was not a natural development. Made from a tree, the cross was a technological advance for the sake of deep evil. Just as great human minds come together to create things like medicine for healing and methods of transportation, when what is wrong in me collaborates with what is wrong in you, human innovation shifts from the inspirational to the diabolical. During the Roman era, human intellect twisted to its evil crescendo to craft a vile means of torture, and what they concocted was the cross. It is to this death that the Lord of life submits.

Justice and the Cross

But the truth about God is revealed on this day too: Jesus's sacrifice is the healing of our callous hearts and the pardon for our sin. In his sacrifice is our forgiveness. The debt of our sin is paid by him. Some may struggle with this, saying, "It's not right that Jesus, an innocent man, would suffer like this!" They look at the injustice Jesus faces, and they see him as a great teacher worthy of pity for dying such a vicious death. But you cannot understand Good Friday, the Cross, or Christianity if you see Jesus's death only through the lens of pity.

Many innocent sufferers were nailed to Roman wood or, in our time, have been hung from poplar trees. Jesus suffered innocently, willingly, and redemptively. Jesus asks not for our pity but for our worship. Yet something inside us still objects, "It's not right that he endured such unjust suffering!" We're correct: It's not right—and that's why we call it good.

It would have been right for God to abandon the type of world that would beat and assault the Lord of life. It would have been right for God to leave us in our rebellion and sin. It would have been right for Jesus to turn his back on the world that scourged his. This day is called not Right Friday but Good Friday. And on Good Friday, the King turns a cross into a throne. He receives insults for praise. He takes nakedness for royal garments. Survey the weighty and wondrous cross, and call this somber but saving day good. In a great twist of saving love, what we did to him was done for us.

In one final twist, it is to this somber good that you must look always. That you must hold in your heart always. What our eyes want desperately to turn away from we must behold. Listen to how one of the ancient voices of the church described Good Friday from Matthew's gospel: "What could be worse than this? What is more abusive? What happened surpasses all telling. When you see him jeered in words and in deeds, the knee bent in mockery, abused, and subjected to extreme suffering, even if you were made of stone, you would become softer than any wax and expel all pride from your soul."[1]

Look to the King enthroned on the cross and behold our rescue. Look to the King enthroned on the cross and behold our God.

Truth to Ponder: The truth about us, sinful yet loved, and the truth about God, all-powerful and self-sacrificing, is revealed in the cross of Jesus.

> Almighty God, we beseech you graciously to behold this your family, for whom our Lord Jesus Christ was willing to be betrayed and given into the hands of sinners, and to suffer death upon the Cross; who now lives and reigns with you and the Holy Spirit, one God, for ever and ever. Amen.[2]

Holy Saturday

In the Silence

Luke 23:50–56

This man went to Pilate and asked for the body
of Jesus. Then he took it down and wrapped it
in a linen shroud and laid him in a tomb cut in
stone, where no one had ever yet been laid.

—Luke 23:52–53

Holy Saturday calls us to sit in the stillness of the starkest heartache the world has ever known: the Light of the world extinguished and the Lord of life dead. Imagine what ran through the minds and hearts of the female disciples, standing just feet away as the Lord's body was sealed in the tomb. Imagine the grief Joseph felt, lifting and wrapping Jesus's lifeless arms and nail-scarred hands, his bruised and breathless body in linen for burial. The Lord who spoke the words of life breathed no more.

Writer John Onwuchekwa says, "Tragedy doesn't ruin us;

hopelessness does."[1] The silence of Holy Saturday combines both in one fatal blow—tragedy strikes, and hope is nowhere to be found. Yet the fact that the Father does not raise Jesus immediately speaks volumes.

Holy Saturday teaches us that wherever we are overwhelmed by hopelessness, silence, or grief, we are not alone. Even in the void, God is present. In our grief and tragedy, the Lord mysteriously works. We neither grieve nor suffer alone. None of these assertions are trite religious clichés—they are truths drawn from the story of Jesus's own life. In the silence, Jesus descended into the bowels of death, snatching away its ultimate power. The hush was real and suffocating, but it was not final. Jesus would speak again, breathe again, rise again.

Holy Saturday teaches us that with God, there is always something on the other side of silence. This something does not bypass pain and grief but engulfs and redeems them. This something is resurrection.

Truth to Ponder: Holy Saturday teaches us that God is with us in tragedy and that neither silence nor hopelessness is ever the final word.

> O God of the living, on this day your Son our Savior descended to the place of the dead: Look with kindness on all of us who wait in hope for liberation from the corruption of sin and death, and give us a share in the glory of the children of God; through Jesus Christ your Son our Lord. Amen.[2]

EASTER

Resurrection Life

The Easter message tells us that our enemies, sin,
the curse and death, are beaten. . . . They still
behave as though the game were not decided,
the battle not fought; we must still reckon with
them, but fundamentally we must cease to fear
them any more. If you have heard the Easter
message, *you can no longer run around with a tragic*
face and lead the humourless existence of a man who
has no hope. One thing still holds, and only this one
thing is really serious, that Jesus is the Victor.

—KARL BARTH, *Dogmatics in Outline*
(emphasis added)

Easter is the power source of the church year. Everything radiates out from the fact that Christ is risen, and every season points back to this triumph. The magnitude of Christ's victory over sin, Satan, and death is so expansive that the joy of this season cannot be expressed in a single day. In Lent, we fast for forty days, but in Eastertide, we feast for fifty days to celebrate the triumph of our salvation. This season gives us room to rejoice in the hope of resurrection and consider what it means to live in light of the empty tomb. In *Surprised by Hope*, biblical scholar N. T. Wright said that up to a week following Easter, we ought to have champagne with breakfast to celebrate God's victory.[1] That might be a bit much, but the point stands: This is a true time of rejoicing. In the kingdom, feasting wins over fasting because God's victory conquers sin and evil.

The resurrection of Jesus changes everything. Riffing on 1 Corinthians 15, church historian Jaroslav Pelikan writes, "If Christ is risen, nothing else matters. And if Christ is not risen— nothing else matters."[2] The gospel promise given in Genesis 3:15 is realized. Our sins are forgiven (1 Corinthians 15:1–3). Death loses its sting (verse 55). Our bodies will embrace immortality (verses 53–54). This decaying world will be remade (Revelation 21:1). Tears will be wiped away (verse 4). Our present lives are tuned to the way of the new creation. Eternal life is ours (John 17:3). All because Christ is risen. The hope of the world is wrapped up in his victory.

Eastertide Spirituality: How to Live the Resurrection Life

One great challenge of the Christian life is learning how to live as if the Resurrection is really true and Jesus really is the risen Lord over all. This is why we need the risen Jesus to instruct us from his Word, uniting resurrection facts and resurrection faith. Most believers know basic facts of the Resurrection—what happened and why. The challenge of Eastertide spirituality mirrors the challenge of the entire Christian life: living out a resurrection faith, a total transformation of our way of being that's explained only by the fact that Jesus did not remain dead.

There's good news for us. The New Testament teaches that Easter spirituality, or resurrection life, is ours for the taking because we are already spiritually risen with Jesus. In Colossians 3:1, when Paul says, "If then you have been raised with Christ, seek the things that are above," the *if* is not hypothetical but rhetorical. In effect, Paul is saying this: "You *have* been raised with him, so live out this glorious new life."

The whole Christian life is lived under the life-giving banner of the Resurrection. Scripture declares we are dead to sin and alive to Christ; thus, the Resurrection patterns our transformation. Scripture urges us to "walk in newness of life" (Romans 6:4); thus, the totality of our discipleship flows from Jesus's resurrection. The risen Christ in us, united to us by faith and the Spirit, means we can embrace not only the truths of Easter but also the transformation pulsating within those truths. Eastertide forms us by calling us to live out the resurrection life gifted to us by the risen Lord.

The first response of people who live out resurrection life—believing truly that Jesus is the resurrected Lord—is rejoicing. The greater the victory, the deeper the celebration. Just as we thought creatively about fasting in Lent, we concentrate now on ways to rejoice in God and his gifts. This reaches its maximal form on Sundays as Christ's body comes together to exult in him. So, come to church with fresh expectation. Greet others with a hearty "Christ is risen!" Dance and rejoice in every way you know how. The promise given in the garden has come true, our enemies are defeated, and life eternal is ours.

The victory of Jesus and the joy of our salvation overflow into a new way of life. If Jesus had remained dead, Peter would have gone back to fishing, you would not be reading this book, we would still be in our sins, and the world would never know the name Jesus of Nazareth. Our way of living can be explained only by the fact that Jesus is risen. Our view of death, our generosity, our endurance in trials, our vigor in prayer, our confidence in God's love, our hope for non-

Christians—everything bursts with new life and new possibility because Christ is risen.

The Sunday after Easter (the second Sunday of Easter) is quietly called Low Sunday. It's the spiritual valley after the Easter Sunday high. The point is that it's hard to maintain a celebration of joy even in this season of Jesus's victory. Don't be surprised if, even in Easter, you encounter this low. You're not strange or alone. In fact, the gospel narratives demonstrate the hesitancy, fear, and confusion the disciples experienced after the Resurrection (Matthew 28:17; Mark 16:8). That's part of the journey of this season: helping our small hearts grasp the truth that renews all creation.

Eastertide Practices

What are the particular practices that mark worship and discipleship in Eastertide? Several could be named, but these three form a helpful starting place for individuals and communities.

Throw many feasts, parties, and celebrations. This is the season of joy. The Resurrection means life triumphs over death in Jesus; therefore, we have much to rejoice in. Cross-pollinate your friend groups—believers, seekers, skeptics—and celebrate in ways that point to the life of the world to come.

Delight in all God's good gifts as signs of the new creation to come. The resurrection of Jesus is proof God loves his creation—and promises to renew it. Find ways to take in the goodness of this world in thankfulness to God. That might mean feasting, hiking, gardening, golfing, or whatever fills your heart with thanks to the Lord. Feast on these good gifts, and bring others along for the ride.

Share the hope you have in Christ. The Resurrection unleashes a torrent of celebration and proclamation. Just look at the book of Acts. How can you show and share that you have a hope that is not of this world? What friend might be willing to come to church with you, read a gospel, or have a robust spiritual conversation? Find ways in word and deed to testify to the risen Jesus alongside other believers.

Eastertide Feast Days

Each season has notable feast days in which the church is called into a deeper experience of the life of Christ together.

Easter Vigil draws us into the celebration of new life through Jesus. Because he died and rose, evil and sin are defeated and God's people and God's world will be made new. The service happens on the eve of Easter and includes the lighting of the Christ candle and many readings that retell the story of salvation. This church service begins on Saturday night, launches participants into the joy of the Eastertide, and is often followed by a large feast into the night to celebrate the Resurrection. In some churches, the vigil has been replaced by an Easter morning sunrise service.

Easter Sunday (first Sunday of Easter): Known as Resurrection Sunday, this is the great day of rejoicing that the Lord is risen, indeed! Alleluia!

Good Shepherd Sunday (fourth Sunday of Easter): This Sunday focuses on Jesus as the Good Shepherd who loves, leads, and gives his life for his sheep.

Rogation Sunday (sixth Sunday of Easter): *Rogation* comes from the Latin term *rogare,* which means to "to ask."[3] A tradition dating back to the fifth century, Rogation Days are times when the church intercedes for the flourishing of agricultural work and God's provision and protection on the earth and its bounty. This day reminds us that the Lord cares for the earth and that humanity has been called to the sacred task of stewarding and cultivating it.

Ascension Sunday (seventh Sunday of Easter): Though Ascension Day occurs during the week, many churches move the feast to the following Sunday to celebrate that Christ now reigns from the right hand of the Father as our high priest, intercessor, and king.

Pentecost (eighth Sunday of Easter): This day celebrates the coming of the Spirit in Acts 2 in fulfillment of many Old Testament promises. Red is the color for this feast day, reflecting the Spirit descending on the apostles like tongues of fire. Because the Spirit has come, the gospel is spread abroad to all nations.

Reading Easter Texts and Devotions

As you read the following Scripture texts and devotions, you'll reflect on the Resurrection and its implications for our grief, our life in community, our identity, and our future destiny. Truly the resurrection of Jesus changes everything.

First Week

Called by Name

Acts 10:34–43
Psalm 118:14–17, 22–24
Colossians 3:1–4
John 20:1–18

Jesus said to her, "Woman,
why are you weeping?"

—John 20:15

Almighty God, who through your only-begotten Son Jesus Christ overcame death and opened to us the gate of everlasting life: Grant that we, who celebrate with joy the day of the Lord's resurrection, may, by your life-giving Spirit, be delivered from sin and raised from death; through Jesus Christ our Lord, who lives and reigns with you and the Holy Spirit, one God, now and for ever. Amen.[1]

Imagine going to the grave of the most beloved person in your life or family, and as you approach, your body quivers as you find the tombstone vandalized and cracked in pieces. Then your throat tightens as you see thick, large piles of dirt next to the grave. You don't need to look in. You know the worst thing next to death has happened. Twisted people have stolen the body.

This is the sort of plight Mary encounters as she approaches the tomb to honor Jesus's body and finds it burst open. Mary doesn't move an inch closer—she sprints to Peter with the horrible news: They killed him, and now they took his body! This is grief upon grief upon grief. Peter and John have their own experience, but Mary can only weep. The crisis is overwhelming. And it is in this dark hour of calamity that Jesus speaks: "Why are you weeping?"

Jesus's question is not a rebuke. Mary has every earthly reason to shed tears. Her Lord and friend has died. He didn't go peacefully in his sleep after a full eight decades. Her Lord died by execution on a Roman cross.

Yet the dark crisis of Good Friday is lit up by the fire of Easter hope. And Mary, through her tears, is about to see that light. That Mary sees and hears Jesus but does not recognize him immediately is one of the more peculiar moments of the Easter story. She mistakes the risen Jesus for a gardener. She cannot recognize the resurrected Jesus—her friend, her Lord, her maker, her savior—until he speaks her name.

When Grief Meets Resurrection

The risen Jesus first approaches not the male disciples but Mary, who stays at the tomb and weeps. To those stuck in the mire of crisis and grief, Jesus is most pleased to bring hope and life. The resurrection of Jesus teaches us that God meets us in our darkest hours. With Jesus, we need not deny or enshrine our grief; we need only trust he will meet us at the intersection of our loss and need.

On this day, we must understand that through the Resurrection, God rescues and restores us at the root, not the symptoms, of our troubles. What is the root of Mary's crisis? Death has taken her Lord. What is the root of our crisis? Death waits for us, has put its hands on our loved ones, and has stained everything in this world. Death is in tandem with sin, human disregard for the One to whom we owe all things (Romans 6:23). Appearances do in fact lie. Our technological advances, our wellness culture, and our brightest accolades are paper-thin shields against the heartbreak of death and the loss of meaning.

Mary feels all of this as we do. So, when the risen Jesus walks in the garden and calls Mary's name, we are copied in on the message. His good news, his resurrection life, his saving power is for us by name too. Recognize the voice of the Risen One who calls to humanity in our crisis. He says Mary's name and he says our names. His resurrection will triumph over our darkest hours and our greatest enemies.

How can Jesus do this? He holds the keys to resurrection life. Perhaps no one can say it better than Saint Athanasius: "He descended that He might raise us up . . . He went down to corruption, that corruption might put on immortality, He became weak for us, that we might rise with power, He descended to death, that He might bestow on us immortality, and give life to the dead."[2] In giving himself up to death for our sakes, Jesus disarmed its hold on those who trust in him. And the sacrifice of the cross is attached to the victory of resurrection. If the tandem of sin and death have been dealt with, the only thing left is new life—the hope of resurrection.

A New World

In the resurrection of Jesus, God ushers into this decaying world a foretaste of re-creation. By rising again, by calling our names in grace, by meeting the world in crisis, the risen Jesus is re-creating us and transforming our relationships to everything. Think about Mary. She probably never looked at a garden in the same way. She likely never thought of a tomb or of running or weeping in the same way.

It's not that she never wept again. It's that her whole relationship to weeping was transformed or, better yet, re-created. It's not that she never visited a tomb again in tears or walked through grief. It's that her whole relationship to these things was remade because Jesus triumphed over death. Every tear Mary cried from that point forward reminded her that Jesus met her in her weeping and turned her mourning into rejoicing (Psalm 30:11). This re-creation is what Jesus in his death and resurrection holds out not just to Mary and Peter but to you, to me, to adults, to children, to thugs on street corners, to CEOs in corner offices. It's the news of life for a dying world.

John, whose gospel starts with "In the beginning," wants us to recognize the importance of the garden. The risen Jesus recovers for us the gifts lost in Eden: knowing God with no fear of condemnation, no fear of death, but only the fullness of life in the beauty of God's good world. All this was lost. But the crisis is being undone. What is unfolding on us through the resurrection of Jesus is the in-breaking of God's new world.

FOR REFLECTION AND DISCUSSION

1. What's significant about Jesus approaching Mary in her grief? What does this say about the gospel message?

2. In what ways does the Resurrection lead to new creation? How can you live into this reality more fully?

3. What situation do you need to see in light of the victory of Jesus?

Second Week

Resurrection Faith

Isaiah 26:1–9, 19
Psalm 111
1 John 5:1–5
John 20:19–31

Then he said to Thomas, "Put your finger
here, and see my hands; and put out your hand,
and place it in my side. Do not disbelieve,
but believe."

—John 20:27

Almighty and everlasting God, who in the Paschal
mystery established the new covenant of reconciliation:
Grant that all who have been reborn into the fellowship
of Christ's Body may show forth in their lives what they
profess by their faith; through Jesus Christ our Lord,
who lives and reigns with you and the Holy Spirit, one
God, for ever and ever. Amen.[1]

Jesus is risen, but the disciples are still locking doors. This fascinating detail in John 20:26 suggests that the disciples remained deeply afraid. The locked doors are proof of fear and belief that is far from victorious. It's Easter for the disciples and the doors are locked? Why? They are afraid of death.

Think about this from the disciples' perspective: The Romans rounded up Jesus and nailed him to a cross. So, who knows whether the authorities are now on the hunt for the rest of Jesus's crew? They took out the leading light; why not extinguish the whole group? Indeed, fear is what keeps the male disciples from fully believing the Resurrection proclaimed to them by the female disciples (verse 18).

This should make the disciples feel even more relatable. Pastor Timothy Keller once told of a woman who was on the brink of faith in Jesus but hesitated because she felt that the gospel message was "scary." According to Keller, she explained that if salvation is by grace through Jesus's death and resurrection and not by her works or goodness, then her whole life would belong in full and loving surrender to the crucified and risen Savior.[2] Fear is the lock that closes us off from belief in the Resurrection. Sometimes it might be the fear of true surrender, but in the case of the disciples, it's the fear of danger.

Jesus Approaches Us in Our Fear

To the hesitant, fearful disciples, Jesus approaches and proclaims, "Peace be with you" (John 20:19). Last we saw, these disciples fled from him and abandoned him at his hour of greatest need. And here he arrives at the hour of their greatest fear, declaring peace to them. The risen Jesus is seeking after us far more than we seek after him, offering the peace of welcome, forgiveness, and eternal life. Jesus proclaims peace with his words and reveals the source of peace by showing his wounds.

The problem is that Thomas is not present. He misses the gathering with the disciples, and he misses out on Jesus. When he does come back, we see that he isn't too quick to believe:

> Now Thomas, one of the twelve, called the Twin, was not with them when Jesus came. So the other disciples told him, "We have seen the Lord." But he said to them, "Unless I see in his hands the mark of the nails, and place my finger into the mark of the nails, and place my hand into his side, I will never believe." (John 20:24–25)

Often we focus so much on Thomas's doubt that we forget that Jesus seeks out this so-called doubter after his proclamation of unbelief. Jesus refuses to let people miss out, so he makes himself known.

How does Jesus come to Thomas? He appears not in the quiet of a solo spiritual retreat but in the ordinary gathering of the fearful, imperfect disciples. In a simple home, they meet together as his people, processing as best they can in light of what Jesus has done. The risen Jesus is pleased to make his presence known to his unimpressive people in transformative ways when we gather in his name, even if we come fearfully like the disciples and doubting like Thomas. If this isn't a testimony for the beautiful simplicity of the church, then what is?

It is a good thing to gather with disciples, particularly on the Lord's Day, because you never know how the risen Jesus might show up—but you can believe that he will. Any and all good that happens when you gather at church is the work not so much of the pastors or people but of the risen Christ making himself known by his grace.

As we see in John 20, the parallels between the first Sunday of Easter and the second are noteworthy. The liturgy, if you will, is the same: Jesus's words and Jesus's wounds. Jesus again says, "Peace be with you," and he offers his wounds specifically to Thomas:

> Eight days later, his disciples were inside again, and Thomas was with them. Although the doors were locked, Jesus came and stood among them and said, "Peace be with you." Then he said to Thomas, "Put your finger here, and see my hands; and put out your hand, and place it in my side. Do not disbelieve, but believe." Thomas answered him, "My Lord and my God!" Jesus said to him, "Have you believed because you have seen me? Blessed are those who have not seen and yet have believed." (verses 26–29)

When actors are given a script, they must make decisions about their voice tones and inflections. Voice shifts meaning. When we read Scripture, we do the same. In what tone do you hear Jesus speaking the words "Put your finger here"? A tough rebuke or a tender invitation? If Jesus wanted to rebuke Thomas, he would have never appeared to him. Doubts about the Resurrection do not disqualify us from faith; they are the starting line of faith. For the doubts we carry are the very places we can move more deeply into faith in Christ.

The wounds of Jesus become the source of life and faith for Thomas. There is no other way to be a Christian. The wounds of Jesus dissipate our fears, for if he was wounded and risen for us, our wounds will testify to his resurrection when our bodies are raised from the grave. The love of Jesus displayed in his wounds transforms Thomas into the church's great confessor, proclaiming the deity of Jesus. William Barclay writes that Thomas's "great virtue was that when he was sure, he went the whole way. 'My Lord and my God!' said he."[3]

Believing in the Resurrection is for all people and all places. Even if we cannot examine his wounds like Thomas, Jesus speaks a further word of beatitude: "Blessed are those who have not seen and yet have believed" (verse 29). In recording these words of Jesus, John "has an eye for his readers, . . . who 'see him no more,' and are assured therefore that their position is not inferior to that of Thomas." To our surprise, Jesus sees us as being in a greater position than these first disciples "since we are extended 'this special blessedness: "though you have not seen him, you love him"' (1 Peter 1:8)."[4]

FOR REFLECTION AND DISCUSSION

1. How have you understood the relationship between faith and doubt?
2. What do you make of Thomas? Do you relate to him in any way?
3. What is Jesus's response to our doubts and fears? What does this mean for you?

Third Week

Resurrection Community

Acts 2:14, 36–47
Psalm 116:11–16
1 Peter 1:13–25
Luke 24:13–35

They devoted themselves to the apostles'
teaching and the fellowship, to the breaking
of bread and the prayers.

—Acts 2:42

Almighty God, you gave your only Son to be for us both a sacrifice for sin and an example of godly living: Give us grace thankfully to receive his inestimable benefits, and daily to follow the blessed steps of his most holy life; through Jesus Christ our Lord, who lives and reigns with you and the Holy Spirit, one God, for ever and ever. Amen.[1]

In terms of achievement, the iceberg principle teaches that under the surface of any visible success lie untold hours of preparation and training. Anything successful or compelling did not come out of nowhere but came from a cause, a power, a source.

Christians are fond of idealizing the portrait of church life depicted in Acts 2:42–47. The passage has something for everyone. Lovers of theology fawn over the faithful devotion in verse 42. Those who hunger for the charismatic marvel at verse 43. Those who yearn for the church to walk in radical generosity exult in verses 44–45. Evangelists and missional folks get hyped over the conversions in verse 47. Luke's careful summation of the early church's life together has something that everyone yearns for. The church is to be a holistic community of *devotion, charismata, generosity,* and *transformation.* Yet what is beneath this ecclesial iceberg?

Built on Resurrection Community

The early church is powered by the reality and proclamation of the Resurrection (Acts 2:22–25). In and through this proclamation, the Resurrected One is present, birthing a resurrection community. Verses 42–47 are a snapshot of the resurrection community formed by the risen Jesus through the power of His Spirit.

This new community begins with devotion. Devotion is about what we anchor ourselves to. This was a process for the disciples, not unlike developing a new way of seeing. If we recall our journey through Holy Week, we see this unfold as the disciples gradually grasp who Jesus is and how all God's promises come true in him. They move from discovery to devotion through many twists, tragedies, and turns. In reading Acts 1 and 2, we see the continued shift in their perspective.

Imagine the thrill of their first meetings as word of the Resurrection spreads. Imagine also the fear.

Even today, the church is continually moving further into devotion as we discover more of what it means to follow the risen Jesus. This is partly why discipleship is not a solo task. The journey into devotion requires others with whom we practice the way of Acts 2:42–47. Indeed, this is a picture of the church's life together powered by the risen Lord.

Life Together in the Hope of the Resurrection

Make no mistake, these verses are not describing generic neighborly care. The apostles' teaching is the word of the gospel and the Scriptures handed down through the ages. The breaking of bread is the Lord's Supper done in remembrance of him. The forms of prayer—like the Lord's Prayer—make us participants in the work of the kingdom. Fellowship is our bond of life as the body of Christ.

What you might see as the ordinary staples of church life are in fact signs of the Resurrection invading the world and constructing new forms of life together in Jesus's name. This is resurrection community. This is a community formed by the ethics of the new era of living hope, a new people who operate by the rules of new life.

The Resurrection gives us a new ethic of gospel generosity. What we give in Christ's name becomes a greater treasure in the world to come while blessing people in this present world. Selling our possessions for treasure in heaven, as Jesus taught, is not simply an option to consider; it is now the real gravitational pull because Jesus is alive. More than likely, there are people in your communal orbit who struggle to make ends meet. A cooked meal, a surprise takeout order, an anonymous gift card, and the shared use of a car are all simple ways that generosity blesses and binds us in community. There's a good chance you have things in your closet—an old phone, clothes, or so forth—that would bless someone. The challenge is a matter not just of generosity but also of need. Acts 2:42–47 presumes a proximity of relationship in which need is known because people are known. Can we say the same? It takes more for us to live this part of life together—and this is where true fellowship happens. Devotion to the Risen One and the people he is forming means a move toward one another, practicing the new way of Christ.

A People of Celebration

The entire tenor of the church's resurrection life is joy and celebration. Karl Barth once wrote, "To believe in Jesus Christ means to become thankful."[2] Thus, celebration isn't simply cultural; it is much more—it is a sibling of praise. Celebration is a spitting image of thanksgiving. In this sense, celebration is a deep theological reality, a thankful act or expression in response to God.

Though the early church faced great trials and scandals (Acts 5; 7; 8; 15), it was also sustained by joy. In *Living into Community*, Christine Pohl comments on the power of joy and celebration: "We tend to think of celebrations as enjoyable but not central. Communities and congregations that last, however, especially in difficult settings, practice and embody gratitude and celebration."[3] Where have you seen God at work in your life, friends, family, or church? What if you planned a small party to celebrate or scheduled a simple meal with friends and shared a few words to honor how God's been working? What if you, with others, held a potluck for Good Shepherd Sunday next week and invited people to share how God has shepherded them over this last year? The possibilities are end-

less. But these sorts of practices become contagious and cultivate a culture of God-centered and people-honoring gratitude.

Resolve to rejoin in the Resurrection, especially in the
context of the ordinary resurrection community in which you
find yourself. Church need not be spectacular; it need only be
a community reaching for the life of resurrection fellowship
together. Acts 2:42–47 is not just a historical record. It is a living text that Jesus is doing in all churches that are seeking to
continually enter the revealed mystery of his risen life and will.

FOR REFLECTION AND DISCUSSION

1. In what ways has Acts 2:42–47 influenced your
   faith and your vision of life together in the church?
2. Which aspect of the resurrection community in
   Acts 2:42–47 is most compelling to you? Most
   daunting? Why?
3. What one action can you take to cultivate deeper
   resurrection community this week?

Fourth Week

Good Shepherd Sunday

Acts 13:13–39
Psalm 23
Revelation 7:9–17
John 10:7–21

I am the good shepherd. I know my own
and my own know me, just as the Father knows
me and I know the Father; and I lay down
my life for the sheep.

—John 10:14–15

O God, whose Son Jesus Christ is the Good Shepherd
of your people: Grant that, when we hear his voice, we
may know him who calls us each by name, and follow
where he leads; who, with you and the Holy Spirit, lives
and reigns, one God, for ever and ever. Amen.[1]

John 10 is filled to the brim with controversy. Prior to this chapter, Jesus is in hot water with the religious leaders for healing a man on the Sabbath. As he often did, Jesus takes the initial dispute and stirs up more drama by launching into a whole sermon with another audacious "I am" claim. Because this is more than a small controversy—with a main dish of supposed blasphemy—the result is an attempt on Jesus's life (verse 31).

For the modern reader, Jesus's claim to be the Good Shepherd is not so contentious. The implicit royal-divine claim of that title is lost on many, so it doesn't provoke a strong reaction. We may even ignore it. If anything in this episode is troublesome to us, it is that we are lumped under the title of sheep, which is offensive to our desire to be self-made, self-sufficient, and self-directed.

But we are sheep. And sheep are not self-sufficient; they are extremely dependent creatures. They are prey, not predators—vulnerable to wolves with an appetite. Sheep, however, aren't vulnerable only to external threats; they're in danger just because they are animals that can be remarkably dull. Apart from external guidance, provision, and protection, sheep don't thrive. They flounder. They wander. They die.

Sheep often need saving from themselves. I've seen a sheep charge its own bucket of water as though it were a mortal enemy. The sheep flipped over the bucket and spilled all the water, which then caused it to launch its woolly body into the air and land with a crash, only to get up and prepare to charge the bucket again. It would be humorous if this weren't a slightly exaggerated image of ourselves. "For what am I to myself without Thee," Augustine once prayed, "but a guide to mine own downfall?"[2] Sheep are dependent and vulnerable, and they need a shepherd. The quicker we recognize ourselves as sheep who need a shepherd, the sooner we move toward the abundant life with God that Jesus offers.

Protection and flourishing do not come through the enlightenment of the wayward sheep but by the arrival of the Good Shepherd. When Jesus lays claim to this title, he explicitly evokes a major Old Testament motif, the promise that God would come and be the shepherd of his people (Ezekiel 34:11). This Good Shepherd loves wayward sheep, even laying down his life for them. Do you feel lost or stuck in a pit of your own making? There's a shepherd who is strong enough to lift you, compassionate enough to heal you, gracious enough to guide you, and powerful enough to save you.

The Sheep's Actions

The Good Shepherd's saving work shapes the way his sheep respond to him. They hear his voice. They are known. They follow. According to the Good Shepherd, these sheepy actions are pieces that make up the mosaic of the Christian life—the life of purpose, connection, and direction with God we were made for. These three aspects are the wonderful work that we're called into in both a definitive (once and for all) and an ongoing (daily) way.

Hearing. Each day, we need to hear the voice of our shepherd. Hear the voice of Jesus who calls all people to life with God, saying, "The kingdom of God is at hand; repent and believe in the gospel" (Mark 1:15). Hear his voice that says, "Come to me, all who labor and are heavy laden, and I will give you rest" (Matthew 11:28). Keep hearing his voice—turning to him in faith and trust—to be renewed by his mercy, which is new and fresh each morning.

Being known. We need to realize that we're known. Know that Jesus knows you—every wound, every fear, every hope, every sin, every need. Know that he is a good shepherd who cares deeply about his sheep; he will tend to you with care and mercy. Know that he knows when to prod and when to protect.

Following. The Lord's sheep follow their shepherd. Resolve to follow him once and for all. Then with each new morning, with your full attention, say, "Today I'll keep giving my allegiance to the Shepherd who gave himself for me."

To hear, to be known, and to follow are our threefold duty and delight under the Good Shepherd. Jesus shepherds us well by making these actions clear to us.

Sheep Under Attack

Clarity is needed because sheep are not the brightest creatures around and because other voices call to them. Any entity that would lead us astray from the voice and way of Christ is an echo of the twisted voice from the garden (Genesis 3:1–7) who shepherded the first humans away from life with God into a life of death.

The apostle Peter tells us the devil prowls like a lion looking to devour (1 Peter 5:8). This is frightening news for sheep. However, the enemy's playbook is small. The devouring he attempts is something as old as Adam, and it's primarily a move of subtle deception. Sheep meet their downfall when the enemy steals and destroys by drowning out the voice of the Shepherd. In *The Land and the Book,* William M. Thomson writes, "The shepherd calls sharply from time to time, to re-mind them of his presence. They know his voice, and follow on; but, if a stranger call, they stop short, lift their heads in alarm, and if it is repeated, they turn and flee, because they know not the voice of a stranger."[3]

Our task as sheep, then, is to train our ears to know the Shepherd's voice. You can condition your ears to hear the voice of God in Scripture by studying what faithful Christians through the ages have believed and why. This will help you discern truth from error by learning from a neglected part of the flock—our spiritual forebearers. Another option is to read Scripture with believers from different cultures and backgrounds to train your ears to distinguish between what is of Christ and what may be cultural presumptions. (If this isn't possible where you live, try using a Global Study Bible to read Scripture.) In this hearing, Jesus will shepherd you by the hand and by the heart so that no trial, no enemy, no evil, and no failure can steal you from his hands.

The Shepherd's Gift

Don't let all the sheep activity fool you. Our primary task as sheep is passive reception—receiving the gift of the Shepherd. As we hear his voice, we receive life eternal through his gospel. Christ the Shepherd gives us a permanence that even death cannot snatch away. As Christians, death does not separate us from the hand of God but brings us closer to his presence. Our suffering does not snatch us from his hand but brings us deeper toward his heart. Because we are held by the Son, loved by the Father, and led by the Spirit, every believer is a sheep that remains secure by the strength of the triune God.

A good shepherd leads by staying close among and in the front of the flock to shield them from danger. Is this not what Christ has done for us? Christ came among us in his incarnation. Then Christ went before us into the land of sin and into the jaws of death in his crucifixion. Christ the Shepherd has gone before us into death and put it into submission, and now he's taking all his sheep with him into the green pastures of life eternal.

The Good Shepherd is also the Lamb of God slain and raised for us. In John 10 we see controversy—but we must also understand the work of the Good Shepherd in terms of this gift: victory. And so, we give the last word to Revelation's heavenly picture of this victory secured:

> After this I looked, and there was a vast multitude from every nation, tribe, people, and language, which no one could number, standing before the throne and before the Lamb. They were clothed in white robes with palm branches in their hands. And they cried out in a loud voice:
>
> > Salvation belongs to our God,
> > who is seated on the throne,
> > and to the Lamb! (7:9–10, CSB)

FOR REFLECTION AND DISCUSSION

1. What stands out most when you consider humanity—and yourself—through the image of sheep?
2. Of the threefold sheep actions—hearing, being known, and following—which comes easiest to you? Which is more difficult? Why might this be?
3. What challenges are you facing right now? What truths about Jesus as the Good Shepherd speak to your situation? What truths do you need to rest in and draw strength from?

Fifth Week

Transformed by the Resurrection

Acts 4:32–37
Psalm 23
1 John 3:1–10
Luke 24:36–49

See what kind of love the Father has
given to us, that we should be called
children of God; and so we are.

—1 John 3:1

Almighty God, whom truly to know is everlasting life: Grant us so perfectly to know your Son Jesus Christ to be the way, the truth, and the life, that we may steadfastly follow his steps in the way that leads to eternal glory; through Jesus Christ your Son our Lord, who lives and reigns with you, in the unity of the Holy Spirit, one God, for ever and ever. Amen.[1]

In his bestselling book *Atomic Habits: Tiny Changes, Remarkable Results,* James Clear argues that the best way to change your habits is to attend to your identity. Want to write more? Believe that you are a writer, then follow that belief with the logical habits and routine. The power for change, he explains, is at the level of identity.[2]

There's wisdom to this advice because the question of identity shapes our destiny—the action and direction of our lives. "Who am I?" (identity) and "Where am I going in the future?" (destiny) are not just matters of new habits; they are fundamental questions of human existence. Thus, it's no surprise that Jesus's resurrection touches on these two foundational aspects. The resurrection of Jesus opens before us a whole new horizon—a new identity and destiny—into which we are to love and live with exuberance and wonder.

The Question of Identity

"See what kind of love the Father has given to us" is John's way of testifying to a love of a different quantity and quality than the world has ever known. In this love, God took rebels and didn't simply forgive them; he brought them into his heart and made them heirs of eternal life with him.

God could have forgiven our sin and then had nothing to do with us. This is why Anglican theologian J. I. Packer writes, "To be right with God the judge [justification] is a great thing, but to be loved and cared for by God the father [adoption] is greater."[3] And this is where 1 John 3 begins, with an overflow of praise. Who are we? We are called "children of God; and so we are" (verse 1). To be adopted as a child of God means a new way of being. Packer describes this as a life of closeness and affection with, to, and from the Father. We have the full-ness of belonging. Never again do we need to question how the Father views or sees us. He is ours, and we are his.

Adoption fortifies our hearts in a world still marked by death, tragedy, and injustice. Howard Thurman, Black theologian and writer, explains that "the awareness of being a child of God tends to stabilize the ego and results in a new courage, fearlessness, and power."[4] Thurman didn't offer this encouragement from an ivory tower. He lived in the jaws of segregation, writing specifically of the relevance of Christianity to those who suffered with their backs against the wall. Adoption is food for the soul and Teflon for the spirit. And adoption will, at the appointed time, lead to the transformation of our very flesh.

The Question of Destiny

John speaks of what we are *and* what we will be, of identity and of destiny, for grace operates in past, present, and future tense. He writes, "Beloved, we are God's children now, and what we will be has not yet appeared; but we know that when he appears we shall be like him, because we shall see him as he is" (1 John 3:2).

Seeing God is what Christians from Roman Catholics to Eastern Orthodox to Protestants have called the "beatific vision." Seeing, gazing, beholding are all metaphors for the euphoric experience of being in the presence of God in the world to come. It's what Revelation, also written by John, speaks of: "No longer will there be anything accursed, but the throne of God and of the Lamb will be in it, and his servants will worship him. They will see his face, and his name will be on their foreheads" (22:3–4). It's what Psalm 27:4 describes:

One thing have I asked of the LORD,
    that will I seek after:
that I may dwell in the house of the LORD
    all the days of my life,
to gaze upon the beauty of the LORD
    and to inquire in his temple.

It's what Jesus affirms: "Blessed are the pure in heart, for they shall see God" (Matthew 5:8). It's the soul-swelling and mind-bending prospect of beholding God in a way we've never done before. And it's to this wondrous finish line that the children of God are moving every second.

When people think of Christianity and destiny, both believers and non-believers think of one word: heaven. And Christians may often feel they must do public relations for heaven. The PR pitch is quite simple:

Don't worry; it won't just be one long worship song! Everything from earth will be present but purified and elevated: feast, drink, build, work, and play. No more darkness, no more evil, and God will be the center of all.

True. But maybe the emphasis is off. The Bible says the best thing about heaven is the ability and capacity to behold the glory of God. In heaven, the best thing is the view.

Would heaven be heaven if there was no sin and death but also no Jesus to behold? The great hope of the children of God is to behold the vision of God. Just a few years back, a total solar eclipse occurred. Folks drove for miles crossing multiple states to catch just a fleeting glimpse of something that can be witnessed only every few centuries. To see the sun eclipsed in midday was staggering. How much more stunning will it be to gaze at the One who spoke the sun into being with a word?

We were made to behold God in this way. It's why we long to see beauty in art, victory in sports, and the spectacular in fashion. Our eyes were made to behold wonder. The joyous end for which all people were made is to behold the vision of God. Anselm of Canterbury, a medieval theologian, wrote of this divine vision: "I was created to see thee, and not yet have I done that for which I was made."[5] The day is coming. Because, through Christ, you will behold the beauty of God, you need to know that no matter what you're facing right now, no matter if your body is breaking down or you feel hopeless, you as a child of God can say with full confidence, "My future is bright."

What does this have to do with the Resurrection? Bearing witness to something beautiful or vile is transformative. Witness enough violence and it's no surprise if, in time, you become what you behold. Witness beauty in art and in character and it, too, will rub off on you, influencing your taste and actions. To behold the glory of God in Jesus is to be transformed. When Jesus appears, we will see him. Christ has died, Christ has risen, and Christ will come again. When he comes and we see him, we will be transformed to be like him.

The ins and outs of the beatific vision are a complex mystery. But in a sense, we experience a sliver of this vision now, when by faith we meditate on Christ and the beauty of God. Scripture is the place where we behold God's beauty, encounter the risen Christ, are purged of vice and sin, and are transformed to be holy and happy in God. Scripture and worship are the dress rehearsal of beholding the beauty that awaits in heaven.

The Resurrection transforms your identity and destination: As a Christian you will behold God. Your life is not one long march of mundanity. You are moving—with all God's people—to the drumbeat of a radiant destiny.

FOR REFLECTION AND DISCUSSION

1. In what ways have you found being God's child transformative?
2. J. I. Packer also writes, "Our understanding of Christianity cannot be better than our grasp of adoption."[6] What do you make of this statement?
3. How might your thoughts about the future change if you consider your destiny with Jesus in light of the Resurrection?

Completion and Beginning

Acts 1:1–11
Psalm 110:1–5
Hebrews 1:1–4
Luke 24:44–53

While they were gazing into heaven as he went,
behold, two men stood by them in white robes,
and said, "Men of Galilee, why do you stand
looking into heaven?"

—Acts 1:10–11

Almighty God, whose only-begotten Son our Lord
Jesus Christ ascended into heaven: May our hearts
and minds also there ascend, and with him continually dwell; who lives and reigns with you and the Holy
Spirit, one God, for ever and ever. Amen.[1]

If you were to move away from your hometown and people rejoiced and commemorated yearly the day of your departure, you'd likely feel offended—and rightly so. We don't usually celebrate the leave-taking of people we care for. So, it's not unreasonable to wonder why believers celebrate Jesus's departure. The ascension of Jesus is a much neglected doctrine, at least in terms of how often it is preached on, and its neglect leads to a dysfunctional spirituality. The first step to remedy the neglect—and to be strengthened personally and spiritually by the Ascension—is to recognize that Jesus's ascension is not so much an evacuation but a coronation.

The Work Completed

The Ascension carries a deep sense of completion: Jesus ascended to God's presence because he fulfilled his earthly mission. He walked in our humanity. He resisted the lies of the world and the devil that ensnared us. He loved God and neighbor in full. He suffered and died for our sin. And God raised him from the dead. He taught his disciples about the kingdom and gave them—and us—marching orders to proclaim and serve in his name. And then he ascended to where the Father is.

The Ascension means Jesus is not on earth in some undisclosed location or in the witness protection program. Jesus has returned to God, with nail-scarred hands, truly human and truly divine, to be enthroned over all. The earthly work of our salvation is finished because of Jesus's sacrifice—his very body—before the presence of God in heaven. Hebrews 1:3 lays this out for us: "After making purification for sins, he sat down at the right hand of the Majesty on high." The Ascension completes the cross-to-resurrection mission by bringing Jesus's saving work done on earth into the presence of God in heaven. Luke's gospel ends with the Ascension for a reason: It is the completion of his saving work done for us.

A New Beginning

In his gospel and Acts, Luke writes of the Ascension to show that it is not just a conclusion but also a fresh start—a hinge of finality (Luke 24:44–53) and a new beginning (Acts 1:1–11). Jesus's ascension and enthronement are both the completion of his work done for us and the beginning of his work done through us.

That the Ascension is both an end and a beginning is evident in the reactions to Jesus's return to heaven. In Luke 24, the work completed leads to praise and shouts of celebration. In Acts 1:9–11, the work about to begin leads to confusion:

> As they were looking on, he was lifted up, and a cloud took him out of their sight. And while they were gazing into heaven as he went, behold, two men stood by them in white robes, and said, "Men of Galilee, why do you stand looking into heaven?"

In essence, the angels are saying, "Don't just look up; look out! Don't replay the good old days with Jesus preaching and healing. Don't just marvel at what you've seen and heard. Don't just gaze up to the heavens. Gaze out on the world, and get ready for the work to be done." We need this word too.

Jesus has left one place (earth) to now be king over every place from the control center of the world (heaven). Therefore, there is work to be done precisely because Jesus reigns. Christ's departure urges us to look up and out with eyes and hearts informed by the ascension of the King.

If you only look out and focus on all the needs of the

world, you'll be frazzled or become numb. You'll miss the One who is enthroned despite the evil on our social media feeds and in our communities. And if you only look up, you'll miss the work the King has commissioned us to do in this world full of confusion and evil. Our task is to get our minds right, our hearts lifted, and our sights fixed. Be ascension-minded with ascension sight so you can be of earthly use in the name of the King who rules heaven and earth.

How do you look up? By lifting your mind and heart in joy that Jesus reigns. Remember that you have an advocate before the Father. Rejoice that you are ascended with Christ. Then, look out: Gaze on the hurt in your community through the knowledge of the Ascension, and work to do something about it in the power of our ascended King.

Looking out on the needs is not for the faint of heart. The number of tragedies and abuses within one's own town is enough to make the strongest of souls faint. The thing is, Jesus does not ask us to work without sorrowing. Our work of bearing burdens and weeping with those who weep is em-powered by the fact that a true human reigns. Theologian Michael Reeves offers this potent insight:

> There is now a man, a real man with our flesh and blood, our experiences of the world, our humanity, in heaven. For all Christ's heavenly majesty, seated on the throne, he is not aloof and unconcerned. He knows, and loves, and intercedes.[2]

Because Jesus is enthroned, we have capacity to grieve, weep, and work. When looking out is unbearable, look up. Know that our cries do not stop at the ceiling; they ascend to the throne where Christ, in full tenderness and fully glory, is. The Ascension means Jesus has gone up, but he has not gone away. In a deeper sense, he has extended his work in this weary and lost world. Truly, the King is here; the King is there; the King is everywhere.

FOR REFLECTION AND DISCUSSION

1. In what ways is the Ascension a neglected doctrine? In what ways is it crucial?
2. Are you more prone to look up or look out? Why?
3. How often do you think of Jesus as your ascended advocate? What might this change about your actions and attitudes this week?

The Wind and the Room

Genesis 11:1–9
Psalm 104:24–35
Acts 2:1–21
John 14:8–17

Suddenly there came from heaven a sound like
a mighty rushing wind, and it filled the entire
house where they were sitting. And divided
tongues as of fire appeared to them and rested
on each one of them. And they were all filled
with the Holy Spirit and began to speak in other
tongues as the Spirit gave them utterance.

—Acts 2:2–4

Almighty God, on this day, through the outpouring of
the Holy Spirit, you revealed the way of eternal life to
every race and nation: Pour out this gift anew, that by
the preaching of the Gospel your salvation may reach
to the ends of the earth; through Jesus Christ our Lord,

who lives and reigns with you, in the unity of the Holy
Spirit, one God, for ever and ever. Amen.[1]

Maybe you've heard the saying "I wish I was in the room."
Fans of the hit Broadway musical *Hamilton* know about being
"in the room where it happened." Out of fascination, some
think of the meeting of the minds in 1776 or maybe a fourth-
century church council and murmur, "I just wish I had been
in the room to see what all went down." Up-and-coming mu-
sicians, full of ambition, wish to be in the room with that one
producer who will give them a shot. Whatever it is, we all
likely have rooms we wish we could set foot in.

The thing about the room in Acts 2 at Pentecost is that it
was ordinary—until it wasn't. It was probably hot, musty, and
sweaty. Although this room is not physically available to us, it
is a place we must get into because our hope of salvation and
transformation draws its earthly source from this room.

A Time to Wait

What were the disciples doing before the wind of God's Spirit
blew? They were in the midst of that horrific activity we humans despise so much: They were waiting. That's hard enough,
but they were also *waiting in crisis.* Judas betrayed his friends
and his Lord. And because the religious leaders did not offer
him help in his remorse and despair, he took his own life
(Matthew 27:3–5). Now the disciples must mourn and replace
a friend, all while wondering what Jesus meant when he said
to wait for "power from on high" (Luke 24:49).

Before they could comprehend all the answers, the Spirit
of God burst on the scene, filling that upper room with the

sound of the mighty works of God in the languages of the nations. At Pentecost, the promise Jesus gave in Acts 1:8 came true, but in a way no one predicted. The disciples were waiting in crisis, but they were also *waiting in faith*—a faith seeking understanding—because who knew when the Spirit-like wind would blow? Who could have known that thousands would come to the 120 disciples and that the world would never be the same again? All from the wind of the Spirit of God rushing down on one single room.

Pentecost teaches us there is a time to wait. But the waiting period is never time wasted, because God is faithful to his promise, even when the Spirit blows in a way we could never imagine. Pentecost is connected to what we celebrated last week, the ascension of Jesus. Luke makes this connection by reminding us that the Spirit comes from heaven (Acts 2:2), which is where Jesus just ascended. The Spirit is sent from Jesus's new (old) address. Jesus ascends, and the Spirit descends. The gift of the Spirit is another bright jewel in the crowning glory of God's radical generosity to this world.

A Time When Heaven Came to Earth

There's a divine precedence to the ascending and descending that triggers and brings remarkable transformation into the world. God has done this radical from-heaven type of gift before.

We've been looking at the day of Pentecost as a waiting time. But while one house is waiting with its small band of 120 disciples of Jesus, the rest of the city is bursting with activity. It's Pentecost, which for Jews is an agricultural feast fifty days after Passover that includes the first offerings of crops. But Pentecost was always another entry point into the great story of redemption from slavery to freedom with God. You re-

member Passover, don't you? It's when the lamb was sacrificed, judgment struck, and God's people were saved and
passed through the Red Sea. Then, fifty days after Passover,
they came thrilled and weary to Mount Sinai. Moses ascended
to God on the mountain (one of many of Moses's ascents and
descents). Then he descended with the Law, God's written
revelation.

Do you see the pattern? God is the great giver! And at
Pentecost, God gives his people new power to live out a new
purpose. Through God's heavenly gift, the time of waiting
becomes a time of working. For Israel, the time of working
was to display, through the Law, a life of light and truth to the
world. But the Law was on tablets of stone. The Spirit blows
like supernatural wind to bring something deeper, something
better, something internal and not external. Jesus went up, and
now his Spirit is coming down—not with tablets of stone but
with the ways of God carved on the human hearts of those
God redeems.

A few years ago, my wife and I went to Switzerland for my
cousin's wedding. I got to see my mom with her brothers,
whom she hadn't seen in years—the hugs, the smiles, the
kisses. But above all, the language struck me. They spoke in
their native tongue—their heart language from Côte d'Ivoire.
In that moment, I saw a side of my mom I never really knew.
She spoke neither in English nor in French but in the language
native to her deepest being. What is the intimate point of contact between God and humanity at Pentecost? It is the point of
language. The people outside the room hear about God's saving power in their native tongues. The power of one's heart
language is a true phenomenon. God reaches the people at
Pentecost in their own language, and he will reach us with
ours too.

We need to remember that every good and perfect gift is

from God. This means you and I are constantly being given signs from God's good hand meant to lead us upward to him. Instead, we get curved in on ourselves. We not only miss the beauty of a neighbor's smile or the kindness or the humor of a friend; we also miss that God is the source of these good things. When we see signs of beauty in the world, both small and large, we might attribute it to the universe, ourselves, or a vague higher power. Everything becomes about itself or us. This is similar to the Babel mistake we read of in Genesis 11. But here's the thing: When something amazing and incredible happens, we still ask the question, "What does this mean?" We're always looking for authorial intent when the wind blows because deep down there is a tremor in our hearts that whispers, "Something more is out there."

The Spirit is like a double gust of wind—he stirs up a *sign* and stirs up a *word,* and both gesture without mistake to the person of Jesus. The Spirit is stronger than the confusion and resistance in the broken human heart.

A Time to Work

Look who stands when resistance and confusion emerge in Acts 2: Peter, freshly restored by Jesus. He sees which way the wind is blowing. But the sign needs a word. The time for waiting has passed; the time for working has come. Empowered by the Spirit, Peter explains the sign by the word of the gospel. At Pentecost, the news that makes the world work, that heals the human soul, that overcomes death, that says our sins are forgiven and our hope is secure, is brought into direct contact with the human heart through the Holy Spirit.

Without the wind, no boat can set sail and no ship in centuries past could ever reach new land. No wind, no power. But with the wind, new possibilities arise. Jesus, ever wise and generous, wants us to know that the Spirit of God is like the wind from heaven. With the wind, new spiritual life is breathed into the dry rooms of our lives, new hope rushes into our despairing hearts, and salvation blows into every corner of the world.

Ever since this Acts 2 moment, the wind has not stopped blowing. The breath of life that worked with the Father and the Son in creation is ever and always blowing, leading us further up and into the gift of redemption in Jesus's name. Without the Spirit, no one would know Christ. With the Spirit, the world will know him through you. The Spirit of Jesus looks at you and says, "Here is my interpretive witness. Here is my small-scale Peter." Your task is to say this adventurous prayer: "Spirit of God, let me discern where you, like the wind, are blowing."

I'm reminded of golfers, crouched and focused, trying to discern the wind before approaching their shots. Disciples do that and more. Whom do you need to pray for? Whom do you need to serve? To whom do you need to speak? All this is more than possible—not by your might or intellect but by the Spirit of God who is among us and in us by faith. Understand this: You are now in the room of Acts 2 because the room has become the whole world, for God is moving by his Spirit to bring heaven's salvation to every human heart.

FOR REFLECTION AND DISCUSSION

1. What does it say about God that the Spirit comes when the disciples are waiting in faith and in crisis?
2. How does the Old Testament background on Pentecost help us appreciate the gift of the Spirit?
3. How can you seek and respond to the Spirit this week?

ORDINARY TIME

Walking the Way of Christ

Take our times, times of love and times of weariness,
Take them all, bless them and break them [. . .]
—WALTER BRUEGGEMANN,
from "Occupy Our Calendars"

When I first heard of the church year season called Ordinary Time, I had to suppress a laugh. Chuckling inwardly, I thought to myself, *The liturgical powers that be actually went ahead and admitted that some parts of the year are straight up boring*. That turned out to be a rookie misunderstanding.

Ordinary Time, I came to learn, derives from the Latin word *ordinalis*, not as in "plain" or "boring" but as in "numerical order." This means the Sundays in Ordinary Time are counted.

Ordinary Time (sometimes called Trinitytide) is ordered time, marking the weeks between Pentecost and the first Sunday of Advent.[1] Unlike Lent, which is a season for fasting and renewal, and unlike Eastertide, which is a season for feasting, Ordinary Time is a season for counting. It is the season of keeping time and following Jesus in love and mission day by day, Sunday by Sunday.

Ordinary Time and Epiphany share the same liturgical

color: green. Green is the color of growth, both bad (think of mold) and good (think of your favorite garden plant slowly blooming). Time reflects growth and change. In Ordinary Time, God reminds us that even when life seems boring, even when it appears that nothing significant is happening, he is always at work, tending and cultivating us with the care of a wise gardener and growing us in ways we won't even notice until sufficient time passes.

Ordinary Time Spirituality

The entire church year is an immersive experience into the life of Jesus. So how does Ordinary Time guide us deeper into Christ and form us into his image? It does so through its distinct emphasis of discipleship in the mundane. Ordinary Time spirituality is spirituality with Jesus in—not apart from—the rhythms that constitute our normal lives.

If this part of the church year is ordinary in the sense defined above, then is the remainder of the year rightly understood as extraordinary? There is substance to such an understanding. As we noted in the introduction, the church year presents us with a framework of three movements:

1. **The Cycle of Light:** Advent, Christmastide, Epiphany
2. **The Cycle of Life:** Lent, Holy Week, Eastertide, Pentecost
3. **The Cycle of Love:** Ordinary Time

Sure, Ordinary Time is less extraordinary in contrast to the Cycles of Light and Life, as evidenced by its fewer sacred and feast days. But Ordinary Time is the season in which all the cycles that have gone before combine to form our daily living. Again, the Cycle of Light is God with us in the Incarnation, the Cycle of Life demonstrates God for us in the gift of salvation, and the Cycle of Love is God working through us in love, service, and proclamation. In Ordinary Time, the previous cycles blossom into full effect.

Think of Ordinary Time as a steady reverberation of extraordinary time, a sort of ripple effect of Jesus's work in his people that stretches out to shape life in all its beauty and mundanity. Drawn deeply into the incarnation, life, death, resurrection, and ascension of Jesus in Advent, Christmas, Epiphany, Lent, Eastertide, and Pentecost, we are now placed into a season in which the cumulative power of Christ through the church year flows forth in the nitty-gritty of our common daily life.

How does this happen? Partly through a different tempo and pace. In Ordinary Time, we slow down. We have space to consider, contemplate, and apply. What or whom? Christ, of course! In this season, we find where the life of Jesus intersects with the daily lives we inhabit. We seek and meet Jesus in the mundane and discover that this, too, is holy ground.

Consider what a gift this season can be. Clergy aren't scrambling to pull off Holy Week services, and families aren't hustling to get back from spring break in time for them. The rest of us aren't bouncing between holiday gatherings, cranky from the gloom of winter, all while trying to keep a holy Advent. The slower pace of Ordinary Time permits us to focus on the day-to-day things we often overlook. Ordinary Time is the season to search out the simple, small moments where we can imitate Christ in tiny, holy ways. In this season, we learn that just as the secular and sacred divide is a flimsy fiction, so too is the divide between one's everyday life and spiritual life.

Most of our forefathers and foremothers in the faith did their living in the midst of this sort of ordinary time. We know the extraordinary things the apostle Paul did, but they were just a sliver compared to the full frame of his existence. We marvel at the faith and advocacy of someone like Fannie Lou Hamer, but what of all the ordinary moments, meals, and conversations that shaped her faith and heart to make such a daring and brilliant stand against lynching and for righteousness? The true example, as always, is our Lord himself. Laura Kelly Fanucci explains the Christ connection of Ordinary Time:

> Jesus did most of his living and working in ordinary time. Thirty years before his ministry became public. We don't know the ordinary stories from those decades, but they must have been filled with the regular routines that fill our own lives: work, family, learning, growth, rest, repeat.
>
> All of Jesus's ordinary time added up, slowly over seasons and years, to make him who he was. A son, a friend, a neighbor, a prophet, a healer, a teacher, a leader.[2]

Fanucci then wonders who we are becoming through the mundaneness of our ordinary time. We are becoming like Christ. The Son of God is shining forth in us—not in spite of our ordinary lives but through them.

Ordinary Time Practices

What are the particular practices that mark worship and discipleship in Ordinary Time? Several could be named, but these four form a helpful starting place for individuals and communities.

Look for Jesus in the small things. "Christ plays in ten thousand places," wrote poet Gerard Manley Hopkins.[3] Where is Jesus at work around you? How can you join him? Attending to these questions requires we adjust our eyes to see where Jesus is moving—in a non-Christian friend curious about Christianity, in a conversation with a stranger at a playdate, in a neighbor in crisis and need, in a niece becoming interested in the faith and her calling in the world—and we join him with joy.

Imitate Jesus in the small things. How can you be tangibly formed into Christlikeness? In which of your daily routines can you imitate Christ in love, humility, mercy, or even obscurity? Maybe you drop kids or nephews off at school. Maybe you have multiple Zoom meetings for work each day. How might you seek and display the ways of Christ in these simple but significant moments that make up your day? Ask Christ for the wisdom to imitate him, trusting that he's with you.

Go deeper in Scripture and study. During this season, it's common for churches to move away from the lectionary and center preaching texts on a particular book of the Bible. This is called *lectio continua*. The lectionary often encourages this approach with continuous readings in a gospel or epistle. Ordinary Time is ideal for focused study on whatever you sense will grow you with Christ. Maybe it's a work of theology, a study of a gospel, or a study of a cultural issue. Whatever it may be, Ordinary Time is a perfect opportunity to further love God with all your mind.

Move out in evangelism and service. Many of the gospel readings in Ordinary Time showcase Jesus on his daily grind among the people, meeting needs, healing the sick, and preaching the gospel of the kingdom. Ordinary Time is our time as Christ's body to move in unison with our Head, declaring and demonstrating the gospel with our lives and lips. In Ordinary Time, rector Aaron Damiani writes, "we walk a long obedience in the same direction, seeking to grow spiritually and serve our community for God's glory."[4] Get specific here. Think real neighbors and needs, local people and places; then follow Christ with love and boldness.

Ordinary Time Feast Days

Each season has notable feast days in which the church is called into a deeper experience of the life of Christ together.

Holy Cross Day (September 14): This day honors and remembers Christ's self-giving on the cross for us and our salvation by focusing on the sign and symbol of the cross.[5] In some traditions, the day also commemorates the discovery of the "true cross" around A.D. 326 by Saint Helena, the mother of the emperor Constantine.[6]

Feast of Saint Michael and All Angels (September 29): This day draws our focus to the mysterious existence and presence of angelic beings and their role in spiritual warfare and God's defeat of our great enemies: Satan, sin, and death. The day is often called Michaelmas, which is a contraction of *Michael's Mass.* We celebrate and remember that God's angels are real, present, and on our side.

All Saints' Day (November 1): This feast honors the godly men and women who in holiness and faithfulness have gone before us. Their examples spur us on to run the race of faith with endurance. On this day, we "honor the example of their lives and deaths and rejoice in the continued communion with them through membership and participation in the body of Christ."[7]

Christ the King Sunday (last Sunday before Advent): This is the last Sunday of the church year, and it celebrates Christ as the true Messiah, true Lord, and true King over all the cosmos. This is a more recent feast day, first instituted in 1925 and placed on the last Sunday before Advent in 1970.

Reading Ordinary Time Texts and Devotions

As you read the following Scripture texts and devotions, you'll hear themes of discipleship, prayer, lament, and freedom in Jesus. This wide range reflects the all-encompassing nature of Ordinary Time as discipleship in real life. May these texts and these reflections open you up for the steady growth of Christ-likeness God desires to work out in you.

First Week

Trinity Sunday

Genesis 1:1–2:3
Psalm 150
2 Corinthians 13:5–14
Matthew 28:16–20

Go therefore and make disciples of all nations,
baptizing them in the name of the Father and of
the Son and of the Holy Spirit.

—Matthew 28:19

Almighty and everlasting God, you have given to us your servants grace, by the confession of a true faith, to acknowledge the glory of the eternal Trinity, and in the power of your divine Majesty to worship the Unity: Keep us steadfast in this faith and worship, and bring us at last to see you in your one and eternal glory, O Father; who with the Son and the Holy Spirit live and reign, one God, for ever and ever. Amen.[1]

Does it really make a difference that God is a Trinity? Sometimes considering the Trinity feels like an advanced, confusing
extracurricular for those with too much time on their hands.
Writer Dorothy Sayers has a wonderful line where she says,
"The Christian faith is the most exciting drama that ever stag-
gered the imagination of man—and the dogma *is* the drama."[2]
Our doctrines, creeds, and truths like the Trinity are the
drama. In other words, theological truth is not dry information, nor is it reserved for experts. It is the true, riveting, and
living story of who God is and how he loves this world.

Theology is dramatic; it tells a thrilling story. From creation to Incarnation to Resurrection, it makes the overwhelming assertion that the same God who made the world lived in
the world and passed through the grave and gates of death.
This is the dogma and thus the drama of the Christian story.
And the thrill and hope of Christianity is inseparable from the
God who is three in one.

Which God Is Love?

Jesus's last words in Matthew reveal the key reasons why the
Trinity matters for your life. The risen Jesus uses his authority
to commission his disciples to spread his kingdom in the triune name: Father, Son, and Holy Spirit. Here stands beautiful
dogma (the triune God in equal status) that is life-giving drama
(the gospel moving out to bring the triune God's saving power
to the whole world).

The name in which this redemptive work is done is not
singular. It's Trinitarian. Jesus's words of commission point to
the great fact that God is, in his being, not simply powerful
but personal. Have you ever said that "God is love"? Unless

God is Father, Son, and Holy Spirit, to say "God is love" is to utter a lie. If God were unipersonal (one person), he couldn't be love, for whom would there be to love? A unipersonal God could be *loving* but only at the moment he created something to love: the world, seals, or creatures like you and me. This God's love would amount to an app upgrade, not an eternal, natural feature of his character from the beginning. This would mean that this God could change. If he could become loving once he created something, then presumably he could become less loving. If Jesus had commissioned the church in a singular name, we would have a unitarian, shape-shifting God, who might be capable of learning or adding love and holiness to his character but not possessing it in his nature and being. We can know that our God is love because, as Matthew shows us, God is triune.

Matthew is the first book of the New Testament and is crafted, like Genesis of the Old, to introduce us to the God who loves and claims this world. That's why Matthew's narrative is told in a Trinitarian frame. In Matthew 3:16–17, at Jesus's baptism, the Father speaks, the Son enters the waters to identify with sinful people like us, and the Spirit descends like a dove. At Matthew's close, Jesus commissions in the Trinitarian name—which teaches us that God is unity and trinity. He is personal and relational in his very being.

This means that God is not fundamentally "power" or "might" or even "creator" but is relational: Father, Son, Holy Spirit. When God comes near to us in mercy and love, it's not as though he's learning a new habit. It's the natural disposition of his heart. Are you lonely? Are you hurting? Are you sick of fickle friends? The triune God is reaching out to you with the eternal, infinite love he has had from the very beginning. Because God is trinity, God is love.

This is why the heart of the gospel is not simply God's rescuing us from judgment but also his bringing us into living connection with him—giving us access to the connection he's had within himself from the very beginning. "As Jesus Christ calls us and is heard by us He gives us His Holy Spirit in order that His own relationship to His Father may be repeated in us."[3] By grace we become children of God, marked by the access, peace, joy, and fullness that Jesus gives and shares with us by the Spirit.

Baptized into His Name

Jesus's commission declares the importance of the Trinity by showing us that the relational God is reclaiming his world. The triune God loves and seeks what's been lost: us. The dogma is the drama, for the Father, the Son, and the Spirit are engaged in a reclamation project that is cosmic and personal, touching creation and individuals (Colossians 1:15–20). In Jesus's commission, the disciples are to announce the way to reconciliation with God and a reunion into the love and grounding we were made for.

This restoration leads to being baptized in the triune name. To be baptized is to be made new and placed into something. Being baptized in the triune name means it's the triune God to whom we now belong. In faith and baptism, God claims us anew. Do you know the claim of love placed on you? The triune God created you by the love of the Father. The triune God redeemed you by the sacrifice of the Son. And the triune God indwells you by the Spirit. There's nothing greater than living in the name of the Father, Son, and Spirit, in the confidence and direction of this divine love.

Called to Love

In Jesus's Great Commission, the relational God calls us to relational work in his name. If God is trinity and thus personal, his gospel cannot be shared in ways that do violence to persons. The relational God who came near to us is calling us to come near to others—not with gimmicks but in embodied love—to declare and demonstrate God's saving grace to them.

Our call to mission will certainly never be more overwhelming than what the first apostles felt with Jesus about to ascend. A handful of Jewish believers were being called to go to "all nations"—namely, the Gentile world full of idolatry and animosity. How would they relate? Would they get contaminated ritually and spiritually by the world's idolatry? The church struggled to live out this mission (Acts 8:1; 15), but they stumbled forth in the triune name. Which means they went in triune power. Remembering that the dogma is the drama gives us strength to see that God is love because God is trinity. The gospel is true because God is trinity. God is for you because he is trinity. God is relational not by accident but by his name because he is trinity. And by his mercy, you are called into knowing the triune God.

FOR REFLECTION AND DISCUSSION

1. How have you thought about the Trinity? How is this truth connected to God's love?
2. In what way is it good news that God is not fundamentally "powerful" or "the creator" but Trinitarian?
3. How can the good news that the triune God seeks and claims you shape your self-understanding this week? What joys and challenges does this truth put into perspective?

Second Week

Mercy or Sacrifice?

Hosea 5:15–6:6
Psalm 50
Romans 4:13–18
Matthew 9:9–13

Go and learn what this means:
"I desire mercy, and not sacrifice."

—Matthew 9:13

Grant, O Lord, that the course of this world may be so peaceably ordered by your providence, that your Church may joyfully serve you in quiet confidence and godly peace; through Jesus Christ our Lord, who lives and reigns with you and the Holy Spirit, one God, for ever and ever. Amen.[1]

What kind of statement does Jesus offer in Matthew 9:13? Something serious is at stake, something that strikes at the center of what God wants from us. To find our way into the meaning of Jesus's words, we must get a sense of the dinner party scene that Matthew records.

This dinner scenario is vivid and dramatic, a continuation of the roaring reputation Jesus has been developing. Earlier in Matthew 9, Jesus has been healing the sick and, most shockingly, forgiving the sins of people—a serious *theological surprise*, for only God can forgive sins. But Jesus adds to his résumé a *relational surprise:* He makes a tax collector his disciple.

Tax collectors cheated their own people through partnership with their oppressors, the Romans. Yet Jesus issues the call of the gospel to Matthew. Matthew then throws away his life's script and rises into a new life with Jesus as a disciple. What type of religious leader would make time for a legal crook in cahoots with the evil empire? Jesus would and did. And Matthew lived to write the story, one that includes his conversion and the festive dinner party that followed.

The celebration shifts to conflict as the Pharisees happen upon the joyful noise. If Matthew were writing a modern memoir, he might say, "It was the best of times, and it was the worst of times. It was the best because Jesus called me. It was the worst because Jesus's first serious fight with the Pharisees happened because of me and all my colleagues. It was a sign of things to come—look at chapter 23 if you don't believe me. But it all started because Jesus embraced me in a way, and I embraced him, and he came to eat and teach all of us sinful folks."

It's not hard to imagine the scene. The Pharisees move around the edge of the party, asking a cluster of Jesus's disciples a fair question: "He says he is God's anointed one, so why is he eating with sinners?" The Pharisees have in mind both Scripture (such as Psalm 1) and history. Biblical history showed how often the people of God were contaminated by idolatry through close connection with sinners. So, the Pharisees sought to course correct. Their motto was "We'll return to God with pure devotion and full obedience, and God will then come to us and free us from our captors like he did before in Moses's day."

Jesus answers them first with street smarts: "Those who are well have no need of a physician, but those who are sick" (verse 12). Then Jesus pushes deeper from an answer rooted in common sense to the same answer rooted in sacred Scripture. He quotes Hosea 6:6 but begins with a rabbinic commission: "Go and learn what this means: 'I desire mercy, and not sacrifice'" (verse 13). Jesus looks at the top religious teachers and says, "You need to hit the books. Go back to the sources. Take up and read." According to Jesus, his presence with and among ungodly, disreputable people can be explained by God's desire.

The Great Divide: Mercy and Sacrifice

The words *mercy* and *sacrifice* are containers full of deep meaning. *Sacrifice* contains the work of holiness, the commandments, the offerings, the things holy people ought to do toward God. Sacrifice is like an act of will that separates the righteous from sinners. *Mercy* is connected to the notion of steadfast love—a link of love that flows from God to us and then from us to others in God's name, looping them into his loyal love.

What we see in Matthew's dinner party is a great divide that is repeated in our lives and churches today. The Pharisees were fixated on sacrifice—so much so that they neglected the reality of God's mercy. When Jesus said "Go and learn," he pointed them to Hosea 6, where God's people were being rebuked:

Your love is like a morning cloud,
   like the dew that goes early away. (verse 4)

Hosea speaks of when God's people kept up their sacrifices and rituals yet gave their hearts' loyalty not to the Lord but to other gods. Hence, the parallel meaning of Hosea 6:6:

I desire steadfast love and not sacrifice,
   the knowledge of God rather than burnt offerings.

Today it's more than possible to go to church, say our prayers, give our money, and then go on our way with no knowledge of God, no living link to his deep love, because our hearts are stuffed full of themselves. In effect, Jesus is saying with subtlety what he will later say explicitly (see Matthew 23): "Pharisees, you look much cleaner on the outside than the people of Hosea's time. But the vital heart is missing. You have focused on sacrifice to the exclusion of loyal love toward God—and the proof is this: You won't go near the very people who need the mercy of God the most." The Pharisees were so fixated on sacrifice and holiness via separation and purity that they needed to go and learn that God desires mercy, not sacrifice. Jesus's words are crucial to remember because it is often in Ordinary Time that we have more and unexpected opportunities to connect with, welcome, and serve the people around us.

Three Ways We Relearn with Jesus[2]

1. Go and learn from Jesus, not modern groups making the same mistake. A well-known proverb says, "History doesn't repeat itself, but it often rhymes."[3] People get burned in churches that preach only works and holiness but not mercy and love. Then we pendulum-swing to the other extreme: all mercy, all grace, no holiness, no commands, no sacrifice. Rather than seeing God's commands as part of God's grace, we shun them. And we become what Dale Bruner calls "the *Mercy* Christians."

In the opposing corner of the ring, we find what Bruner calls "the *Sacrifice* Christians." They see the lack of commands and the shrinking attendance of the Mercy Christians' churches because the churches often have no discernible Christian features. Then the *Sacrifice* Christians puff out their chests and double down, cranking up the volume on holiness, faithfulness, discipleship, and separation.

These distortions turn the church into two rival crews: one shouting "Mercy" and the other "Sacrifice," one saying "Grace" and the other "Holiness." Over time, some of us may even get burnt out on one and flip sides to join the other. Either way, we miss the picture by falling for an either-or binary when Jesus strikes a different note of emphasis. What's the way forward? Don't miss that Jesus's prescribed remedy is to point the Pharisees back to Scripture. In effect, Jesus instructs them to relearn everything by looking to him (John 5:39).

When it comes to how we relate to God and to others, Jesus is our example. In fact, as our teacher, Jesus quotes this line from Hosea twice (Matthew 9:13; 12:7). Negative experience can inform us, but it is a flawed instructor. It is time to go and learn from the Teacher.

As we study and learn under Jesus, we quickly see that mercy and sacrifice need not be separated but placed in proper connection, which will help us follow Jesus's emphasis without buying into a false binary. Notice that at the dinner party, Jesus does not relativize holiness. He actually calls the tax collectors and sinners "sick" in front of their faces. He embodies mercy and truth. Jesus is not afraid to call a spade a spade or a sinner a sinner—he just won't abandon people to their fate under the guise of purity. So, spend time with Jesus in the Word and with others following him in the life of the church; in this way, your soul and imagination will feed on Scripture and be reminded daily and weekly that mercy and truth live harmoniously.

2. Go and learn from Jesus, who never separates what God joined together. Holiness and sacrifice matter. "I desire mercy, not sacrifice" is a Semitic form of speech that means "I desire X *more than* Y," emphasizing the former without abolishing the latter. It's not one or the other. The reason mercy matters more is because it's part of God's character. When Moses encounters God, God passes before Moses and proclaims his name as "the LORD, the LORD, a God merciful and gracious, slow to anger, and abounding in steadfast love and faithfulness" (Exodus 34:6). In the testing of Abraham's faith in Genesis 22, what mattered more to God—that Abraham sacrifice Isaac or that Abraham display loyal love to God? Mercy matters more than sacrifice.

At Matthew's dinner party, this charge from Jesus to go and learn matters greatly because we often divide what God has joined together. We're not different from Matthew; we, too, are sick and in need of healing. But once we receive grace, we are prone to become unmerciful to the people who were just like us. We violently divide the covenant loyalty of mercy and sacrifice in pieces, butchering what God has always wanted held as one. Jesus is our strong and gentle teacher, with whom class is always in session, the mercy is flowing, and the chance to turn from our divided ways is ever available. Will you turn to him and be taught? Will you admit where you are divided—or where your heart is simply numb? Will you let his grace revive you so that mercy and sacrifice, grace and holiness come alive in you?

3. Go and learn from Jesus by worshipping him. The primary way we learn from Jesus is by worshipping him. Worship consists of beholding and adoring. If we look primarily to the ways that we—or other Christians—have failed to be merciful and formed by holiness, our gaze is broken. Like a plant that never takes in sunlight, we'll fail to grow into what we're meant to be. For this reason, prayerful reading of the Gospels is vital for learning from and worshipping Jesus. When we behold Jesus—his merciful way with sinners like Matthew and his sacrificial death for the world—we gaze at the bright glory of God revealed. By grace, we become what we behold and adore.

For this reason, the crucifixion of Jesus looms large in all four gospel narratives. Only in proximity to the Cross do we learn to worship Jesus and to follow his counterintuitive ways. From a heart of deep loyalty to God and love for this world, Jesus joined together mercy and sacrifice for the sake of sinners. This is a sacrifice without comparison. And it is this sacrifice that is mercy. He sacrificed himself because of God's loyal love, and as a result of his sacrifice, mercy flowed down to us. God desires mercy more than sacrifice so much that he will sacrifice himself in his Son to cover us in mercy from start to finish and make us people of mercy to a watching world. What our Teacher and Savior has joined together, let no one separate.

FOR REFLECTION AND DISCUSSION

1. How would you describe the relationship between mercy and sacrifice according to Jesus's words?
2. Do you tend toward mercy or sacrifice? Why?
3. What relearning is Jesus calling you toward? How can you pursue this with others?

Third Week

The Serious Surprise
of Discipleship

Exodus 19:1–8

Psalm 100

Romans 5:1–11

Matthew 9:35–10:15

He called to him his twelve disciples and
gave them authority over unclean spirits, to
cast them out, and to heal every disease
and every affliction.

—Matthew 10:1

O Lord, from whom all good proceeds: Grant us the inspiration of your Holy Spirit, that we may always think
those things that are good, and by your merciful guidance may accomplish the same; through Jesus Christ
our Lord, who lives and reigns with you and the Holy
Spirit, one God, for ever and ever. Amen.[1]

Most days, we glide right past one of the most essential Christian truths: Jesus calls his followers to do what he did. At a basic level, this is what all great teachers do. Have you ever had to teach something you were unable to do? No matter your explanatory prowess, whether you're teaching algebra or how to change a car's oil, at some point, a student gets tired of the theory and asks for a demonstration. We see this in Matthew 10, when Jesus shows that he is the type of teacher who explains and shows. His followers are not meant to be analysts—operating in theories alone—but disciples who practice what they've heard and seen. The surprise is that novice disciples can also truly share in the work of the kingdom.

Defining a Disciple

Jesus is serious about calling us disciples, so he is always prodding us to move from a faith that is theoretical to one that is lived out. Christian writer and philosopher Dallas Willard observes that a disciple is "simply someone who has decided to be with another person, under appropriate conditions, in order to become capable of doing what that person does or to become what that person is."[2] Everyone is therefore a disciple; the question is to whom most exclusively. I remember wanting to be discipled by a seventh grader when I was in fifth grade. This seventh grader—LeVar—was cooler than the other side of the pillow. He had a swagger, a way with words, and fresh clothes, and he seemed quite confident talking not only to teachers but most notably to girls. In every way, he felt like the opposite of me. So, I decided to be like him by following him everywhere I could and asking lots of questions. I learned what brands to wear and how to at least project confidence. I didn't know it at the time, but I became his disciple.

The decision to follow is where discipleship begins, humanly speaking. But the offer is the true catalyst, and this comes from Jesus himself. What a gift when he says, "Follow me!" God in Jesus decides to be near the twelve disciples to mold them to be like him. God in Jesus decides to be near you to mold you to be like him. Jesus possesses a joyful seriousness about making people his fully formed disciples. Jesus looks out on people and sees more than the messes of their past or the problems of their present; he sees the potential of their transformation through him.

It's clear that true discipleship is serious business to Jesus because he calls his disciples into work with real stakes. Jesus commissions them to be laborers in the harvest, co-laborers in the work God yearns to do in every inch in the world, starting with the house of Israel.

We speak about this passage in Matthew for World Mission Sunday in Epiphany, but notice that the source of the commission to go preach is the heart of compassion. The commission is first local and then global, but the source for both is the same: Deep in Jesus burns a love for the people who are standing on the razor's edge between life and despair. The commission Jesus gives is a call for his disciples to share in his compassion through proclamation. The serious surprise of discipleship is that his heart of compassion can take root in us.

Our Savior and Teacher

Jesus calls us to push back the effects of evil and sin by speaking, serving, and showing the way of the kingdom. To do what he did, his disciples first needed to agree with his assessment. The world both then and now contains more than what meets the eye. Far from being regressive or making us fanatical, Jesus's assessment of the world helps us make a difference.

In his book called *The Death of Satan,* Andrew Delbanco, a scholar at Columbia University, argues that "a gulf has opened up in our culture between the visibility of evil and the intellectual resources available for coping with it."[3] He asserts that secular people often, understandably, attribute all human cruelty to psychological deprivation or social conditioning and, in so doing, trivialize the terrible wrongs people are capable of. Christianity, however, offers us real intellectual and spiritual resources to understand the wrongs we see in the world and in us. Jesus teaches his apprentices the world is not a flat space but a contested arena. It is not simply God and humanity but God, humanity, and the powers of sin and death—and Jesus is recasting us into this story on the right side of things, as agents who possess authority to push back on the effects of sin: "Jesus . . . gave them authority to drive out impure spirits and to heal every disease and sickness" (Matthew 10:1, NIV). The serious surprise continues as Jesus's followers share in his compassion, his commission, and his authority.

Our Apostolic Authority?

We can often read these verses, nod quietly, and think, *That's nice, but what does it really have to do with me? Yes, I'm a Christian, but I'm an accountant (or a schoolteacher or a stay-at-home parent). I'm not really fighting evil head-on or something. We have missionary friends working in hard local or global settings—they are living out this reality. But me? Not so much.*

The call of Jesus comes to the Twelve, and then through them—surprise!—Jesus knocks at our doors. Now we, too, have authority to do what he did. Authority is the power and capacity to make a difference. Sadly, it is often squandered, exploited, or withdrawn. Matthew knew about exploitation as a tax collector, using his power to steal and cheat the weak. But look at how Jesus reforms him. The man who stole money now goes out on mission with no money bag. Jesus seeks to reform our stories too.

How do we walk in his authority? By grace, by his Spirit, we do what he said and we do as he did. This is how we push back against sin and evil. Your vocation? Work in it as Christ would if he were in your shoes. This world? Pray for it as Christ taught, for the Lord's Prayer is participation in God's gracious kingdom revolution. Lies from the enemy roam this world like evil spirits. Speak Christ's truth and grace.

The final surprise of discipleship is the greatest. Before Jesus sends us, he himself is the sent one. In compassion, he heals us from the great affliction: our separation from our Creator. And with all authority, he gives us his Word and his Spirit to teach us and guide us. Just as we read in our Exodus reading, let us answer the Teacher's call by saying, "All that the Lord has spoken we will do" (19:8).

FOR REFLECTION AND DISCUSSION

1. How would you define a disciple? What nuances does Willard's definition add to your understanding?
2. What does it mean to share in Jesus's compassion and authority?
3. How is God calling you to change or respond to the surprise of discipleship?

Fourth Week

Measures of Fear
and Rejection

Jeremiah 20:7–13
Psalm 69:1–15
Romans 5:15–19
Matthew 10:16–33

A disciple is not above his teacher,
nor a servant above his master.

—Matthew 10:24

Lord of all power and might, the author and giver of all good things: Graft in our hearts the love of your Name, increase in us true religion, nourish us with all goodness, and bring forth in us the fruit of good works; through Jesus Christ our Lord, who lives and reigns with you and the Holy Spirit, one God, for ever and ever. Amen.[1]

Have you ever been deep asleep in a dark room, and someone comes in and flicks the light switch? Suddenly your eyes and senses are flooded with a blaze of light. If you're like me, you yell, "Turn off the lights!" You're angry. The light is too harsh, too much; it's not gradual, and it's an unexpected disruption to everything about your former state—asleep, warm, quiet, and in the dark.

There is a darkness in the world so strong that the light of God's grace feels like death. And the just way of God's kingdom provokes vicious backlash from the systems and powers at work for evil in the world. The light of the gospel in word and in deed stirs up drama, rejection, and offense. Even though we may be dim lights, believers are lights of Christ all the same.

Think about all the strange things that are permissible in our world—but to speak the claims of Jesus is, in some places, anathema. Many of our neighbors desire a form of kingdom virtues—justice, peace, equity, compassion—without the King. Christians can be pesky reminders of what is perceived as the lingering residue of a hateful age. Though America is not among the fifty countries where it is most dangerous to follow Christ, many of us as Christians are afraid of social rejection. No matter how compassionate or culturally astute a disciple is, some form of rejection for Jesus's name is unavoidable. Jesus is not teaching us something we are to escape; he's telling us what we must endure.

How to Rightly Order Our Fears

After detailing this rejection requirement, Jesus says to have no fear of people who will do this. There is every reason to be a bit nervous and more than a little reason to be afraid. Jesus's discipleship lesson, however, takes a surprising plot twist: Disciples are to expect a real measure of animosity but to do so without a measure of fear.

The judgment of God often produces fear in us, but in this case, it banishes fear. Jesus calls us to have no fear of those who reject or harm us because God's judgment will bring everything to light. Disciples fight fear with the fear of God, which will put everything to scale. The fear of God will banish all lesser fears, sending them to their room for a long time-out.

So, disciples are fearful creatures whose fears are rightly ordered toward God and little else. Jesus's lesson on fear is straightforward: People can kill your body and harm your reputation, but they cannot touch your soul. Fear God who can save or condemn you in both body and soul. Others can destroy the part of you that is temporary, but God can destroy the you that is temporal *and* eternal. This is a spectacular and shocking teaching that can change your whole life if you let it sink in.

What exactly is this fear of God? Jesus turns to birds to explain:

> Rather fear him who can destroy both soul and body in hell. Are not two sparrows sold for a penny? And not one of them will fall to the ground apart from your Father. But even the hairs of your head are all numbered. Fear not, therefore; you are of more value than many sparrows. (Matthew 10:28–31)

This is different than just being afraid of God. The fear of God is knowing his holy love in such a way that it begins to control your way of being—even your fears. You recognize that the same God who can give and take life is the one who loves the smallest of his creation, the cheapest thing sold in the market—the sparrow.

No sparrow "will fall to the ground apart from your Father," Jesus says. This means when the sparrow dies, God is there—not just in sovereignty but in care and presence. So, how much more do you mean to this God? Every one of your hairs is counted by him. If you suffer, he will be there. Nothing will befall you apart from his will and apart from his personal, tangible presence.

Beyond the object lesson of the sparrow, there is a greater place that puts the fear of God in us and banishes all lesser fears. It is the place where Jesus was rejected for us: the cross on which he chose to suffer, where he was stretched to bear our rejection so we would know the Father's embrace. To fear God is to know he's got his gaze on you—and it's full of eternal holy power and mercy. We learn this not only from the Lord's teaching but also from the life he lived and laid down and took up again.

FOR REFLECTION AND DISCUSSION

1. Why is rejection a part of following Jesus? What forms can this take?
2. What are you most afraid of when it comes to following Jesus?
3. How is the sparrow a lesson about fearing God by knowing his love?

Fifth Week

The Terms of Allegiance

Isaiah 2:10–17

Psalm 89:1–18

Romans 6:1–11

Matthew 10:34–42

Do not think that I have come to bring peace to the earth. I have not come to bring peace, but a sword. For I have come to set a man against his father, and a daughter against her mother, and a daughter-in-law against her mother-in-law.

—Matthew 10:34–35

O God, your never-failing providence sets in order all things both in heaven and on earth: Put away from us all hurtful things, and give us those things that are profitable for us; through Jesus Christ our Lord, who lives and reigns with you and the Holy Spirit, one God, for ever and ever. Amen.[1]

When was the last time you read a business's or website's terms and conditions? Hardly anyone does. We just scroll until we can click "I agree." A few years back, twenty-two thousand people did this when they joined a free public Wi-Fi network—and inadvertently agreed to a thousand hours of community service, including scrubbing toilets and "relieving sewer blockages." The company said they added this service clause "to illustrate the lack of consumer awareness of what they are signing up to when they access free wifi."[2]

Matthew 10 is where some skimming happens. People linger on the Sermon on the Mount, Matthew 5–7, captivated by the vision of discipleship to Jesus and the ways of the kingdom. But we skim at our own risk when we move into the following chapters. Where companies put the terms of service in fine print to bury inconvenient details, Jesus does the opposite. He's clear-eyed and up-front about the troublesome aspects of what it means to be his disciple. He prepares us, his friends, for the wild ride of discipleship that awaits.

The terms of discipleship Jesus presents consist of relational division. Recall that a disciple is simply a person who apprentices under a teacher to learn their wisdom and ways up close and personal, with the goal of being like them in attitude and actions. Therefore, disciples share—by faith, grace, and decision—in Jesus's compassion for the world, his commission to the world, and his rejection from the world.

Allegiance: The "Sword" of Division

When Jesus hits the scene, the result is less like an era of peace and more like the unsheathing of a sword. Jesus brings in his wake tidal waves of division. This seems strange for one deemed the Prince of Peace. What's the deal? In a sense, Jesus brings an ultimate peace in the end and a felt peace in the heart, while at the same time causing an immediate division. Why? Choosing to follow Jesus is a daily shift in loyalty, direction, and allegiance.

The decision of discipleship produces division. For many Christians around the world, it strikes at the most intimate level of family. Listen to one Christian writer reflecting on this very passage:

> While attending two different Seminaries I sat alongside students from all over the world; some of them were first generation Christians who knew firsthand what Jesus describes in this passage. One classmate from India shared about not being able to go home to see his family because they had turned their backs on him. Even worse, he knew a young man who had been beaten to death because he became a Christfollower. These perils are real for many of our brothers and sisters around the world.[3]

There's a saying that good friends are your "found family." Allegiance to Jesus can sever those bonds too. All disciples feel this in one way or another. And unless you constantly keep the "terms of discipleship" before you, this division will throw you for a loop. Earlier in the sermon on mission, Jesus makes clear that his disciples will share in his rejection (Matthew 10:22). This of course is balanced with people seeing the disciples' good works and praising God (5:16). It's both. Still, the daily decision to be a disciple of Jesus means that in some measure, you will experience rejection for his sake.

I'm reminded of a friend who recently renewed their commitment to follow Jesus and then noticed, gradually, that one of their friends stopped responding to texts and calls. It took a while to unearth the cause, but the culprit was faith. Though my friend had not been obnoxious about their new commitment to Jesus, this change was visible enough to make their friend second-guess the relationship. This was a painful form of rejection—not from stupidity or hypocrisy but from a desire to center one's life on Jesus as his follower. Though this is a far cry from the rejection of physical persecution that many believers face today around the world, even these seemingly small waves of rejection are real and seen by our Lord.

Admirers Versus Followers

Danish philosopher Søren Kierkegaard was an intense man who thought much about allegiance to Jesus. Kierkegaard wrote of the difference between admirers and followers of Jesus, observing, "What then, is the difference between an admirer and a follower? A follower *is* or strives *to be* what he admires. An admirer, however, keeps himself personally detached. He fails to see that what is admired involves a claim upon him, and thus he fails to be or strive to be what he admires."[4] Jesus has called us not to admire him from a distance but to worship by following him up close—and through his grace to become like the one we follow.

One great threat to disciples is the temptation to detach from Jesus because the social or physical rejection is too much to bear. In Frank Herbert's sci-fi classic *Dune*, the main character must put his hand in a mysterious black box, a container of excruciating pain. He must keep his hand in it long enough to prove he is worthy of the training he seeks. Everything in him wants to pull his hand free. At one point it seems that, despite all his preparation, he will withdraw and detach because the pain is simply overwhelming.

Can we admit that the pain of losing relationships on account of Jesus makes us want to disconnect from Jesus because the terms of discipleship are too unbearable? How, then, can we grow in allegiance to Jesus if division and rejection are the basic terms of discipleship?

Take comfort that this is the narrow way Jesus himself walked. He walked the terms of his discipleship before we ever moved a muscle. Jesus's mission divides his own family (Matthew 12:46–50). Yet later, at the cross, he will entrust his mother to the care of his disciple John (John 19:25–27). Jesus knew the sting of the sword of relational division because he walked in full allegiance to the will of the Father. Indeed, he felt worse than the sword; he took the pain of the cross.

Whatever family—found or biological—that you lose in following Jesus, he gives you back "a hundredfold" in his global body (Mark 10:29–31). Whatever you've lost or stand to lose when you put your allegiance in his hands, Jesus presents a greater reward to you in the life to come, such that you'll say, "I'd do it all again if only I could give up more for the One who gave his all for me."

FOR REFLECTION AND DISCUSSION

1. In what ways might we be prone to apply this passage about division in ways Jesus did not intend?
2. What's the difference between admiring and following? Does fear of rejection keep you from following Jesus more fully? How so?
3. In what ways is Jesus's own experience the ultimate fulfillment of this Matthew passage?

Sixth Week

Freedom Time

Isaiah 61:1–3
Psalm 16
Galatians 5:1, 13–25
Luke 9:51–62

For freedom Christ has set us free;
stand firm therefore, and do not submit
again to a yoke of slavery.

—Galatians 5:1

Grant us, O Lord, we pray, the spirit to think and do always those things that are right, that we, who can do no good thing apart from you, may by you be enabled to live according to your will; through Jesus Christ our Lord, who lives and reigns with you and the Holy Spirit, one God, for ever and ever. Amen.[1]

During their 1990s multiyear championship run, Michael Jordan and the Chicago Bulls had a mantra for the pregame huddle. With all hands placed in the circle, one teammate would shout, "What time is it?" and the team would scream, "Game time! Whoo!" This rallying cry—liturgical in its own way—stoked the team's passion and supplied emotional clarity: It's not playtime, leisure time, or even practice time. It's the real thing—it's game time. There's a similar rallying cry in the apostle Paul's letter to the Galatians. It's an exasperated and worried cry, but a rallying cry all the same. It is time, Paul writes, *to live free.*

What Time Is It?

Ordinary Time is an appropriate time to discuss freedom, especially in an American context. During this season, our civil calendar remembers the Fourth of July and Juneteenth, two vital days in our country's history where we celebrate the gift of freedom. Yet Paul speaks of a freedom different from our common ideas. He speaks not of a personal freedom or of a political freedom granted by a government. Instead, the apostle proclaims a freedom that comes to humanity from Christ. It's the freedom of cosmic rescue from the ways of evil in this age (Galatians 1:3–4).

The Chicago Bulls' rallying cry was controlled by the arrival of the game. The rallying cry announced by Paul and declared to us is controlled by the arrival of God's Messiah come to set the captives free. It is freedom time because it is Messiah time (4:4). We are no longer under the law and its guilt but under grace. This is why Galatians, and chapter 5 in particular, drips with such passion. What's at stake is the freedom of God's people. The Galatian Christians were on the brink of losing it all, tossing their freedom aside by turning back the clock to the era of seeking God through Old Testament law.

The Galatian believers received the message of the true gospel but were drawn toward another gospel that told them, "You're not really free or truly a part of God's people. You have Jesus, but you do not have the sufficient obedience to belong to God. You need Jesus plus following the law." If Paul were writing his warning today, it would be in all caps: "You are severed from Christ, you who would be justified by the law; you have fallen away from grace" (5:4).

This means, in a very real sense, the Christian life *is* about freedom. For freedom Christ has set us free:

1. Jesus by his death and resurrection sets us free from idols.
2. Jesus frees us from the penalty of sin.
3. Jesus frees us from thinking we obey to be saved.
4. Jesus frees us to step into the life for which we were made.

Self-Rule, Self-Bondage, Self-Awareness

The great crisis in Galatia still exists today—the disregard of this gift of freedom.

If the Christian life is about freedom, human life away from Christ is self-selected bondage. In the film *The Usual Suspects,* one of the characters says, "The greatest trick the devil ever pulled was convincing the world he didn't exist."[2] If that's true (and it probably is), then the second-greatest trick the devil ever pulled was convincing us that freedom is doing whatever we please apart from God. That is not actual freedom. That is fleshly freedom—it's defined as self-rule. This form of freedom is alluring, but how much trouble in your life has come from you listening to you? We ought not loathe ourselves since we are made in God's image, but we ought not overinflate ourselves either. You and I are glorious and unstable, wise and foolish, capable of great things and able to wreck our lives with one bad choice made on a whim and an empty stomach. We cannot even understand ourselves and the reasons we sometimes do what we do. Why, then, would we blindly submit to ourselves? This is not self-deprecation; it is self-awareness.

What I've outlined for us gently, medieval Christian Saint Bernard states boldly: "He who makes himself his own master, subjects himself to a fool."[3] Another deceptive trick of this present evil age is the perversion of God's good gifts. Evil cannot create things, so sin and death deform God's gifts by (1) warping the gospel into Jesus plus work and (2) warping freedom into self-rule controlled by the flesh. The flesh makes life apart from God and his ways feel like freedom.

The Freedom to Be Bound to Love

In Jesus, you are free. But Christ's freedom creates a new bondage, the right type of enslavement: "Through love serve one another" (Galatians 5:13). It brings a new set of chains—that of mutual love. True freedom is not liberation from a yoke but submission to the right yoke—the yoke of life. Let Jesus make you a servant in love, both to God's people in the church and to his image bearers in the world. That's gospel freedom.

This love for which we are freed doesn't consist of polite manners and forced smiles. It is encapsulated by the list of the Spirit's fruit (verses 22–23), as well as by this phrase from verse 6: "faith working through love." This is the true fulfillment of God's law: love of God and love of neighbor. Gandhi is said to have quipped, "I like your Christ; I do not like your Christians." While such a sentiment can be a way to evade reckoning with the claims of Jesus, to deny that Christians have often failed spectacularly to love God and neighbor is its own form of religious evasion. The point is that we cannot guarantee that Christians will step into the bondage of this true freedom. A person can claim the name of Christ without putting on the chains of Christlike love. The flesh is strong even in believers, and it will not go down without a battle. True freedom is a fight.

Indeed, this section of Galatians 5 has strong military undertones, particularly the statement "Only do not use your freedom as an opportunity for the flesh" (verse 13). The language evokes the idea of giving up ground or territory to the flesh like a beachhead. A beachhead occurs when an army gets a few soldiers behind enemy lines and sets up a small camp to slowly and quietly take more and more ground. Once the outpost is strong, the army launches a full assault. Of all the ways the flesh works, which would be the first soldier over the line, drawing you away from Christ and from grace? Don't think only of "big sins"; consider the "small" ones that might slip past your defenses. Take anger, for instance. Anger wages its most potent attacks not only in violent outbursts but also in the silent, internal flame of hatred that begins the entire descent in the first place. Frederick Buechner says it well:

Of the Seven Deadly Sins, anger is possibly the most fun. To lick your wounds, to smack your lips over grievances long past, to roll over your tongue the prospect of bitter confrontations still to come, to savor to the last toothsome morsel both the pain you are given and the pain you are giving back—in many ways it is a feast fit for a king. The chief drawback is that what you are wolfing down is yourself. The skeleton at the feast is you.[4]

Through the beachhead of the flesh, we bite and devour ourselves and others. The works of the flesh dehumanize us while the Spirit's fruit rehumanizes us, calling us into the higher life that gives light in a dim and dark age. This is freedom's fruit born and grown through Christ. Freedom's fruit is social; instead of self-rule, it binds us to one another in love. It is the fruit that holds a church together through political elections. It is the fruit that makes the irreligious say, "My Christian neighbor has some weird beliefs, but she's the kindest and most generous person I know."

The stakes are high, but God is with us and supplies a promise for us: "I say, walk by the Spirit, and you will not gratify the desires of the flesh" (verse 16). Stand firm because the Spirit of God will empower you, even today, as you set your mind on Jesus. It is not by our strength or goodness that we are freed unto life but only by the gift of Jesus and his life-giving Spirit.

FOR REFLECTION AND DISCUSSION

1. What competing ideas of freedom exist today?
2. How is true freedom connected to faith and love?
3. In what ways does this passage in Galatians encourage you to receive and respond to Jesus?

The Great Seeker

Isaiah 1:10–20
Psalm 32
2 Thessalonians 1:1–12
Luke 19:1–10

The Son of Man came to seek
and to save the lost.

—Luke 19:10

Let your merciful ears, O Lord, be open to the prayers of your humble servants; and, that we may receive what we ask, teach us by your Holy Spirit to ask only those things that are pleasing to you; through Jesus Christ our Lord, who with you and the same Spirit lives and reigns for ever and ever. Amen.[1]

Every person has a backstory. When you encounter someone, behind what you see rests unseen chapters of complexity and beauty, as well as dormant layers of silent hope and secret fears. Each person carries multitudes of experiences and emotions. Every person is a long, winding narrative of how they arrived at this very moment.

Have you ever thought about Zacchaeus's backstory? Children's Bible classes over the years have filled in his life narrative in a simple way: "Zacchaeus was a wee little man, and a wee little man was he." There is, of course, more for us to contemplate about Zacchaeus. The man was short, but his money was long. Luke 19:2 tells us Zacchaeus wasn't simply a tax collector—he was the chief tax collector. Not only did he collect fees against his own people for Rome, but he also defrauded them at higher rates than Rome asked to line his own pockets. As if that were not sufficiently lecherous, as a chief tax collector he likely took a cut of all his subordinates' profits, which also came by way of cheating others. Zacchaeus's multi-level marketing pyramid scheme was on point. It's not too much of a stretch to think of Zacchaeus as something akin to an Israelite turned Roman tax mafia man.

Jericho was a big city, and likely not a soul in that place had an ounce of care for Zacchaeus. Not only was Zacchaeus a hated man; he was also a tragically lost man. The name Zacchaeus is derived from a Hebrew word for "pure, innocent."[2] With a name carrying such meaning, I wonder: Every time a stack of cash hit his hands and a cheated Israelite said with venom, "Here, Zacchaeus," did Zacchaeus feel in his gut how far he had wandered from God? The man was named for innocence but living for greed.

The Man Who Forgot Himself

Zacchaeus had forgotten himself. That is, until the rumors of Jesus's arrival. Jesus is one who teaches with divine authority, and most shocking of all, Jesus has told a doozy of a parable about how a repentant tax collector was justified rather than an obedient Pharisee (Luke 18:9–14).

Here might be the one person in all the region who has a speck of concern for Zacchaeus. The next thing you know, the wee man scales a sycamore tree to get a glimpse of this Jesus. Don't you like how Luke puts it? "He was seeking to see who Jesus was" (19:3).

It's easy for us to forget that Luke has crafted his account as a holistic project. Imagine reading Luke's gospel in one sitting and encountering this description of Zacchaeus in verse 2— "He was a chief tax collector and was rich"—after reading these stories:

- In Luke 6:24, Jesus declares, "Woe to you who are rich."

- In Luke 12:15–21, Jesus teaches the parable of the rich fool, a man who is immensely wealthy but dies suddenly and is called to account by God.

- In Luke 18, Jesus encounters a rich young ruler who refuses to part from his goods, leading Jesus to ruefully declare, "How difficult it is for those who have wealth to enter the kingdom of God!" (verse 24).

By the time we come to Luke 19, we are rhetorically primed and prepped. The setup and payoff are placed for Zacchaeus like a trapdoor of judgment. Sure, Jesus told one little parable about a tax collector who prayed for mercy and got it, but Zacchaeus is the *chief* tax collector. He is the very best at being the very worst. He's looking for Jesus, and as sharp literary readers of Luke's narrative, we might think Jesus is about to issue a smackdown. But Jesus surprises us. The only thing

Zacchaeus has coming for him is God entering his home and heart.

The God Who Seeks

Zacchaeus is chomping at the bit to find out who Jesus is—and in his search, he learns Jesus is actually seeking him. Jesus is the God Who Seeks, and his criteria for seeking is not our own. He operates by a different set of prerequisites than you or I do. We're looking for those who are a mess but not too messy, who are difficult but not too difficult, who are needy but not too needy. Hear it from Jesus's own lips: "I came not to call the righteous, but sinners to repentance" (Mark 2:17, KJV).

Pause to remember this truth today: Jesus seeks you not to judge you but to heal you. He seeks you not to curse you but to free you. He sought Adam and Eve in the garden, covering their shame and promising salvation. He seeks you this moment in your regret, bringing the hope of the Resurrection that everything sad will, by his tender touch, come untrue (Revelation 21:4).[3] He seeks you this moment in your discouragement and in your self-inflicted ruin. He is the God Who Seeks.

You Are Called by Name

When Jesus spies Zacchaeus clinging awkwardly to the sycamore tree, Jesus says his name. He's not afraid to call him pure, righteous, or innocent, for Jesus will make him what he is not yet. Jesus will make us what we cannot be on our own. He is determined to grace us: "I *must* come to your house," he says. The God Who Seeks does so boldly—he comes to Zacchaeus's home and sits at *Zacchaeus's* table. He brings salvation—

himself—into Zacchaeus's life. Jesus is unafraid to identify with the worst of the worst, the people with shady backstories. The arrival of Jesus at Zacchaeus's home, the arrival of Jesus on this earth that is humanity's home—this layered homecoming makes the primal truth of the Christian faith unmistakable: God in Jesus cherishes sinners. Never believe anything different. He cherishes us with a sinner-seeking love. He comes and says, "I'll find you and heal you from the inside out."

Those of us who are especially attentive may be wondering about Jesus's judgment—the vengeance for disobeying the gospel that we read in 2 Thessalonians and is clear throughout the remainder of the New Testament (and even in Luke's second volume, Acts). And we are right to wonder. Think about it this way: What if Zacchaeus had responded to Jesus with a simple, stubborn, "No. My house is not clean"? Or, "No, I think you're no good"? C. S. Lewis is right, in part, to say that "the doors of hell are locked on the inside."[4] To close the door to the gospel is to not obey, heed, and receive Christ's call. Luke is clued into this unbelief as well. Remember the rich young ruler? Some answer the knock of grace, while others cling to their idols—money, self, sex, comfort, success—and slam the door shut.

Even still, Jesus is seeking. If Jesus was just a seeker of sinners, a locator of broken people, that would be fine. But Jesus does this and more. Because of Jesus, you can have hope for yourself, for your friends, and for your family. You can have hope that your prayers mean something because Jesus is the great seeker, the great finder, and the great savior.

Sought and Found at the Table

This seeking happens in the home, which means it happens at the table. Luke's gospel is filled with Jesus partaking of meals (chapters 10, 11, 14, 19, 24). Luke gives the impression that we can feast our way into the kingdom of God. (How wonderful is that?) It is at the table where the sinner from Jericho meets the Seeker from heaven.

Jesus seeks us through the table, just as he does with Zacchaeus. There is a rich tradition of medieval Christians who reflected on Scripture as a table and food, where we feast on the sweetness of Scripture (Psalm 119:103).[5] At the table of the Word, we are fed by the truth of Scripture. At the table of the Lord, we are fed in communion with the very body and blood of Jesus (1 Corinthians 11:23–26).

To be sought, found, and saved is to be healed. It is to become the person God made you to be. When this happens, God molds a new creation, and the response is sheer wonder. Sought by Jesus, Zacchaeus is now living in sync with the pattern of God's righteousness found in Isaiah 1:16–17, which is fitting because Zacchaeus's name alludes to righteousness. Like Zacchaeus, you possess a backstory and a future story. That future is unfolding today—Jesus is seeking you now to bring the fullness of salvation into the home of your heart. The result will be mercy. The response will be wonder.

FOR REFLECTION AND DISCUSSION

1. In Graham Greene's novel *The Power and the Glory*, a character realizes that "hate was just a failure of imagination."[6] What sort of imagination did Jesus have toward Zacchaeus?

2. Based on this, what sort of imagination does Jesus

have toward you and those whom you struggle to embrace?

3. How might Jesus's encounter with Zacchaeus inform how you follow Christ and seek those around you with the grace of the gospel? What changes can you make this week to live in step with the God Who Seeks?

Eighth Week

Lamenting Losses

Isaiah 55

Psalm 60

Romans 8:7–17

Matthew 13:1–9, 18–23

You have made your people see hard things.

—Psalm 60:3

O God, you declare your almighty power chiefly in showing mercy and pity: Grant us the fullness of your grace, that we, running to obtain your promises, may become partakers of your heavenly treasure; through Jesus Christ our Lord, who lives and reigns with you and the Holy Spirit, one God, for ever and ever. Amen.[1]

Disaster has struck God's people. The desperation in Psalm 60's first verses makes it clear. The superscription shows that this psalm pairs with Israel's victory over a military rival, but the verses pull back the curtain to show that the victory was nearly defeat. The psalm's cry for help describes an opportunistic invasion of David's territory by Israel's unfriendly neighbors and kinsmen, the Edomites, while he was campaigning elsewhere. Just as Israel finally had a good king, finally began to enter the land, and would soon become a light and blessing to the world, they faced unexpected disaster. As they are about to walk in their purpose, they experience devastation.

"You have made your people see hard things." Because we inhabit a world vandalized by brokenness and chaos, each of us can relate to this cry and echo this verse on a personal level. I think back to a string of hard things in my life at the height of the Covid-19 pandemic. My family was suddenly forced to move out of our rented home; my son broke his foot and elbow at our first outdoor church service; my mother suffered a stroke; and then our large church began to leak people and staff like a broken faucet. I remember thinking, *Lord, why are all these hard things happening?*

Lament Your Losses

The first movement of Psalm 60 is to teach us what to do when we see hard things: We are to lament our losses. Do not stuff the pain; express it. Do not numb it; name it. But do so in the language of lament. Notice the onslaught of "you" in the first three verses:

> O God, *you* have rejected us, broken our defenses;
>   *you* have been angry; oh, restore us. . . .
> *You* have made your people see hard things;
>   *you* have given us wine to drink that made us stagger.

How does this language strike you? Perhaps you can't handle confrontation. Perhaps you're used to friends and family who can't deal with a full dose of honest emotion. But God can. You are free to name your losses and hurts truly and honestly before him.

Lamenting is not the same thing as venting. Venting is the act of naming your pain to anyone but God—whether it be filling in your parents or the Trader Joe's cashier or flinging your hurt into the deep abyss of the internet via social media. Lament primarily takes our losses and hurts to God. "A lament is a prayer in pain that leads to trust," writes Mark Vroegop.[2] Mingled inside the psalmist's lament are prayers of desperation hoping for restoration and repair.

Lament can handle what feels like a walking contradiction. This is important because there is an ordered path of lament. Seek the whole journey, not simply the first step. Some fail to enter the full journey of lament because they fear to be honest. This is spiritual bypassing that stays silent before the God who knows every thought of our hearts. Others view lament as simply honesty before God and thus never seek the real reward of hope by trusting God in their pain. This is a mistake in the other direction. Resolve to seek the entire journey. Speak the whole language of lament: "God, you rejected me, so please restore me."

Lament and Listen

The Lord replies to the cries of his people. In Psalm 60:6–8, the Lord "in his holiness" speaks to the lament and fear of his people. The Lord declares that all things belong to him and that he will be true to his promises. He details a catalog of places that may be foreign to us but were sacred to his people.

Shechem and Succoth are locations where, in generations prior, God was faithful to a wayward man, Jacob. Manasseh and Ephraim refer to his people enslaved and then redeemed in the Exodus. When God speaks of Moab, Philistia, and Edom, he is talking trash to the mighty enemies of his people. These fierce nations will be brought low before the Lord of hosts.

What does this mean for us? It means we lament our losses to God and also listen to his promises. At the heart of Psalm 60 stands God's pledge to his people. It's of special note that God speaks in his holiness, with a voice of triumph.[3] The reason we can lament and know our cries do not hit the ceiling and die—the reason we can see hard things and still have hope—is because of the holiness of God.

Perhaps that last sentence seems strange. However, holiness is relational. It is God—Father, Son, and Spirit—in all his perfections binding himself to the world in commitment and love. This language of binding is all over Psalm 60:

- "beloved ones"
- "your people"
- "for those who fear you"

In speaking his promises out of his holy nature and from his holy place, the Lord reminds us that he is bound to us and we are bound to him—not by our merit but by his holy mercy.

Yet how bound did Israel feel as disaster struck? How bound do you feel now to the Lord even as you read this? Life in the world is full of trouble. Our losses—those deep pains that make us think God is fundamentally against us—must be interpreted by listening to God's promises. The devastating loss Israel faced led them to believe understandably that their sin had caused God to reject them forever. They needed to lament but also listen to the promise: "Upon Edom I cast my shoe" (verse 8). God will triumph over their foes.

What about for you and a world that seems to be on fire in more ways than one, you ask? Lament and listen to the promises: "God so loved the world, that he gave his only Son, that whoever believes in him should not perish but have eternal life" (John 3:16). "If God is for us, who can be against us?" (Romans 8:31). Nothing "in all creation, will be able to separate us from the love of God in Christ Jesus our Lord" (verse 38).

Who Will Bring Us Victory?

The promise was not hypothetical, for Israel needed to go up to Edom to defeat them. Edom was a uniquely fortified place. It featured an inaccessible mountaintop sort of fortress where attacks could come only through a few visible roads that limited the size of the invading army.[4] It seemed a guaranteed loss. This is why Psalm 60:9 ponders the question, "Who will bring me to the fortified city? Who will lead me to Edom?" The turning point is verse 11: "Grant us help against the foe, for vain is the salvation of man!"

Psalm 60's golden lesson is that whatever battle or loss you face, you are not self-made or self-saved. It is God who delivers and restores. How long would it take you to trace all the voices, songs, and influences that have taught you that life is what you make it, so hope is a self-generated reality? The Psalms form us in a different way, pointing us to the truth that deliverance ultimately comes from God. Consider this: Every time Psalm 60 was sung in the temple, the Israelites rehearsed the lesson that life was not them against the world; it was God for them in their battles so they would bless the world (Genesis 12).

This is our lesson too. This is the lesson you need. What sort of battle would you say you're facing? A battle to make ends meet? A battle for your marriage? A battle against a sin or addiction? Whatever it is, if you are looking in the mirror for deliverance or looking to another person for hope, you're already on the path to defeat.

The wisdom of Psalm 60 is not at odds with preparation or personal action. King David was a tactician and military genius. But David knew it was God or nothing at all. Losses help us realize what we needed all along: to graciously come to the end of ourselves and trust in the loving care of God who binds himself to us before we ever look for him. And it is when this happens—and we lament to God, listen to his promise, and reach the end of ourselves—that against all odds, we are lifted up to share in God's victory (verse 12).

The holiness of God means even devastation will give way to victory. The gift God desires to implant deep in our hearts is that we are not alone—it is God who will turn pain into victory, loss into triumph by his power. We will lose, but God will restore. We will stumble, but God will repair. Our losses lead us to the end of ourselves, which leads us to rely on God's promises alone, and at the right time this lifts us into his victory.

FOR REFLECTION AND DISCUSSION

1. How have you understood lament, and in what ways has lament shaped your prayer and life with God?
2. What losses and hurts do you need to name, truly and honestly, before God?
3. What promises and truths do you need to listen to in the process of lament? What word does Jesus seek to speak to you?

Ninth Week

A Mixed Body

Isaiah 6:1–6

Psalm 86

Romans 8:18–25

Matthew 13:24–30, 34–43

The kingdom of heaven may be compared to a
man who sowed good seed in his field, but while
his men were sleeping, his enemy came and
sowed weeds among the wheat and went away.
So when the plants came up and bore grain,
then the weeds appeared also.

—Matthew 13:24–26

Almighty and everlasting God, you are always more
ready to hear than we to pray, and to give more than
we either desire or deserve: Pour down upon us the
abundance of your mercy, forgiving us those things of
which our conscience is afraid, and giving us those
good things for which we are not worthy to ask, except
through the merits and mediation of Jesus Christ our

Savior; who lives and reigns with you and the Holy Spirit, one God, for ever and ever. Amen.[1]

The parable of the weeds is a strange one. We can be thankful the disciples begged for an explanation. Its plot is downright petty: After a man sows good seed in his field, an enemy sabotages his work by sowing bad seed. Such treacherous acts were common enough in Jesus's time for the Romans to impose laws against them. It seems if you saw an inordinate number of weeds spring up in your field, you'd suspect a nefarious neighbor was at work.

The plot thickens when we grasp what Jesus's audience would have understood. Wheat and these particular weeds (called "tares" in some translations) looked almost identical. In Jesus's parable, the weeds sown are a poisonous type—darnel—that is nearly indistinguishable from wheat until it matures.[2] And the weeds and wheat are inextricable, tangled together. The separation of the two will be costly and require painstaking labor.

This mixed field is not only a picture of what the kingdom is like but also, in reality, a relevant picture of the church. The parable then carries three levels of meaning—personal, communal, and cosmic—meant to shape our view and actions as we live within a kingdom that is like a mixed field.

Personal Watchfulness

A critical lesson Jesus presents in this parable is the necessity of watchfulness. A lack of watchfulness enables the enemy's plan to go off without a hitch:

The kingdom of heaven may be compared to a man who sowed good seed in his field, but while his men

were *sleeping*, his enemy came and sowed weeds among
the wheat and went away. (Matthew 13:24–25)

Sleep is a gift from God. But sleep is also a symbol of death
and sloth. Here sleep leads to a crop spoiled. Watchfulness is
critical because of two truths: First, there's a real enemy at
work in the world, and second, in his patience God is not
eradicating evil quite yet. All disciples must stand on guard.
Disciples must realize an enemy may want to poison the
church through us. We must know the sort of temptations and
lies we're prone to swallow like bait. We must know the spiritual disciplines that keep us close to Christ and his people and
the things that pull us away. We must be on watch. This is not
paranoia; this is reality. To be called to Christ is to be called to
watchfulness until his kingdom comes in full.

Communal Realism and Church Hurt

Sadly, too many of us have experienced the tragedy of church
hurt. Being hurt by the people who know God best always
stings the most. Finding rot and weeds among the people of
God has shipwrecked the faith of many. If you ever get up
close to such things, it is devastating.

At a communal level, this parable speaks to the glory and
grime of the community we call the church. Indeed, Jesus
speaks with a dose of realism that can help us hope again.

In verses 27–30, the servants realize the weeds have infil-
trated and mixed in with the good crop. It's a total mess. They
ask, "Master, did you not sow good seed?" In other words,
they want to know whether something was wrong at the
source of the master's work. Because the plants are contaminated, the seed must have been bad. The answer is that the

chaos they see is the work of the enemy. It is not Jesus's doing. An unintended corruption has taken root.

The field of poisonous darnel mixed with good wheat is a picture of the people of God. The church, on this side of Jesus's return, is a mixed bag, a *corpus mixtum*, a mixed body. In our ecclesial body are both healthy and deadly cells; we are sinners and saints in whom the line between good and evil, flesh and spirit, runs down the middle of each human heart. If we add the reality that the "weeds" in the field can also represent those in the church who do not truly know Jesus, we're confronted with a vision of how mixed the church really is.

What about such a message is hopeful? It's the hope of realism. No longer will we gasp when inside the kingdom of God people act out of pocket or do something that brings shame on his name. Why? We've paid attention to what the Teacher said: Let both weeds and wheat grow together until the harvest (verse 30). It's as if Jesus is warning us against being overly discouraged when opposition to the gospel comes even from within. Realism is accompanied by a cosmic spiritual awareness: The health and wholeness of God's people are opposed by a real enemy, Satan. Unable to get Christ to turn away from the Cross, he seeks to corrupt the people and the world who are redeemed by it.

For those of us who have experienced church hurt, Jesus's parable does not gaslight us or call us to cheaply "forgive and forget." It suggests what we know by experience: that even among God's people, sin and harm are perpetrated. Rather than give up on the church or the world, we must become disciples who resist evil and keep hope in Christ even when his body is a mixed field.

Resisting Evil, Awaiting Final Judgment

Instead of choosing to uproot the weeds immediately, removing the work of the enemy onsite as his servants suggest, the master opts to leave them, "lest in gathering the weeds you root up the wheat along with them" (verse 29). If God purified the kingdom and world right now, uprooting evil in all places, who could stand? But in his tenderness, the Lord awaits the proper moment, the fullness of time—when the multitudes have come to him for mercy—to then bring the final hour of sorting and judgment. The Lord does not rush to judge; judgment comes in slow motion.

The willingness of Jesus to tolerate brokenness in the church and world is a sign of his patient mercy. His patience teaches us that we are not the ones responsible for judgment. He has not asked us to discern wheat from tares so we can then root out all people who appear morally or spiritually poisonous. We do not cast the final word about someone's eternal destiny. We are not responsible to uproot evil from the church or the world, because we cannot uproot it from our own hearts.

To acknowledge our limited defense against evil and the Evil One is not an act of surrender. It is motivation to resist evil and to plead with the One who can heal and remove what we cannot. Politicians offer us a promised utopia, but a Christian cosmology recognizes lies for what they are, even in their most inspirational form. We strive for a more just world, all while recognizing this is an achievement only Christ can secure—and one that arrives only by his hand at the time of the world's harvest.

FOR REFLECTION AND DISCUSSION

1. Do you have a history with this parable? What insights are you contemplating as you consider Jesus's words today?
2. Do you find the image of the kingdom and the church as a mixed field or mixed body encouraging or discouraging? Why?
3. How does this parable discourage us from judgmentalism? How does this parable show the patience of Jesus?

Tenth Week

The Ripple Effects of the Mustard Seed

Ezekiel 31:1–18

Psalm 119:121–136

Romans 8:26–34

Matthew 13:31–33, 44–50

The kingdom of heaven is like a grain of mustard seed that a man took and sowed in his field.

—Matthew 13:31

Almighty and merciful God, it is only by your grace that your faithful people offer you true and laudable service: Grant that we may run without stumbling to obtain your heavenly promises; through Jesus Christ our Lord, who lives and reigns with you and the Holy Spirit, one God, now and for ever. Amen.[1]

If you dropped a mustard seed in the dirt, it would be extremely difficult to find. While it's not the tiniest seed in the world, it was the smallest known to the people of Jesus's day and time. Jesus says the kingdom of heaven—the rule and reign of God on earth—is like this tiny seed. Though miniscule, a mustard seed can grow into a brushy plant standing more than eight to ten feet tall, with many a branch or perch for birds to claim as their own. That's what the kingdom of God is like.

As fascinating as this teaching is, Jesus's parable has an impact beyond its immediate words. Jesus spun parables to paint the truth of God's kingdom on his hearers' imaginations. They were his chief strategy to shift the way we see the world. This parable is so visual and provocative that it worms its way into our minds and, like a rock thrown into water, sets off ripple effects for how we see everything.

Clarifying the Difference

The first ripple effect of this parable is a sharp distinction. When Jesus says, "The kingdom of God is like . . ." he is clarifying the difference between the kingdom of heaven and the kingdoms of the world. Just as each house, each block, each culture possesses a distinct way of being, so too do the kingdoms of this world. In Jesus's day, the Romans ruled. Caesars were akin to gods. One Caesar boasted of enslaving and crucifying a million people, and while the numbers were inflated, such brute force was revered as true power and greatness. Not unlike some nations today, the Romans mastered power and violence as the operating system of their kingdom.

Many countries possess an operating system of spectacle, always desiring bigger, better, faster, stronger. This way of being is so seductive that even Christians buy into this system, believing God is at work only when church attendance is high and getting higher. Or believing the kingdom will advance only when Christians get all the positions of power and prominence. Jesus's parable teaches something different. The kingdom of God does not run the same operating system as the world. God's rule on earth does not extend through the power of might; it grows through the power of a seed.

Like a simple seed planted in a nondescript patch of dirt, the kingdom of God exists and advances. It's nothing you'd marvel over at first glance. But then, quietly, slowly, powerfully, the kingdom grows. The small seed yields unimaginable results.

This difference that Jesus clarifies also places before us a choice. We must choose between the way of the spectacle or the way of the seed. Will we believe that God wants to work by bigger, better, faster means in churches, families, and our lives? Or by the quiet, steady, almost imperceptible work of a seed slowly coming to bloom?

Countering Discouragement

In the early 2010s, my wife and I served as church planters in Boston. New England is not an easy place to start a church, which is precisely why we love the place and wanted to be there. I remember being filled with that first-time church planter enthusiasm and holy naïveté, putting flyers all over the city for our first public-interest meeting. We invited everyone we knew. And most of all we prayed. Then the event came. I believe fourteen people attended, four of whom shared our last name and five others who were already part of our core group. Afterward, I was crushed. How would we join with the churches of the area to impact a city of nearly five million for the kingdom with only fourteen people?

Jesus set before his disciples a grand mission: to change the world through the spread of his gospel. At the same time such a mission would invigorate the disciples, it must have also discouraged them. How could a band of twelve flawed apostles change the world? What did it feel like once they understood that Jesus wanted to accomplish this through them?

Because the kingdom is like a mustard seed that becomes a tree, we should never be discouraged by simple, small, and ordinary beginnings in the life of faith. Biblical commentator Leon Morris says it best: "Jesus teaches [the disciples] not to be hypnotized by size."[2] In the kingdom, size isn't king. Jesus is. And Jesus uses the small and foolish things of this world to bring about the purposes of God. To understand the kingdom is to understand that impact is not about spectacle and size; it's about the power of Jesus at work in ways so ordinary and seemingly small to the human eye that they become, in God's timing, a full-blown experience of the rule of God on earth as it is in heaven.

Once the disciples began to understand the meaning of the mustard seed, discouragement must have fled from their hearts. This is exactly what Jesus desires for you today. Don't be hypnotized by size and spectacle. Would a small change in your life perhaps be the seed to spiritual flourishing? Maybe it's a return to church after a hiatus, a season of doubt, or a move to a new town. Maybe it's a slight adjustment to decrease social media scrolling and increase moments of silence and prayer. Maybe it's a tweak to your budget to be more generous in Jesus's name. Maybe it's an effort, even inconsistent, to pray with your children and pass on the faith. Don't be discouraged by the size of your efforts. Be encouraged by Jesus's words. For what starts small in his name can end glorious because of the power of the King.

Creating True Diversity

Jesus must have been a bird-watcher because birds are common illustrations in the Sermon on the Mount and appear again in this parable about the mustard seed. Jesus's word on the birds is the last ripple effect. What precisely is he referring to here? I'd venture that Jesus may be drawing from Ezekiel 31, in which kingdoms are described as trees and the nations as the birds that find a home among the branches. Verse 6 says:

> All the birds of the heavens
>   made their nests in its boughs;
> under its branches all the beasts of the field
>   gave birth to their young,
> and under its shadow
>   lived all great nations.

This is speaking of Pharaoh, who had gathered the nations to himself through violence and enslavement. In verses 10–12, God says he has caused Pharaoh to be cut down for his wickedness. And now we see in Jesus that a new tree will come and gather the nations in righteousness, holiness, and joy unto God. This ripple effect highlights that Jesus creates a true diversity, for the kingdom of heaven is not for one people but for all peoples. The gathering of nations that former kingdoms achieved through injustice Jesus will achieve through his peaceable reign.

Here we find an echo of the New Testament's final word on the Cross of Christ in that Jesus died to purchase people from every tribe, nation, and tongue (Revelation 5:9). Indeed, the Cross is like the small mustard seed of the kingdom. Do you know how many people died by crucifixion under Roman rule? Crucifixion was horrific but wildly common. From this common death, Christ was planted in the soil like a seed. Then, three days later, the Father raised him from the dead, and through him all can find a home in his eternal kingdom.

What was foolishness to the Greeks and a scandal to the leaders of Israel was in fact the power of God to save and establish his kingdom on this world's sin-stricken soil. We need only the gift of faith—a new imagination—to see this kingdom breaking in among us even now.

FOR REFLECTION AND DISCUSSION

1. How can this parable expand your imagination for the kingdom?
2. Of the ripple effects in this parable, which is most challenging for you to embrace? Why?
3. What small step of discipleship do you need to be encouraged by in light of this text?

Eleventh Week

The Economy of Attention

Jeremiah 23:23–29
Psalm 82
Hebrews 12:1–14
Luke 12:49–56

You hypocrites! You know how to interpret the
appearance of earth and sky, but why do you not
know how to interpret the present time?

—Luke 12:56

Almighty God, give us the increase of faith, hope, and
love; and, that we may obtain what you have promised, make us love what you command; through Jesus
Christ our Lord, who lives and reigns with you and the
Holy Spirit, one God, for ever and ever. Amen.[1]

What do you consider your most valuable resource? We might
jump to money. But money, possessions, and even our bodies,

though they matter, are not the most important. Perhaps your most valuable resource is your attention, the very thing that directs everything else about you. Experts call the world we live in—with all its screens, streaming services, and gas-station-pump ads—an attention economy. Every corporation you can think of is waging war for our attention. Attention is our most precious resource because it's limited, and our gaze determines how we spend, how we act, and how we live.

Attention and Devotion

The poet Mary Oliver captures this idea well, writing, "Attention is the beginning of devotion."[2] This pithy statement gives rise to a host of questions: Where is your attention? Who's got your gaze? Oliver's searing poetic statement holds theological truth. Could this be the interpretive key that unlocks the meaning to Jesus's strange and seemingly cold words in our gospel text?

This is not Jesus gentle and mild. This is Jesus bothered and calling names. What's happening? The issue is a matter of attention, specifically interpretation. Attention and interpretation go hand in hand. When you notice someone walking toward you, seeing them is the act of attention. But then you must interpret the manner in which they are approaching: Will they walk by, say hi, or ask for directions? Attention and interpretation are inextricably linked. In Luke 12, Jesus is grieved that the crowd's attention produces an interpretation that leads not to devotion but to distraction: "You know how to interpret the appearance of earth and sky, but why do you not know how to interpret the present time?" (verse 56).

What exactly is the present time of which Jesus speaks? Luke made it clear in chapter 9: Jesus has set his face to Jerusalem because it is time—he is marching to endure the cross.

His work began with a baptism in water, but now he is moving toward a baptism of blood. It is the time for redemption and salvation. Think about the swirl of foretold events hovering over Jesus and the people. A young preacher has come proclaiming God's salvation and healing the blind and the sick. Then he opened the scroll and read Isaiah 61, boldly declaring that the prophecy was about him (Luke 4:16–21). The signs are clear: The time of God's rescue has come.

These events are like clouds that need attention, interpretation, and ultimately response. Instead, many in the crowd are undecided and indifferent, with souls in the posture of a shrug. Jesus uses harsh language to graciously wake them from their slumber. They can read the clouds but fail to read all the salvation-critical events concerning him.

Jesus's words are about a historical moment, but they reveal a human problem. Isn't it odd that the human mind can make connections between all sorts of things in the surrounding world, yet some will look at the movement of Jesus's life, death, and resurrection and say that such events are not worthy of investigation? The fact that Jesus calls this warped attention hypocrisy is important. Hypocrisy is like playacting, pretending to be what you are not. Some of the crowds were, as one commentator put it, "unable to see the true character of the times because they did not want to see it."[3] We fear to see what we cannot control, don't we? In refusing to see the times, the crowds did not have to give attention to Jesus and therefore could convince themselves they were right in not giving him their devotion.

Attention as Beginning and Continuation

Hebrews 12:1–4 adds an important aspect to this crucial reality of attention. From this text, we learn attention is not just devotion's beginning but its continuation. Attention means continued devotion or, in the language of Hebrews, endurance to keep running the race of faith. Once more, we encounter clouds. Pay attention, Hebrews says, to this cloud of witnesses, the faithful women and men of God who comprise the so-called hall of faith (Hebrews 11). We look to them because, if we pay attention, we realize we are caught up in the same story. Your life, simple as it may be, is—through Jesus—another chapter in the story that houses the flawed yet faithful lives of the great saints who came before us. Pay attention and realize you are in the company of the cloud. Fix your gaze on God's action in Jesus and be reminded that your life is not aimless. You're a sacred soul running in the race of redemption. To borrow the running imagery of Hebrews, realize you are a relay runner following the compassionate Champion who blazed the path, opened the way, and leads us home.

Hebrews 12:2 layers the language of attention by using the phrase "looking to" or "fixing our eyes on" (NIV)—in other words, we are to *consider*. To grasp this idea, think of what you often do with your smartphone. You skim and scroll through newsfeeds and articles with a simple and often mindless flick of your thumb. To consider is to do the opposite—it is to pay attention with settled concentration.

We must stomach a hard question. Could our weariness be the result of skimming Jesus rather than considering him? From Luke 12, we learn attention that is interpretation leads to devotion that responds to Jesus with trust. From Hebrews 12, we learn attention that concentrates on Jesus leads to endurance to keep going with him despite hardships. Taken together, we encounter the heartbeat of the Christian life: devotion and endurance with Jesus through concentrated faith set on Jesus. As a nineteenth-century theologian once said, "For every look at yourself, take ten looks at Christ."[4] That's the key to discipleship in any era or context. Do not make your hardships, sins, or failures the concentrated center. Rather, consider, with all your might, Jesus.

Today, are you weak and weary? Take what little strength you have, and consider him who endured hostility for us. Another scroll through the painful mental catalog of all you've been through and all you're facing today will do little unless you consider Jesus, the author and perfector of our faith.

FOR REFLECTION AND DISCUSSION

1. How does the story of the gospel fill our ordinary lives with deep significance? Do you find this encouraging or overwhelming? Why?
2. Have you seen Christians "read the times" in unhealthy and unbiblical ways? How might we think more biblically about these things?
3. What do you attend to most? How can you attend more to Christ, his Word, and his kingdom?

Twelfth Week

Exclusion and Embrace

Isaiah 56:1–8

Psalm 67

Acts 8

Matthew 15:21–28

I will give them an everlasting name
that shall not be cut off.

—Isaiah 56:5

Keep your Church, O Lord, by your perpetual mercy; and because without you the frailty of our nature causes us to fall, keep us from all things hurtful, and lead us to all things profitable for our salvation; through Jesus Christ our Lord, who lives and reigns with you and the Holy Spirit, one God, for ever and ever. Amen.[1]

Years ago, I overheard some well-meaning but dangerous Bible teaching at a coffee shop. A young man was being taught

Scripture by a kind older gentleman. The latter gestured at his
Bible and explained in a somber voice that everything in the
Old Testament was about God's "anger" and salvation by
"works." Then the gentleman's voice lightened as he explained
that the New Testament is about grace because it is about
Jesus. The young man nodded and took notes while I debated
whether it was my pastoral duty to intrude on their study and
correct this erroneous lesson.

A persistent misconception in the world and in the pews
is that the Old Testament is the tale of exclusion and effort and
the New Testament is the story of embrace and grace. This
view is a serious misreading of Scripture. Isaiah 56 is one of
many glorious counterproofs that show how the Christian
gospel offers a healing word about exclusion and embrace.

Good News Announced

Imagine a people in ruins, enslaved in a far-off land. Their
backs are bent. Their souls are broken. Then imagine that to
these weary people comes a glorious announcement: Their
God is coming to rescue and renew. This is the backdrop for
the good news in Isaiah 56. The Israelites are in exile because
they followed idols, didn't do justice, and broke God's covenant. Yet their sin won't be the final word. God's righteousness
will burst on the scene.

When God comes to rescue, he doesn't give suggestions.
He makes an announcement: "My righteousness will be revealed" (verse 1, CSB). As we saw in Advent, righteousness
here is shorthand for the fulfillment of God's saving purposes.
Righteousness is not simply a status God grants; it's a saving
action God performs. The Lord's announcement is the declaration of his action. And while our actions get us into our
messes, his action gets us free. The good news of Christianity

is the announcement of God's action for us, not advice performed by us. From Old Testament to New, God's saving plan is the announcement and victory of his action.

The Response to the Good News

As God shouts his gospel announcement, it's met with a fearful question: Is this really for me? The foreigner and the eunuch express doubt that they are embraced by God's good news. The foreigner says, "The LORD will surely separate me from his people" (verse 3). The eunuch says, "I am a dry tree"—in other words, "I can produce no offspring. I'm impure and worthless."

Why would the eunuch think this? Leaders of nations would create eunuchs by forcibly castrating the enslaved so they had no choice but to become loyal servants. By eliminating a eunuch's ability to procreate, especially after removing him from his home country and severing any possible ties to his community, a ruler would ensure that the eunuch had nowhere else to turn.

Among the Israelites being restored, there are some who have been castrated. They know that this means they cannot worship at the temple (Deuteronomy 23:1). So while God declares, "My salvation is coming," these people hear, deep in their hearts, "We're excluded." They hear the good news as a message of exclusion, not embrace. But as we'll see, this is not the Lord's message.

The Gospel for the Uns

Almost every person has felt like at least one type of "un" or another in their life. Unwelcome, unworthy, unprivileged, undesired, ungodly, unaccepted, unimportant, unseen, unforgivable. The foreigner mentioned in Isaiah 56 is a parallel to those who just don't fit in church despite their best efforts and no matter the form or denomination. But the eunuch has parallels that are especially sensitive and heartbreaking. Jesus helps us grasp the range of meaning in this term by adding a new category. In Matthew 19:12, Jesus speaks of marriage, making the point that it's not for every disciple:

> There are eunuchs who have been so from birth, and there are eunuchs who have been made eunuchs by men, and there are eunuchs who have made themselves eunuchs for the sake of the kingdom of heaven.

Jesus teaches that some choose singleness and celibacy for the kingdom ("made themselves eunuchs"). For some, this is part of their way of living out faith allegiance to God's good news.

Jesus wants us to consider who feels this "un" status in the church today. There are the single men, the single women, the widow(er)s, and the sexual minority (those who are same-sex attracted or not attracted to either sex). They can feel unwelcome in the church because marriage and family are far too often prized as the ultimate goal of the Christian faith. At times in church contexts, believers even make jokes about certain communities, not realizing that members of these groups may be among them, wrestling internally with thoughts of being unwelcome. Because self-selected singleness and celibacy are so odd in our time (especially for the sexual minority who purposefully and faithfully make this choice), these "eunuchs for the sake of the kingdom" often experience debilitating self-talk like the historical eunuchs mentioned in Isaiah. It's a tragedy when those seeking to follow Christ faithfully among God's people feel like unwelcome outsiders.

No matter what you've faced or seen, God sees your history and hears your fears. He's watched the footage of your rejection, and he says, "They might exclude you, but in Christ, I embrace you." The Lord offers a life-giving heavenly hush to our deepest fears:

> Let *not* the foreigner who has joined himself to the LORD say,
>   "The LORD will surely separate me from his people";
> and let *not* the eunuch say,
>   "Behold, I am a dry tree." (Isaiah 56:3)

The good news announcement is applied directly and personally to the fears of the unsure and the unwelcome:

> Thus says the LORD:
> "To the eunuchs who keep my Sabbaths,
>   who choose the things that please me
>   and hold fast my covenant,
> I will give in my house and within my walls
>   a monument and a name
>   better than sons and daughters;
> I will give them an everlasting name
>   that shall not be cut off." (verses 4–5)

The Lord reaffirms his gospel announcement directly to the uns. Now notice the language of embrace coming from the human side: "Keep," "choose," and "hold fast" are all ways we respond to the good news through faith and allegiance. To those who think the Lord's kingdom is not open to them, God offers full entrance with the dignifying language of covenant—a binding, lasting relationship. The Lord doesn't insult the foreigners and the eunuchs by dumbing it down and dimming the stakes of allegiance because they are uns of a particular sort. God offers full invitation and desires our full allegiance because he offers to *all* his full embrace. In the kingdom, there are no second-class citizens.

How does Christianity rebuild in the rubble, in our moment of exile that we've created through our scandals and idolatry? One corner of the church says to welcome all the uns—but *without* any of the language Isaiah 56 offers: to keep, bind, serve, love. Beware a gospel that includes no challenge and no cross to carry. Beware a gospel that degrades you and degrades God's grace by saying allegiance and holiness don't matter and aren't possible.

The other corner of the church world is desperate to rebuild by insider exclusion. They say uns have no place. Want to enter God's house? Become an ex-eunuch, an ex-foreigner. You can't struggle with temptation. All your sins need to be past tense.

I'll never forget hearing a Christian attracted to the same sex once quip that when they went to "progressive" churches, they didn't hear much about the Bible and when they went to "Bible" churches, they felt like they were a disease to be cured, a project gone wrong in every way. They wanted to follow Jesus and be cared for but found only extremes. Of course, this is a radical example, yet it's real and isn't a one-off experience. Will we participate in receiving and building something better, something that aligns with God's pronouncement here?

The Lord says to that searching person and to all of us, "Hold fast to my gospel promise, for you're moving toward a legacy and honor that will outshine the sun." Whatever price we pay to follow Jesus is not just worth it; it's a living legacy that will never fade. How can this be? Isaiah has one eye on the present and one on the future, for the saving action of God has now touched earth in Jesus.

There is a new exclusive inclusion—a new gospel embrace—

because the righteousness of God spoken of in Isaiah 56:1 has arrived. This righteousness of God started in Mary's womb, laid his head in a dirty manger, then lived out the gospel Isaiah announced. Where's the proof? How about the Ethiopian eunuch who is both a eunuch *and* a foreigner. A double un is welcome home to God. All around you the gospel promised is being realized. God's righteousness is on the move to the unwelcome, the unseen, the ungodly—even us.

FOR REFLECTION AND DISCUSSION

1. In what ways does the theme of exclusion and embrace run through all our Scripture readings?
2. What's most surprising to you from Isaiah 56? When have you felt like an un?
3. In what ways does the gospel create a new "exclusive inclusion"? How does this change our sense of the gospel and our relation to others?

Thirteenth Week

The Grand Question

Isaiah 51:1–6
Psalm 138
Romans 11:25–36
Matthew 16:13–20

He said to them, "But who do
you say that I am?"

—Matthew 16:15

Let your continual mercy, O Lord, cleanse and defend your Church; and, because it cannot continue in safety without your help, protect and govern it always by your goodness; through Jesus Christ our Lord, who lives and reigns with you and the Holy Spirit, one God, for ever and ever. Amen.[1]

"The medium is the message" is a well-known communication maxim. The medium casts an undeniable interpretive filter on the message. For example, the same message received via phone call, text, or in person can have a range of interpretation. Location can be part of the message too. How we hear something is deeply influenced by the place in which we hear it.

Jesus, in our gospel passage, has gone where no Jewish teacher would dare to go, and he's brought his crew too. They've undertaken a twenty-five-to-thirty-mile trek north to Caesarea Philippi, the land flowing with idols and pagan temples. This city, at the foot of Mount Hermon, rested against a large cliff called the "Rock of the Gods." Shrines to deities like Pan were all built on this rock.[2] In Jesus's day, this place still held to the lingering memories of child sacrifice and sexual perversion, all performed at the site in the name of idol worship. At the bottom of the Rock of the Gods stood a massive cave from which water flowed. It was called the "Gates of Hell (or Hades)" because people believed that idols would enter and leave the underworld through caves with water like this.[3]

The Revelation of Christ

Amid a region rife with pagan idolatry, Jesus asks a critical question about his identity: "Who do you say that I am?" In response, Peter makes the gospel confession on which Matthew's gospel hinges: "You are the Christ, the Son of the living God" (Matthew 16:16). This confession communicates the core of Jesus's identity, but the location also speaks. God unveils who Christ is in a place full of idolatry and debauchery. This is a sign of what the church is to be in the world: light in confusion and darkness, through our confession of Christ.

When believers turn away from the confession of who Christ truly is, the light of our witness is extinguished. Sadly, this happens when churches and believers seek to make Jesus in our own image rather than to build our faith on the gospel confession. Consider what Peter does after this episode. When Jesus foretells his deep suffering, atoning death, and resurrection, Peter says, "No way!" He rebukes Jesus (verse 22), for Jesus's vision does not fit Peter's understanding. A crucified Jesus is not the Jesus he wants.

Before we lambast Peter, we must recognize this tug-of-war over Jesus's identity as the continual challenge of discipleship. Even after we trust in Christ, do we not struggle to conform our lives to his words, his way, and his will? Are we not tempted at times to make Jesus into what we wish he would be for us? As we read some of Jesus's words in the Gospels and the writings of the apostles he handpicked (hello, Saint Paul), do we not effectively pull Jesus to the side to offer some rather significant revisions to his teachings?

So, the same question Jesus asks of his disciples then he asks graciously of us daily: "Who am I to you?" The Lord's question is an invitation to continual faith. He is not an idol we fashion; he is no object. He is the Son of the living God. Jesus's crucial question and Peter's gospel confession set the record straight. One commentator puts it this way: "Jesus is the visibility of God, and Peter is his first privileged witness."[4] In the land of idols, God has made himself known.

The Promise Given

Then we must consider Matthew 16:18: "I tell you, you are Peter, and on this rock I will build my church, and the gates of hell shall not prevail against it." These words have generated more books than one can count. They have created a "storm center of exegetical controversy"[5] as Roman Catholics and

Protestants wrestle to show their reading is correct. What is the rock that Jesus refers to?

One interpretation is that "this rock" refers to faith, pointing to the confession Peter makes. In this view, Peter's faith represents a type of faith that all subsequent disciples must follow, for the church will be built on the faith of those who confess their belief in Jesus.

Roman Catholics believe "this rock" refers to Peter, since Jesus plays on the words "rock" (πέτρα, *petra*) and "Peter" (Πέτρος, *Petros*). This interpretation includes the notion of apostolic authority: Peter, as the first bishop of Rome, is the "rock" on which Jesus would build his church; a succession of "rocks" (popes) would then occupy the see of Peter in Rome.

Then there is the Christ-centered reading, which believes "this rock" is Christ himself—the object of Peter's confession of faith. Jesus would build his church on his own life and work. The Old Testament often refers to God as a rock: "Their rock is not as our Rock" (Deuteronomy 32:31). "There is no rock like our God" (1 Samuel 2:2). "The LORD is my rock and my fortress and my deliverer" (2 Samuel 22:2; Psalm 18:2). "Who is a rock, except our God?" (Psalm 18:31). "It is as if Jesus said: 'You are Peter; and on myself as rock I will found my Church; and the day will come when, as the reward of your faith, you will be great in the Church.'"[6]

We must also consider communication in the context of location. In the shadow of the Rock of the Gods, Jesus promises that his church will be built on him. Christ is the solid rock, no matter how dire and dark the state of the world. With all our strength, we need to take in the invitation of Jesus's question, the faith of Peter's Christ confession, and Jesus's promise to build his church. Without inhaling these truths, our location amid an idolatrous world will overwhelm us.

Overwhelmed believers tend to do the most regrettable things. We think the rock is weak, so we try to build the church and our faith on all sorts of rival rocks—the personalities of our favorite preachers, a faith mixed with political idols, or bite-size religious teaching that keeps us comfy—all of which turn out to be glittering sand, alluring but quick to crumble.

The Gates That Won't Prevail

Jesus promises the church will prevail because it is built on himself. "*The gates of Hades* is a familiar Semitic expression for the threshold of the realm of death."[7] (See Job 38:17.) Yet Christ is building something that will confront and defeat death. The church becomes the "gates of life" that overcome the "gates of death," by the Rock who went beyond the threshold of death and straight into its morbid heart.

This is the stunning beauty of the gospel: "Christ died for our sins in accordance with the Scriptures" (1 Corinthians 15:3), but he didn't stay dead. He broke through the gates of death, disarmed its permanent power, and was raised by the Father. Our faith is built on nothing less than this gospel. The church is built on nothing less than this gospel.

FOR REFLECTION AND DISCUSSION

1. Can you recall a time where the location shaped the message you received or gave? How does the location of Caesarea Philippi help us better grasp this passage?
2. What sort of "rival rocks" might we be tempted to

build our churches and our faith on? Have you seen this happen? Why do you think this is a temptation?

3. Why is Jesus's crucial question one we should answer daily?

Fourteenth Week

The Body Tells the Story

Jeremiah 15:15–21
Psalm 26
Romans 12:1–8
Matthew 16:21–27

I appeal to you therefore, brothers, by the
mercies of God, to present your bodies as a
living sacrifice, holy and acceptable to God,
which is your spiritual worship.

—Romans 12:1

O Lord, we pray that your grace may always precede
and follow after us, that we may continually be given to
good works; through Jesus Christ our Lord, who lives
and reigns with you and the Holy Spirit, one God, now
and for ever. Amen.[1]

Did you know that "just sitting quietly, doing nothing at all, your brain churns through more information in thirty seconds than the Hubble Space Telescope has processed in thirty years"?[2] The human body is remarkable. Even when our bodies betray us, are marked by accidents, or feel at war with us, our bodily existence remains a site of tremendous beauty and wonder. But what is your body for? Philosopher Alasdair MacIntyre reminds us that we can't know who we are or what to do unless we first know what stories we are a part of.[3] In Romans, the body tells the story of human beings. A brief tour of the body in earlier chapters helps us marvel at what Paul says of the body in chapter 12.

Romans 1–3 outlines how human beings have strayed from our purpose and plunged ourselves into a bleak cycle of death and destruction. This fall has occurred because rather than offer our bodies and minds to God, we've turned away from him to idols (1:21). In chapter 3, the body tells a tragic story. In refusing to offer ourselves to God, we give ourselves to something besides God, and notice what becomes of our bodies:

We have already charged that all, both Jews and Greeks, are under sin. . . .

"Their throat is an open grave;
     they use their tongues to deceive."
"The venom of asps is under their lips."
     "Their mouth is full of curses and bitterness."
"Their feet are swift to shed blood;
     in their paths are ruin and misery,
and the way of peace they have not known."
     "There is no fear of God before their eyes." (verses 9, 13–18)

This portrait shows humanity ruined through idolatry. Shooters rush into stores and schools to shed blood. Co-workers curse and slander one another. Politicians seem to sit on a throne of deceit constructed with the tongue. This sickness plagues us, too, in ordinary yet devastating ways. Have you ever surprised yourself with your capacity to damage others with your lips, your hands, or your heart? When I was an undergrad, I surprised myself on a basketball court when, out of nowhere, I decided to trip a rival player. Who does that? To this day, I don't know what got into me, but I know that was the ill of which Romans speaks.

The Mercies of God

What causes the shift from humanity's death-dealing ways in Romans 1 to the bright possibility of offering our bodies in worship to God in Romans 12? The mercies of God. A new reality has broken into the world by the sheer power of God's mercies, which orbit around one body, Jesus, and then spread. Some of God's mercies we see are as follows:

- **Justification is graciously granted to sinners.** "All have sinned and fall short of the glory of God, and all are justified freely by his grace through the redemption that came by Christ Jesus" (3:23–24, NIV).

- **Peace with God is ours in Jesus through mercy.** "Since we have been justified through faith, we have peace with God through our Lord Jesus Christ, through whom we have gained access by faith into this grace in which we now stand. And we boast in the hope of the glory of God" (5:1–2, NIV).

- **Union with Christ in his death and resurrection through faith and baptism marking our bodies is yet another gift of God's mercy.** "We were therefore buried with him through baptism into death in order that, just as Christ was raised from the dead through the glory of the Father, we too may live a new life" (6:4, NIV).

- **The gift of the Holy Spirit and adoption into God's family are mercies that remind us salvation is not simply a status but a transformed relationship.** "You did not receive the spirit of slavery to fall back into fear, but you have received the Spirit of adoption as sons, by whom we cry, 'Abba! Father!'" (8:15).

These are not the merits of humanity. These are not abstract mercies. They mark us, body and soul. All mercy, all through Christ, all offered like a crown of grace to you and to me. Now by the mercies of God through Jesus, our bodies live out a different story. Our altars are altered. We can offer ourselves back to God through his saving mercy.

The saving mercies of God make it possible for us to become living sacrifices. The term *living sacrifice* can sound like an oxymoron. But when we offer ourselves to God through a life lived in faith and worship, this is the living sacrifice. This is the response to God's transforming mercy—it is our spiritual or reasonable worship. It's the only sane thing to do. Why return to our dead ways when mercy has altered the altar and brought us back to God? Can a living body go through life like a corpse? It's perverse and impossible. The same logic holds here. We are alive to God, so how can we act dead by offering ourselves to anything but the One who made us alive in Christ?

Conformed or Transformed?

The tragic complication is that the world seeks to conform us to its ways. J. B. Phillips captured the complication of Romans 12:2 in a fresh translation: "Don't let the world around you squeeze you into its own mould." In a 2010 book called *The Shallows,* Nicholas Carr argued that while the internet has its benefits, it essentially makes us stupid. The thing is, the internet isn't merely a time drain or a brain duller—it's a soul molder. It's often a malformation system, rewiring how we think and respond to the real-life world, shaping us to react first and think last. The online world—along with our smartphones—even molds our waking and sleeping, often squeezing God out of the frame without us really noticing. Day and night aren't random parts of the day; they form the very frame of our daily existence. To whom do we present these times? In recent years, I've heard pastors deeply discouraged to find out how many in their churches begin and end the day with social media and Netflix. Rather than being squeezed into the world's mold, we are to seek transformation from Christ.

This transformation is bodily, just as our living sacrifice is bodily. A picture of what it might mean to be a transformed living sacrifice emerges by turning upside down the litany of vices in Romans 3. Theologian John Stott paints the picture:

> Our feet will walk in his paths, our lips will speak the truth and spread the gospel, our tongues will bring healing, our hands will lift up those who have fallen, and perform many mundane tasks as well like cooking and cleaning, typing and mending; our arms will embrace the lonely and the unloved, our ears will listen

to the cries of the distressed, and our eyes will look humbly and patiently towards God.[4]

This is a new humanity remade by God's mercies. Whatever your relationship is to your body, by God's mercy, you can honor him in it and with it. Will you let Jesus make you a living sacrifice that spreads the aroma of wonder and worship? Jesus can do this for us because he is the true living sacrifice. Who else but Jesus has offered themselves fully—body and heart—to God? His offering turned an ordinary Roman tree into an altar of life for the world. He made atonement for all our false offerings, all our idolatry. He was the sacrifice who died but lived again to no longer die. And his body, with its resurrected wounds, will forever tell this gospel story.

FOR REFLECTION AND DISCUSSION

1. What's the relationship between your body and your faith? Is this something you've considered? If so, how has that changed over time?
2. What bodily practices shape your faith? How might these practices—like kneeling in prayer upon waking—help you live into God's mercies and avoid being molded by the world?
3. Which of God's mercies outlined in this reading do you find most encouraging? Why?

The Song of Jesus

Genesis 18:1–14
Psalm 15
Colossians 1:15–29
Luke 10:38–42

He is the image of the invisible God,
the firstborn of all creation.

—Colossians 1:15

O Lord God, grant your people grace to withstand the temptations of the world, the flesh, and the devil, and with pure hearts and minds to follow you, the only God; through Jesus Christ our Lord, who lives and reigns with you and the Holy Spirit, one God, now and for ever. Amen.[1]

Christians often speak of mountaintop experiences—moments of transcendent joy where the presence and power of God feel real and euphoric. While these experiences are lovely, their rarity requires we not base our faith on them. Scripture, however, is full of mountaintop passages. In these texts, the glory of God leaps off the page in power that's poetic and staggering. Colossians 1:15–20 is one such pinnacle of scriptural glory, offering us the chance to experience the wonder of Christ this very moment.

After opening in prayer for the church at Colossae, the apostle Paul takes them to the mountaintop, sharing what was likely an ancient hymn about the glory of Jesus. The mountaintop is itself a soundtrack, a carefully crafted hymn that speaks of Jesus as the revelation of God:

- the creator and sustainer of all things
- the Lord of the church and of the new creation
- the reconciliator who brings peace to the cosmos through the Cross

Speaking of Jesus this way so early in his letter is deeply significant. Paul has prayed for this young church to increase in the knowledge of God, endure in the faith, and live worthy of the grace they've received (verses 3–14). And the way that all these prayers will be answered is by the Colossians staying rooted in Jesus and what God has done through him.

Being grounded in the gospel is both basic and advanced. It is simultaneously the basis of the Christian GED and Christian PhD. If you're around the church for any extended period, you will realize how easy it is to shift and drift from the exhilarating Jesus of whom Paul sings. Years ago, while pastoring in a megachurch context, I remember calling congregants I hadn't seen in a while, just to check in. Speaking to one member, I asked how she was doing spiritually. Her reply shocked me. She said she was doing great and feeling closer than ever to Jesus because she had added the use of various enchanted fortune-telling cards to her Bible reading. While an extreme drift, it illustrates an unholy fusion of Christ with worldly wisdom and not being grounded in the gospel.

Another more subtle drift is this sense that can emerge in Christians: "I know about Jesus already. Can we move on to weightier doctrinal matters?" It is possible to dive into doctrine while forgetting Jesus. For the Colossians, the threat of a shift and drift from the centrality of Jesus was vicious and real. What was the remedy? For them to deeply know the song that they'd already learned to sing, to live under it, to live in step with its beat, and to marvel at the One of whom it sang. This, too, is our task.

The Song at the Center

"Is God really like Jesus?" A young dying soldier asked this question of T. F. Torrance, a theologian turned World War II military chaplain.[2] This same question lingers in the depths of our own hearts. Torrance assured the dying soldier that yes, God is really like Jesus. And Colossians 1 also offers a resounding choral *yes*. Irenaeus, the early church father, put it this way: "The Father is the invisible of the Son, but the Son the visible of the Father."[3] These insights find their source in the mountaintop song of Colossians 1, which finds its source in the enfleshing of God in Jesus.

Do you want to know God for the first time or afresh? Turn in no other direction except that which points to God made known in Jesus. The great hope of the dying soldier and the great hope of the world is that God is indeed made known in Jesus. Truly, he is the image of the invisible God. He made the heart of God visible when he became man to redeem us (Galatians 4:4–5). He made the compassion of God visible when he welcomed sinners and ate with them (Mark 2:13–17). He made the grace of God visible when he said, "Father, forgive them" (Luke 23:34). He made the mercy of God visible when he healed the sick (Mark 8:22–25). He made the power of God visible when he told the winds and waves to settle down (4:35–41). He made the holiness of God visible by being tempted in every way yet remaining without sin (Hebrews 4:15). He made the love of God visible when he died on the cross (Romans 5:8). At the heart of true humanity and true divinity, real spirituality stands for you, today and always: Jesus Christ.

Revelation and Creation

The Christ hymn of Colossians 1 reveals many breathtaking notes. It emphasizes Jesus not only as the revelation of God but also as the Lord of creation. All creation, visible and invisible, is "by him . . . through him and for him" (verse 16). These prepositional phrases are radiant jewels in Jesus's crown as the Lord of creation. In other words, Jesus is the cause, the means, and the end—or *telos*—of all the world, all the cosmos, every square inch of the universe.

By whom, for whom, and *to whom* comprise the set of questions at the center of every human person in every era, sometimes assaulting us each morning upon waking. *Who made me? Why am I here? What's the purpose or goal of all this?* Apart from God's grace, our answers to such questions are bleak. We respond to "By whom?"—the question of our origins—with cold science devoid of theism, claiming we're here only by chance and chaos, meaning we don't matter all that much. The answer to "For whom?"—the question of guidance and authority—usually becomes a fatal glance in the mirror. We live for ourselves or a vague notion of kindness because that's the life we choose. We twist "To whom?"—the question of purpose—into a depressing fill-in-the-blank statement: Life is short, so find your purpose in _____ before the clock runs out. All this is what writer Alan Noble calls the burden of self-generating meaning. Bertrand Russell puts it more sharply, drawing unbelief in the divine to its honest, logical conclusion: "Only on the firm foundation of unyielding despair, can the soul's habitation henceforth be safely built."[4] This is true only if Jesus is not Lord.

These alternative answers to the deep questions of existence are a false song claiming to be the true one. When we forget the nearness, goodness, and truthfulness of Jesus, we synchronize our lives and hearts to the wrong song. Like all creation, you were made through Christ, for Christ, and to Christ.

FOR REFLECTION AND DISCUSSION

1. Of all the titles and descriptions of Jesus in our Colossians passage, which speaks to you the most right now? Why?

2. Pastor and writer Tim Keller wrote, "The gospel is therefore not just the ABCs of the Christian life, but the A to Z of the Christian life."[5] How does this insight relate to the temptation to drift from Christ in Colossians 1 and 2? Do you sense any temptation to drift from the centrality of Christ?

3. How does our Colossians reading encourage you to go deeper into Christ and his grace? How can you apply this to your life this week?

Sixteenth Week

Scripture as Divine Encounter

Genesis 32:3–8, 22–30
Psalm 121
2 Timothy 3:14–4:5
Luke 18:1–8

All scripture is inspired by God and is useful
for teaching, for reproof, for correction, and for
training in righteousness, so that everyone who
belongs to God may be proficient, equipped
for every good work.

—2 Timothy 3:16–17, NRSVA

O God, because without you we are not able to please
you, mercifully grant that your Holy Spirit may in all
things direct and rule our hearts; through Jesus Christ
our Lord, who lives and reigns with you and the Holy
Spirit, one God, now and for ever. Amen.[1]

How should you approach the Bible? For some, it is a moral handbook. To others, it is an inspirational text. Some people study it deeply so they can use it as ammunition for doctrinal debates. But there is a more excellent way to approach it. The key phrase is that all Scripture is "inspired." Really this means "God-breathed." This unique phrase would have caught Timothy's eye as he poured over this last letter from his imprisoned spiritual father. The statement that Scripture is God-breathed is another way of saying that Scripture is the breath of God.

What's striking here is the relationship between God and Scripture. The reason Scripture is authoritative for believers is that it is an encounter with the God who makes himself known through the poetry, history, sin, suffering, and redemption of the world as the story of salvation captured in this written text. Marvel for a moment at that.

Why does Paul, imprisoned and facing execution, tell this to Timothy, his pastoral protégé? Why use his last breath to speak about Scripture as God's breath? Because he knows Timothy has a hard task in front of him, one that will require a strength he does not possess. In an age of false teaching, confusion, sensuality, and inequity, Timothy is to establish God's people in goodness and truth (2 Timothy 4:1–2). Living and serving in an era where people "will accumulate for themselves teachers to suit their own passions" and "will turn away from listening to the truth and wander off into myths" (verses 3–4), Timothy needs to draw meaning and strength from somewhere beyond himself. So, Paul points him to inhale God's breath through God's Scriptures. Timothy needs to "continue in what [he has] learned and . . . firmly believed" (3:14). The Greek word for "continue" is the same one Jesus uses in John 15:1–9 when he says we are to abide in him.[2] Paul wants Timothy to stay rooted in Jesus by being rooted in

Scripture because Scripture is an encounter with the living God who speaks, reveals, and instructs.

We are not establishing church communities in the first century like Timothy was, but in our own way, each of us stares down a series of hard tasks daily. You wouldn't be reading this if you believed yourself strong enough to face life equipped only with the power of your own resolve. The strength we need is not Scripture as a rule book but Scripture as divine encounter.

Understanding Scripture as an encounter with the living God is crucial to a whole and holy faith. Think about it: If Scripture is only an authority, then it's a power we can yield as we please. If it's a powerful reality—like a nuclear material—then it's a power that can be leveraged for good or ill, depending on the character of the one who possesses it. But understanding Scripture as an encounter with God can protect us from making these tragic mistakes. If it is an encounter with God, then it's an authority that blesses us but does not answer to us. It's not our breath—it's God's.

Scripture is a site of divine encounter where God meets us through the revelation of himself in the realm of human affairs. As Saint Augustine wrote, "For now, treat the Scripture of God as the face of God. Melt in its presence."[3] As such, we don't just read the Bible; rather, through the Bible, God reads us. When a person captivated by the idol of money and means hears or reads the story of the rich young ruler, who is reading whom? The breath of God is reading them, calling them to life. When you feel trapped by a hard situation or self-pity and you hear the words of Psalm 23:1, "The LORD is my shepherd," who is reading whom? What voice is calling out to you? The breath of God is urging you into life and faith, a new way of seeing and not being controlled by your circumstances. In

churches, when we say, "The Word of the Lord" after the
Scripture passages are read, we are reminded that through the
Word, the living God addresses us.

Reading and Wrestling

If Scripture is a divine encounter, it then makes sense why its
words can at times be confusing. We should expect Scripture
to be hard to grasp, for it speaks of God. God is infinite and other,
a reality too immense for human minds to conceive apart from
the glimpses of his nature that he condescends to reveal to us.
In this way, Scripture shows us a real glimpse of God's infinite
nature and ways. Because his ways are so great and so deep,
when his Word confuses us, we can take comfort that the Lord
whom we encounter in this holy text is beyond our full com-
prehension. This is why Scripture teaches us to pray that we
grasp God's love (Ephesians 3:18–19). His ways are indeed infinite.

Do you know how Peter describes Paul's letters? In 2 Peter
3:16, he says, "There are some things hard to understand in
them. The untaught and unstable will twist them to their own
destruction, as they also do with the rest of the Scriptures" (CSB).
If we acknowledge only this verse, we will be suspicious readers. If we acknowledge only 2 Timothy 3:16, we will be un-
discerning readers. We need both lenses when we read: discerning
the ways Scripture can be twisted and declaring it to be God-
breathed. But we also need a third lens, one from our Old Testament reading—the lens of adoration. This lens emerges when
we recognize Scripture as the location where God meets us.

We learn from Jacob's encounter with God in Genesis 32
that sometimes we must wrestle with Scripture, refusing to let
go until it blesses us. This grappling may be difficult if we have
experienced the Bible only through others as a violent cudgel

or a harsh rule book. But perhaps we need to encounter God's grace in the text for ourselves, even daring to wrestle prayerfully and communally with the texts that give us pause or make us sweat. Quite often, believers struggle to navigate the immensity of the Old Testament. But the Scripture Paul refers to in 2 Timothy 3:16 is certainly the Old Testament, since the New Testament was still being written. This means we need to recognize all of Scripture as a God-breathed encounter—the written Word pointing to the living Word, Christ (John 5:39). He is the encounter of God for us. If we refuse to wrestle, we lose the possibility of help by turning away from the breath of life. And this is why God has revealed himself: for the sake of life. Scripture is the result of God's desire to breathe life into a dead and dying world.

FOR REFLECTION AND DISCUSSION

1. In what ways has Scripture been hard for you to engage? In what ways has it been life-giving?
2. What does it mean for you that Scripture is inspired?
3. How can you better engage Scripture as an encounter?

Seventeenth Week

Resurrecting Literacy

Jonah 3:10–4:11
Psalm 145:14–21
Philippians 1:12–25
Matthew 20:1–16

Yes, and I will rejoice.

—Philippians 1:18

O Lord, you have taught us that without love, all our deeds are worth nothing: Send your Holy Spirit and pour into our hearts that most excellent gift of charity, the true bond of peace and of all virtues, without which whoever lives is counted dead before you; grant this for the sake of your Son Jesus Christ, who lives and reigns with you and the Holy Spirit, one God, for ever and ever. Amen.[1]

Talk to any counselor who knows their stuff, and at some point they'll mention these two important categories: your experience and your interpretation of that experience. Two people can interpret the same tidal wave at the beach in completely different ways. For one, it's a gnarly event to wish for again, but for the other, it's a moment of sheer terror. Life is in part a matter of experience and interpretation. In other words, it's a matter of reading. How do we read what happens to us? Jesus once said that to enter the kingdom of God, we need to be born again. To endure in life—with all its beauty and crisis, joy and death—we need to learn to read again.

Facing Crisis

In our Scripture reading, the apostle Paul is experiencing a three-headed monster of a crisis. Each head is a form of death. He faces a crisis in his vocation: He was called to be an apostle to the Gentiles, but he is imprisoned (Philippians 1:7, 13). He faces a crisis in his reputation: He's given his life for the gospel, but now he's being slandered (verses 14–17). And he faces a crisis of existence: He's on the threshold of death, facing execution (verses 21–25).

In crisis, Paul radiates a joyful confidence. He's no superhero, for you can hear the weight on his psyche. Yet he possesses a joyous confidence to face life and death. As we learn to read again in light of Christ, God produces in us a stable confidence within our vulnerable humanity to face crisis without entirely wilting.

Recently, I heard a podcast about literacy and reading that featured an appalled parent. Their child was not being taught to read by learning sounds and sounding out words; they were being taught to read by guessing the words in question. Too often we read our life experiences in the same way—just guessing, intuiting, or going with what makes sense to us. Saying something like "It will all work out in the end" is a guess unless it's rooted in something real. How can you learn to re-read your crisis, your situation, your experience in light of Christ?

Reading Crisis

Paul reads his crisis through the event of Christ's resurrection. Christ has so seized the apostle that the apostle now reads suffering, crisis, life, and death through his relation to Jesus. Reading this way is more valuable than the world's weight in gold.

Most of us read backward. That is, we often read God through our crisis and success—if crisis comes, we think God can't be good or can't exist, and if success comes, we think it's the sign of divine presence and blessing. It's almost as if something in us wants to believe the presence of God is about making life smooth and making us successful and glorious. It's almost as if we've forgotten that at the heart of the Christian gospel stands a crucified Savior.

Crisis reveals how we read the world. It peels back the layers to the definitive, personal core of our beings, which for Paul was "to live is Christ, and to die is gain" (Philippians 1:21). What exactly is Paul saying? We're off the mark if we think he is immune to fear. Reading rightly means we see death differently. Death is not only an enemy but also a gateway, an appointed time for those in Jesus to be released into the presence of God. Elsewhere, Paul writes, "Whether we live, we live unto the Lord; and whether we die, we die unto the Lord: whether we live therefore, or die, we are the Lord's" (Romans 14:8, KJV). It's not that there is no fear but that there is full confidence alongside any trepidation. And this confidence rests on Christ. He's gone ahead into the jaws of death before us. He stands ready to lift us from its hold and into his embrace.

Paul's story is what happens when an individual human life is revamped by the Resurrection and seized by the gospel of God. Paul's reading of his crisis is not the product of an individual. It is through the prayers of the Philippians and the help of the Spirit that Paul learns to read and hope (Philippians 1:19). We don't live into the truth of the Resurrection alone. Together we learn how to read again under the shadow of Jesus's victory. Resurrection confidence is deepened by resurrection community.

When the famous evangelist Dwight Moody was dying, he offered a word of resurrection hope. Moody said, "Soon you'll read in the Chicago newspapers that Dwight Moody is dead. Don't believe it. I will be more alive than I am now."[2] Moody was learning to read again—rereading even the great enemy death through the truth of the Resurrection. Because of the power of Christ, we can read our lives through the same hope.

FOR REFLECTION AND DISCUSSION

1. Have you noticed a default lens through which you interpret or read events in your daily life?
2. How would you describe the way Paul reads his crisis?
3. What new ways of reading through the Resurrection can you inhabit this week?

Eighteenth Week

The Posture of Grace

Ezekiel 18:1–4, 25–32
Psalm 25:1–14
Philippians 2:1–13
Luke 18:9–14

He also told this parable to some who trusted in
themselves that they were righteous, and treated
others with contempt.

—Luke 18:9

O merciful Lord, grant to your faithful people pardon
and peace, that we may be cleansed from all our sins
and serve you with a quiet mind; through Jesus Christ
our Lord, who lives and reigns with you and the Holy
Spirit, one God, now and for ever. Amen.[1]

Jesus tells the parable in our Scripture reading to correct and
heal the human posture of the arrogant. Considering the con-

text, hear the crystallized truth of the parable: "Everyone who exalts himself will be humbled, but the one who humbles himself will be exalted" (Luke 18:14). Now, visualize a split-screen comparison showcasing the posture of the parable's two characters, the Pharisee and the tax collector. One is a devout member of the religious establishment, and the other is a scammer, a corrupt employee of the oppressive Roman Empire. One is respected for his holiness, and the other is despised for his treason. Yet what matters is not their perception by the public but their posture before God.

Words can reveal posture. The Pharisee's words disclose a posture of conceit, a deep-seated pride. "The Pharisee did not really go to pray," one commentator notes. "He went to inform God how good he was."[2] Did you note the continued use of the pronoun "I," particularly as the Pharisee thanks God for how righteous he is? This is a posture of pride.

Meanwhile, the tax collector's words and physicality reveal a posture of contrition, a deep-seated humility. The posture of his heart is reflected in his body. He stands far off and does not lift his eyes. He beats his breast in an act of self-abasement and remorse. Some today might accuse him of not having enough self-esteem. But the posture of the heart revealed in his body is confirmed in his words, "God, be merciful to me, a sinner!" (verse 13). A more proper translation would read, "God, be merciful to me, *the* sinner."[3] As far as the tax collector is concerned, the chief sinner in the world is himself.

Whereas the Pharisee speaks of God, himself, and others, the tax collector deals strictly with God—no comparisons, no excuses. Evelyn Underhill writes:

> He stood afar off, saying "God be merciful, be generous, to me a sinner!" . . . He was a realist. That opened a channel, and started a communion, between the

rich God and the poor soul. But the Pharisee's accurate statement of his own excellent situation made no
contact with the realities of the Spirit, and started no
communion. He was dressed in his own spiritual self-
esteem. . . . The dew of grace could not get through.[4]

Grace runs downhill to those who trust not in their goodness but in God's mercy. Jesus spoke parables to shock listeners
into the truth. This one functions like a verbal slap in the face.
Replace *Pharisee* with *churchgoer* and *tax collector* with *agnostic,*
and perhaps we get a slice of the shock of this parable for its
original audience. For the familiar, this story can feel a tad
stale since we are already on the side of the tax collector. The
real temptation, then, is to read it and think, *Thank you, God,
that I'm not like the Pharisee.* Ironically, this temptation highlights the challenge of a right posture before God.

Receiving a New Posture

A parable is typically "an expanded analogy used to convince or
persuade."[5] In this context, Jesus seeks to convince us to not trust
in ourselves for right standing with God, as well as to not treat
others with contempt because we think they are unrighteous
and we're righteous on our own merit. So, how is Christ calling
us to respond to this vivid parable? There are at least two ways.

First, we need to see the connection between our posture
before God and our capacity to love people. You can look
down at others only if you have an exaggerated view of yourself. The kingdom logic of mercy, forgiveness, and compassion
is that those who have received and still need these gifts are
those who extend them. Get the gospel deep in your bones,
and your posture to others will expand to be merciful in ways
you think impossible.

Second, and most critically, Jesus calls us to honesty. We must be honest about our deep need—you and I are the sinners. And we must be honest about our sense of superiority—about whom do you or I say, "Thank you, God, that I'm not like them"? In these two invitations, Jesus seeks to shift the posture of our hearts and our orientation to people—the prickly, needed, and proud.

Missiologist Lesslie Newbigin wrote that the church is the hermeneutic of the gospel. The world knows the gospel is true and non-ignorable insofar as the gospel shapes the lives of believers in community and thus becomes visible.[6] The parable of the tax collector is therefore of vital importance for not only individuals but also churches. What happens if you have a community of people filled with the posture of conceit? What happens if you have a community of people filled with a posture of contrition? None of us has the power to shift the tide of a whole church, but we can embody the posture we want to see more of in our local participation in the body of Christ. Who do we desire to be, by God's mercy, in the church for our sake and for the sake of a watching world?

A change of physical posture is not easy, but it's not impossible. Harvard Medical offers a listicle with numerous tips, promising results in six to twelve weeks.[7] If only the posture of our words and hearts were such a quick fix. Anyone who has sought to evict pride or self-righteousness from the heart knows it's a battle with no expiration date. How then do we make any real progress toward the posture Jesus wants? Here is the secret: Our posture is healed by his, as our eyes and our hearts are lifted to him. We have considered the posture of the tax collector and the Pharisee, but what of the posture of Jesus, the speaker of the parable?

What is Jesus's posture? How does Jesus relate to us? For centuries, artists of all backgrounds have been enamored with the posture of Jesus, depicting the place where it was revealed most clearly: the cross. There we find Jesus with his arms open wide, stretched out from his body, to embrace both those who sin greatly and those who trust they are better than the great sinners. The cross reveals the posture of Christ.

And so does the empty tomb. In his resurrection, Jesus's posture is victorious: He is lifted up, then ascends in glory. Here, then, is the gift of Jesus to us: Trust not in your righteousness but his mercy—and treat others with that same mercy in his name. His posture heals our own.

FOR REFLECTION AND DISCUSSION

1. How has your familiarity with this parable helped or hindered your ability to engage with what Jesus teaches about our postures?
2. How would you describe the posture of your soul of late?
3. What type of alignment does Jesus wish to bring to you?

Nineteenth Week

Endurance Wisdom

Isaiah 5:1–7
Psalm 80:7–19
Philippians 3:14–21
Luke 21:5–19

By your endurance you will gain your lives.

—Luke 21:19

Keep, O Lord, your household the Church in continual godliness, that through your protection it may be free from all adversities, and devoutly serve you in good works, to the glory of your Name; through Jesus Christ our Lord, who lives and reigns with you and the Holy Spirit, one God, now and for ever. Amen.[1]

In the passage of Luke from this week's readings, we find some gloom and doom words spoken by Jesus. He speaks of the temple's destruction, of false saviors, of wars to come, of famines, and of the earth itself convulsing. Later in this chapter, he tells of his glorious, fearsome return. He speaks of the gravity of final things. Jesus speaks these fateful words as a means of prophetic preparation. And these words from Jesus can prepare and guide us into a resilient faith that can endure hardship with wisdom, no matter what comes our way.

Prophetic Preparation

Luke tells us that Jesus is in the temple and that some around him are floored by its size and beauty. The historian Josephus confirms the temple's splendor, saying its golden outward face, "at the first rising of the sun, reflected back a very fiery splendor, and made those who forced themselves to look upon it to turn their eyes away, just as they would have done at the sun's own rays."[2] This seemingly indestructible glory will become dust and rubble, Jesus says coolly. (This is what happens in A.D. 70 when Rome invades and destroys Jerusalem. War erupts, and all is lost, leaving Israel as a people and the disciples as a band of Jesus followers at an utter loss for what to do, where to go, and what it all means.)

"Do not be terrified," Jesus says, "for these things must first take place, but the end will not be at once" (Luke 21:9). Catastrophic upheaval is not the end. It is the middle ground in which his disciples must live. Jesus in essence says, "My disciples are to live in the doom and glory. And somehow in the disaster of political, social, and religious chaos, they are to endure."

What does this mean for us? Certainly, we must respect the original context that Jesus is speaking to. Yet there is, by the power of the Holy Spirit, a living word in this prophetic preparation for all eras, ours included. Though the temple and the church are not the same, though America and the people of Israel in the time of Scripture are not the same, in a way, this passage is a word on target for our time.

Over the last several years, it feels as though the American church has been toppled, existing in a figurative state of fracture and rubble. Pew Research shows that 64 percent of U.S. citizens are Christians, down from 90 percent decades ago, and likely to be under 50 percent in the decades to come.[3] Add to this our tumultuous and often violent political climate, including the January 6 insurrection, threats of global warming, and escalating world conflictions. You can look in any direction, and it seems things are, to put it mildly, crumbling. Yet we are not the first age to face serious upheaval.

Jesus speaks a word of preparation to his church in every age; he does not leave us without endurance or wisdom. But Jesus's wisdom in the upheaval is quite jarring. Listen to how he prepares his followers for the disaster to come: "This will be your opportunity to bear witness" (verse 13). According to Jesus, his disciples will live in disaster and be persecuted, arrested, and harmed—and all such dire straits will be our opportunity. Honestly, to me this sounds more like tragedy. Clearly, Jesus seeks to produce a fundamental shift in the minds and hearts of his people: from a passive victim complex to an active witness posture.

Without this shift, endurance is impossible and the church will fixate exclusively on what it experiences rather than on its task to endure and proclaim. There is a brand of American Christian discipleship that has a fixation on persecution. This often produces a vicious cycle where churches obsess over the loss of our rights while losing sight of our call to bear witness. Such a posture is often not much different than an athlete who spends most of their time complaining to the referee rather than doing the hard, urgent work of playing the game. Even great athletes like Luka Dončić and Caitlin Clark fall prey to this obsession. That disciples do the same is a cause not for shame but for adjustment.

Witness in Disaster and Adversity

The deeper truth Jesus speaks is that disaster is the great context for Christian witness. We think the opposite, don't we? Only when our bills are paid and relationships are strong, happy, and healthy do we feel we have a worthwhile testimony that God is good. However, when we speak the good news in bad times, it becomes evident to all who hear that the power belongs to God alone. Only the living God can cause such a witness in such a time. The witness goes out in jars of clay during times of pain so that the power is known to be God and eyes are opened to him, not us. Falsely, we think that only when society is thoroughly Christianized can the gospel truly flourish and find a hearing. Church history, especially in the first century, proclaims the opposite. The great time of witness is not prosperity but adversity. Indeed, witness in adversity is an indication of divine mercy, a tangible sign that God has not abandoned the world to its own chaos and destruction.

Rather than human preparation, our witness relies on holy improvisation. Jesus says, "Settle it therefore in your minds not to meditate beforehand how to answer, for I will give you a mouth and wisdom, which none of your adversaries will be able to withstand or contradict" (verses 14–15). Far from a ban on thoughtful responses, Jesus prohibits his disciples from resting on the crutch of preplanned, self-generated answers. Remember that Luke's gospel is accompanied by a second volume—what begins in the gospel of Luke is continued in Acts. Jesus's promise to "give you a mouth" is fulfilled in what he has done in the life of the church. It is fulfilled all throughout Acts, particularly in chapter 2. Peter, often portrayed as the loudmouth disciple, becomes Jesus's mouth, seizing the moment and proclaiming amid adversity and confusion: "Let all the house of Israel therefore know for certain that God has made him both Lord and Christ, this Jesus whom you crucified" (Acts 2:36).

In our own simpler way, Jesus calls us to witness not simply on the strength of human preparation but in holy improv. When speaking with friends this week, take Jesus up on his wisdom. Enter the conversation, praying in your heart, *Here I am, Lord. How should I listen? How should I speak?* To do so is to embrace the Lord's endurance wisdom in our witness.

The Word That Overcomes

There's a deeper reason behind the call for the disciples to not determine ahead of time how to answer people. Perhaps Jesus limits their prepared answers because he has yet to be crucified. It's as if Jesus says, "The answer will come, and it'll be a message you wouldn't believe. . . . It will involve my body, a Roman cross, an empty tomb, and a glorious return." By saying, "Don't determine the answer yourself," Jesus is keeping the disciples from being led astray by any word other than his gospel. For it is the word of the gospel that overcomes our adversaries. Indeed, the gospel that is God's wisdom—though the world sees it as foolishness—turns God's adversaries into his family (Ephesians 2:1–8).

Even so, this endurance wisdom is difficult to stomach, even for the most faithful believers. Jesus speaks words we wish were not true. We will incur hatred for his name's sake, and even families will divide because of him. For some, physical persecution is reality. Amid such sobering facts, Jesus says not a hair of our heads will perish (Luke 21:18). Is this not a paradox, declaring that some will be put to death but not a follicle

will expire? How can this be? One word: resurrection. The
journey of the disciple begins by embracing the hard wood of
the cross and ends in the sure hope of rising again. Take comfort that the path of endurance Jesus places before us is the
road he himself first walked.

FOR REFLECTION AND DISCUSSION

1. How do Jesus's words function as a gift of grace?
2. What shifts need to happen in your understanding
   of witness to live in light of this passage?
3. In what ways do Jesus's life and sacrifice empower
   our endurance as disciples?

Twentieth Week

The Good Life

Jeremiah 17:5–10
Psalm 1
1 Corinthians 15:12–20
Luke 6:17–26

Blessed is the one who
does not walk in step with the wicked . . .
but whose delight is in the law of the LORD,
and who meditates on his law day and night.

—Psalm 1:1–2, NIV

Almighty God, look mercifully upon your people, that by your great goodness they may be governed and preserved evermore; through Jesus Christ our Lord, who lives and reigns with you and the Holy Spirit, now and for ever. Amen.[1]

Psalm 1 is instruction and inspiration toward the good life with God according to God. "Blessed is the one" (verse 1, NIV) translated into modern speech means "Here is a person that in the middle of a fractured world is truly experiencing the good life." The way into this good life is about knowing what to embrace and what to reject. The power of contrast between opposing realities—*this*, not *that*—is part of the gift God gives us throughout this psalm. Two ways of living are presented in verses 1–2: the way of the wicked and the way of God's law. Then we encounter two images of what each of us will become based on the path we choose: grounded or groundless (verses 3–4). Finally, there are two ultimate outcomes: divine embrace or divine rejection (verses 5–6). The stakes are high.

The Good Life with God

Psalm 1's instruction is a gift because countless competing ideas on the good life are presented to us and warring inside us. How often has your concept of the good life, true flourishing, changed and shifted? Are you glad that what you thought was the good life back then you no longer think is the good life now? This proves that to really flourish, we need instruction and revelation from outside ourselves. The good life is, as our collect prayer states, being governed by God.

Psalm 1 warns us that the "step" (or "counsel" in the ESV) of the wicked is exactly the opposite of this God-governed view. The counsel of the wicked can be boiled down to thinking the good life is found through any strategy except God's ways. It's easy to think wickedness means immersion in the "big" sins: physical assault, adultery, murder. Sure. But this isn't the full picture. At its root, the counsel of the wicked is life governed by human folly—ours or others'—through the rejection of God. That's what "sinners" and "scoffers" do. A scoffer is like a person who is drowning yet manages to spit in the face of the one offering them a lifeline. The terms *sinners* and *scoffers* represent people who double down in their disregard of God, not simply people who are prone to wander. To flourish in life means to take seriously the diversity and popularity of the good life according to the counsel of the wicked, to remain open to God's counsel, and to thus check yourself before you wreck yourself.

The Modern Good Life

In a modern consumeristic society, the good life is often understood as getting everything you want, with as many variations as there are people. For some, the good life is achievement and success. For others, it is happy hedonism, a life without needs and full of exotic travel. Some equate the good life with family values—a nice house, a good spouse, and kids who don't run their mouth. Others view the good life as being conscientious citizens, a life rooted in making society's wrongs right. There are traces of true goodness in each of these visions of the good life, but apart from God, they are futile projects in self-definition.

An Invitation to Delight

Because the good life involves being governed by the good ways of life with God, the doorway is to delight in a particular law or instruction. People determine the value of instruction based on the nature of the teacher. No one is lining up to learn the laws and ways of gymnastics from yours truly. But many folks would drain their bank accounts to get that counsel from Simone Biles. Take the invitation into flourishing: Delight and meditate on the Lord's law. This meditation is not an emptying of the mind but a filling up. Whenever my sons and I see a great sports highlight, whether an acrobatic Kyrie Irving layup or a vicious dunk from Anthony Edwards, my sons will demand we watch the replay over and over. By the time I'm ready to move on, they are just getting started, asking to see it from a new angle. They are practicing meditation. Meditation is a turning over, a chewing on, a continual reflection.

Why do we meditate on the Lord's law? Because it is the Lord's revelation of his saving love. God's law teaches that we were made in, by, and for love. God does not despise what he has made—he made humanity in love, he showed his redemptive love in the Exodus, and he brings that rescuing love to the nations in Jesus. From Genesis to Revelation, this is the through line of Scripture across its manifold genres. The counsel of the ungodly seeks to flee from God and enthrone oneself. But meditation on the law—Scripture—brings one over and over again, from each and every angle, into and under the joyful ways of God from head to toe, for all parts of life and living.

Which will you seek? Scripture becomes the way to flourishing, a remedy for the confused and sinful human heart, because the life-giving medicine of the Word leads us to the living Word—Christ himself. Remember Saint Augustine wrote, "For now, treat the Scripture of God as the face of God. Melt in its presence."[2] Psalm 1 tells us that as we seek his face, we flourish, and rather than melt, we become rooted like a tree planted by streams of water.

The Whole Story in One Psalm

The imagery of the flourishing tree shifts this psalm from instruction to inspiration. Do you want to be a tree that bears fruit or chaff blown away in rejection? The entire story of God and humanity is found in Psalm 1's vivid imagery, stirring our hearts to receive the gift of God's grace and wisdom. Each key image functions like a scriptural hyperlink:

- The tree carries us back to the Garden of Eden and the purpose that you and I were made for: to flourish with God as his co-rulers, governed by him, and to steward the world under his rule.

- The water points us to Christ the living water (John 4) who heals and restores.

- The fruit reminds us that the fruit of the Spirit (Galatians 5:22–23) is the blessing we are to extend into the world through virtuous lives of love. The good life is not only about us but also about becoming those who help God's goodness come to full bloom in the lives of the hurting all around us.

The life we were made for, which in sin we lost, is now returned to us: life with God in fullhearted love of God and neighbor. The good life is not freedom to act as we please; it is the gracious invitation to receive what was lost. The first humans—Adam and Eve—walked in their own counsel and brought ruin into God's good creation (Genesis 3:1–7). Yet the flourishing that was lost is being restored.

The good life according to the Christian gospel is wide open for all because it is tied not to wealth, intellect, achievement, personal resolve, or the absence of suffering; it is tied to receiving the grace and goodness of God through his Son and then by his Spirit walking in the ways of his kingdom. It is life governed by the just and peaceable rule of Jesus.

A question remains: What gives Jesus the right to remix Psalm 1 and expand the borders of "blessing" in such a radical way? Jesus can expand the teaching of this psalm because he is the one who brought it to life. For us, Psalm 1 is instruction, but for Jesus, it is fulfillment. As a faithful Israelite, Jesus knew and loved this psalm. But he also lived it. Unlike us, Jesus—though truly man and truly tempted—never walked in the way of sinners. Hounded by Satan to reject God and take glory for himself and tempted by his best friends to turn from the Cross, Jesus resisted by quoting the truth of God's law. And delight in the law of the Lord led Jesus to the cross, where the good fruit of his work leads to our salvation.

Jesus is the Psalm 1 man who delighted in the law of the Lord even to the point of death. He was the tree uprooted, crucified, and judged like chaff for our sake—then raised by the Father in victory. Our Psalm 1 biography is the opposite. Who among us can say we've not walked in the counsel of the wicked? On our own we are chaff, but with Jesus we've become trees. Jesus is gathering chaff, and when touched by his blood, it becomes a tree planted by living water. Sinners are healed, planted, and bearing fruit, and humanity can flourish again. His grace turns chaff into trees and scoffers into saints.

What is the good life? It is knowing that you are *chaff* but that through the power of the Lord you've been made a *tree*—planted, rooted, and flourishing. That is the good life for which we were made.

FOR REFLECTION AND DISCUSSION

1. What is your understanding of the good life? How has this changed over the course of your life?
2. What is the good life according to Christ? In what

ways is the kingdom version of the good life both uniform and diverse?

3. How have you experienced meditating on Scripture? Try a method such as praying through a passage, lingering on each phrase, or asking how a passage points to Christ and the gospel.

Twenty-First Week

More Grace

Exodus 34:1–9
Psalm 103
James 4:1–6
Mark 9:30–36

He gives more grace.

—James 4:6

O God, our refuge and strength, true source of all godliness: Graciously hear the devout prayers of your Church, and grant that those things which we ask faithfully, we may obtain effectually; through Jesus Christ our Lord, who lives and reigns with you and the Holy Spirit, one God, now and for ever. Amen.[1]

James 4:6 is possibly the most wonderful and overlooked verse in the New Testament. It points us to the reality and promise

of grace in the midst of real-life failure, temptation, and sin. To set the stage, we need a quick overview of James as a letter.

The book of James, traditionally believed to have been written by Jesus's brother, is perhaps the most commandment-dense letter of the New Testament. It contains nearly sixty imperative commands in 108 verses. Many of these commands deal with the hard truth about the divided loyalty of James's audience:

- They are hearing the Word but not doing it. (James 1)
- They are tempted to fawn over the rich and degrade the poor. (James 2)
- Their faith in Jesus has been polluted by envy and selfish ambition. (James 3)
- And the desires warring within them are causing infighting among God's people. (James 4)

The summary charge is levied in James 4:4: "You adulterous people!" As much as we'd like to chomp our popcorn and say, "Yes, James, let them have it," it's quite clear that in telling the truth about them, he's revealing the truth about us. And this will enable us to grasp grace.

The truth that James points out is that we are divided and disloyal creatures. Christianity teaches we are made in the image of God, so our dignity is not extinguished by the failure of our morality. Glory and beauty are forever etched on us by God. But sin—our choice to turn from God's love and wisdom—has resulted in each of us being a marred and mixed walking contradiction.

We were made for fellowship and union with God, but we trade that royal gift for a love affair with deadly things: money, comfort, power, ease.

We spurn God, the giver of every good thing, to find fullness on our own.

We divvy up our allegiance, giving portions both to God and to the world that encourages us to live as if God does not matter.

We reject the One for whom we were made—and then wonder why we feel so empty on the inside while being successful by all accounts on the outside. This is the tragic human story.

Yet notice the good news that breaks in verse 6: God "gives more grace." Were a person to only understand sin, they could not understand Christianity. The central word of the Christian gospel is not *sin* but *grace*—a grace that shines brightest in the arena of human sin and failure.

Grasping Grace

What is this thing or reality called grace? The context of James 4 teaches us that whatever grace is, it is a decisive turn in a new direction, a new dimension ripped open by the action of the triune God. Whatever grace is, it's the best news for the worst people.

Why? We might have expected James to move from the charge of spiritual adultery to the verdict and sentencing by saying something like, "You adulterers are now judged and condemned." Instead, we receive a life-altering declaration from Holy Scripture: "He gives more grace." Again, your grasp of Christianity cannot be stronger than your grasp of grace. But if you grasp grace, or rather as grace grasps you, the person you were made to be—alive to God, shedding pride, and shucking off despair—will come to full bloom. That's the power of God's grace.

The problem is that with something like grace, we often

use human categories to understand a divine reality. A human-centered view of God's grace reduces it to a bit of slack granted to us from heaven, sort of like a divine do-over. In this view, grace is like failing an algebra test, but the teacher lets you take it again even though you don't deserve to. Is grace just another chance to break everything again?

God's grace is much better than we can imagine. We learn what grace is, not primarily by looking at acts of human kindness and pity but by staring at God's relation to us. James reveals the obvious thing that is therefore the first thing we might overlook: *Grace comes from God*. He gives it. Marvel at this. The sin and contradiction and brokenness that ensnare you, that have been in you and hounding you since you first inhaled and exhaled outside your mother's womb—God desires to gift you something to remedy those elemental illnesses. Grace is a gift from God that deals with our sins and contradictions, our situations and our conditions.

Grace is God's unearned favor that gives spiritual life to the spiritually dead, true pardon to the guilty, and real transformation to wayward sinners. What changes our status before God? What changes our nature as creatures made by God but marred by brokenness? God's saving grace.

God's grace possesses a diamond-like beauty. Imagine a diamond that gets larger and more captivating and beautiful as it is beheld. That's God's grace. Held to the light, it shines in ways diverse but unified, with endless radiant angles of power and beauty. Let's consider just a few aspects of these.

The timing of grace. *When have you last considered the beauty of grace's timing?* Romans 5:8 says, "While we were still sinners, Christ died for us." God's grace seeks us before we seek him. Grace is beautiful in its joyful pursuit of the lost and wayward, the sick and the sinful.

The more of grace. *When have you last considered the beauty of grace's more?* A little bit of a great thing makes you hungry for more. The saying that "all good things must come to an end" is true of many things, but not the grace of God. We need to believe James when, by the Spirit's inspiration, he writes the truth about sin. There is a lot of sin in us, even as those redeemed by Christ. But there is more grace in God than sin in us. It is impossible to out-sin the grace of God.

The recipients of grace. *When have you last considered the beauty of grace's selection?* Who are the beneficiaries of grace? Grace is given without regard to the recipient's worth. Grace has never met its equal. The forgiveness, love, mercy, and transforming work of God are all unearned and given to those who, in fact, deserve only the opposite.

The power of grace. *When have you last considered the beauty of grace's power?* Grace forgives and transforms. Theologian Michael Horton puts it powerfully: "Grace is not self-esteem, moral uplift, or therapeutic recovery. It is nothing less than God's favor on account of Christ: a new Word (justification) that generates a new creation (sanctification and glorification)."[2] Grace can turn spiritual adulterers and divided disciples into fullhearted people who love God and neighbor in a way that makes neighbors stop and stare and question their whole worldview.

God's grace can work these wonders in, on, and through you because grace is not a substance that God uses like a master physician pouring medicine into a bottle. Not at all. In grace, God gives us himself: He is the gift and giver. Saving grace to the world is enfleshed in the person of Jesus and brought to our souls by the Spirit. Grace has a face and a name: It is Jesus, crucified and risen. That's the act of grace that flows from the heart of God into the world, a gift with no end for all who receive.

FOR REFLECTION AND DISCUSSION

1. How have you understood or thought about grace?
2. How does James 4 and the devotional add to your conception of grace and its relation to Jesus and us?
3. If grace possesses a diamond-like, multifaceted beauty and depth, which aspects of grace speak most powerfully to your current needs, hopes, challenges, or fears?

All Saints' Day

The Grace of Blessed Examples

Revelation 7:9–17

Psalm 149

Ephesians 1:15–23

Luke 6:20–26

For this reason, because I have heard of your
faith in the Lord Jesus and your love toward all
the saints, I do not cease to give thanks for you,
remembering you in my prayers.

—Ephesians 1:15–16

Almighty God, you have knit together your elect in one
communion and fellowship in the mystical Body of your
Son: Give us grace so to follow your blessed saints
in all virtuous and godly living, that we may come to
those ineffable joys that you have prepared for those
who truly love you; through Jesus Christ our Lord,
who with you and the Holy Spirit lives and reigns, one
God, in glory everlasting. Amen.[1]

"The saints are not our way to God," writes theologian Robert Jenson. "He is our way to them."[2] This saintly maxim is important. With it in mind, All Saints' Day reminds us that the Lord wants to transform us through the contemplation of those who have served him faithfully.

All Saints' Day is thought to have originated in the fourth-century church but was formally established in the early 600s.[3] While every Christian is a saint—someone made holy by God's grace to us in Jesus—this day focuses on exemplary Christians, those in whom the transforming grace of God shone brightest throughout history. Because God is our way to being like the saints, the saints are not our bridge to God. They are a shining beacon we may one day resemble. For this reason, our collect prayer speaks of the grace of blessed examples. Saints are models to follow in our journey to heaven.

The Saints in Heaven and in Ephesus

What blessed examples do we find in our Scripture readings? In Revelation 7, we find the example of faithful martyrs. This final book of Scripture details the vision John received, one meant to strengthen believers who were violently persecuted by political powers. Revelation shows that amid immense suffering, Jesus still prevails. Like an otherworldly gust of wind, chapter 7 lifts us into the reality at the center of all things. We float beyond earth and into heaven, where the saints and the martyrs who died give praise to Jesus, the Lamb who was slain.

What is the blessed example here? It is that the worship of God is the great joy and center of human living. Despite the cacophony of suffering, the sound of reality is praise. The saints in heaven sing "Holy, holy, holy" (4:8). In our worship, we join their chorus. And our future is reunion with them and our God. Their example is worship and faith. Jesus and the Resurrection were so real to them that they were willing to stake their lives on this truth.

Where the saintly example in Revelation unveils heaven realities, Ephesians 1 displays a saintliness that is more readily grasped in everyday life. Saint Paul demonstrates the blessed example of prayer and love, writing, "For this reason, because I have heard of your faith in the Lord Jesus and your love toward all the saints, I do not cease to give thanks for you, remembering you in my prayers" (verses 15–16). The recipients of the letter are everyday Christians, as regular as you and me. The author is a radiant, exemplary saint dramatically changed by the grace of Jesus (Acts 9). Perhaps your faith feels thin, the opposite of Paul and the martyrs of Revelation. Perk up, then, as we behold the believers in Ephesus. When we look at these ordinary saints, what do we see? Paul reports that these believers trust their Savior and love his body—their fellow saints on the journey. Don't let this slip past you: It is easy to love Jesus, but it is sometimes hard to love his people. But if we would love the Savior, we are to love his body, warts and all. Saint Paul is especially fascinating, though, if you consider his example in this context. We are made saints by grace through faith, and we become radiant in our holiness as we do the hard work of loving God's people.

Through Paul's example, God urges us to do what saints do: to be devout in prayer for the good of others. A saint in the making is a person persistent in prayer. Scholars note that Paul did his "theology on the run," so it's safe to say Paul prayed on the go (or in a dim, dank jail cell, given his many imprisonments). With many plotting to kill him and endless work to be done, Saint Paul's ceaseless prayer reminds us that we can commune with God in constant dialogue in our hearts even as we career through life's chaos. Busybodies can live out ceaseless prayer. Saints commune with God even while bound in jails and even when we live on the go—whether running errands, running for office, or running from persecution. A breath prayer like this can be repeated in our hearts upon inhaling and exhaling: "Lord Jesus Christ, have mercy on me, a sinner" or "Good Shepherd, lead me and those around me." Such prayers shape us and bring us into divine communion. To pray in accordance with God's heart for yourself, those around you, and the flawed yet glorious body of people known as the church—that is saintly work.

The Prayers of the Saints

A saint wars against the cynicism that believes prayer is the dress rehearsal for the real deal: activity, accomplishments, and actions. Prayer is in fact the real work that fuels everything else. A saint is one who recognizes they need to know this truth more and seeks examples to follow to attain it.

The holiness of prayer is something that even those outside the formal walls of the church seem to grasp. Kendrick Lamar, a Pulitzer Prize–winning rap artist, offers a staggering example. On his 2017 concept album *DAMN.*, he describes the state of abject despair and hopelessness through a single haunting line: "Ain't nobody praying for me."[4] When we pray for others, as Saint Paul stayed on bent knee for the Ephesians, holy work occurs. Rambling prayers, sobbing prayers, even drowsy prayers are holy work. Your one-word prayers are perhaps holiest of all, since even in the immensity of emotion and trial, your soul still turns to God to muster up whatever utterance you can. Whether eloquent or mumbled, lengthy or brief, all your prayers offered to God in Jesus are full, strong, and pleasing to his sight.

Just as a road trip makes no sense without a destination, the prayers of the saints have a goal in mind. Saint Paul does not pray that the Ephesians would have a simple life. He prays for them to have the ineffable joy of knowing the love and hope of God in Jesus. Did you know that you are hearing about Jesus today because someone has done saintly work on your behalf and prayed you to this moment? We remember Saint Monica because she prayed in this Christ-ward way for her wayward son, Saint Augustine. The prayers of the righteous avail much.

Perhaps the greatest comfort a saint can have is that Jesus prays for us. Paul writes that Jesus is at the right hand of the Father and is interceding for us (Romans 8:34). To know this is to take courage. Robert Murray M'Cheyne wrote, "If I could hear Christ praying for me in the next room, I would not fear a million of enemies. Yet the distance makes no difference; He is praying for me."[5] The saints are not our way to God; he is our way to them in courage and in prayerfulness.

The grace at work in them is freely at work in you, for that grace is a person: Christ by his Spirit. The blessed examples exist not because of the discipline of people but because of the thick and potent power of God. That same power raised Jesus from the dead and is at work in all who believe. "The saints are not our way to God; he is our way to them." To believe this about yourself is not to trust in your resolve but to bank on the power of Jesus to make a saint of you—a project he's invested in until we join all the saints around the throne with the fullness of the church, saying, "Blessing and glory and wisdom and thanksgiving and honor and power and might be to our God forever and ever! Amen" (Revelation 7:12).

FOR REFLECTION AND DISCUSSION

1. What do you make of Robert Jenson's saintly maxim? Why do we need saintly examples in the journey of faith?
2. In what ways are you already a saint in Jesus?
3. In what ways do you wish to see Jesus transform you to more fully embody the life of a saint?

Christic the King Sunday

The Hands of the King

Ezekiel 34:11–20

Psalm 95

1 Corinthians 15:20–28

Matthew 25:31–46

The LORD is a great God,
and a great King above all gods.

—Psalm 95:3

Almighty and everlasting God, whose will it is to restore all things in your well-beloved Son, the King of kings and Lord of lords: Mercifully grant that the peoples of the earth, divided and enslaved by sin, may be freed and brought together under his most gracious rule; who lives and reigns with you and the Holy Spirit, one God, now and for ever. Amen.[1]

In a crowded marketplace, recommendations are everything. As much as you and I try to restrain our consumerist impulses to buy, around this time of year Cyber Monday and Black Friday remain alluring. Either way, in that moment, reviews and recommendations become indispensable. Who wants a 4.0-star printer when you can have a 4.8-star option that a thousand more people swear by?

The marketplace of consumption is boldly in the foreground today, and the marketplace of worship stands in the shadows. But as the American civil calendar collides with that of the church, with Christ the King Sunday near to Black Friday, we see how much we need to think about worship.

In Psalm 95, the marketplace of the gods is made clear, which helps us see things as they really exist. All people must inevitably make a choice of worship. Indeed, we do this each day, bowing to either God, ourselves, or false gods or idols. This psalm gives full recommendation and invitation to worship the Lord who gives life. Some psalms feature words spoken by God, to God, or about God. Psalm 95 is the recommendation from the people of God who have tasted and seen that the Lord is good, so they call out, "Come praise the Lord. Come worship and bow before him."

This call to worship is filled to the brim with unrestrained enthusiasm because it's rooted in the truth of who God is. Joyful noise is most fitting as we come before God the great king. Exuberant worship, fullhearted delight, is not really a matter of emotion or personal temperament. It's grounded in the "rock of our salvation" (verse 1). Israel understood that in the marketplace of the gods, the Lord alone stands true and worthy, "a great King above all gods" (verse 3). How far "above" is a human to their pets? They inhabit two different planes of existence. When we speak of God, we are not just speaking of the best human qualities with a louder voice. We speak of the One who is king over all, enthroned in a glory that thrills the heart and shatters our wildest imaginations. And the evidence in this psalm is his hands.

The King's Hands

What do you hold in your hands? What's in your possession? What do you control? Life reminds us daily that our hands hold far less agency and power than we wish. Yet God holds in his hands the deep recesses of earth and the tops of the highest mountains. The whole world is in his hands. He formed it, he made it, and he upholds it.

By virtue of this might alone, the Lord is the king worthy of our praise. For all these reasons and more, this psalm has been used often to begin worship services throughout church history. In the Anglican tradition, Psalm 95 is read every morning in morning prayer. It is called the *Venite*, a Latin term for "come," a word of invitation. The daily use of this psalm teaches us that worship is not only the songs we sing but also the posture of our lives, bowing in joy to the King of kings. Through this worship, by God's hand, we are shaped to live in such a way that our lives are each transfigured into a recommendation and invitation for others to know this God. Your life becomes a *Venite*. Will you today bow down and kneel— that is, will you bring your whole existence under the hand of our Lord and Maker?

Christianity does not wag the finger and say "bow" just because. God woos us with beauty and truth. The human heart will inevitably bow to something or someone. Why bow to false gods? At this time of year, we can easily look at how foolish people become when they bow to politics. At any time, we can look out—and look in—and see how gradually unhinged people become when they bow to themselves. There is relief and life in bowing to the Lord through joy, submission, and faith as "the people of his pasture, and the sheep of his hand" (verse 7).

This is the third mention of the King's hands, and the point is crucial. First, his hands teach us of his might (verses 4–5), and then his hands preach his tenderness (verse 7). Take comfort here: The Lord who holds the whole world in his hands in divine *might* also holds you in divine *tenderness*. The world is held by him, and so are you. The people of God are held like the sheep of his hand. The Lord is both mighty king and tender shepherd. The gospel is the word of God the King's might and tenderness. Jesus is mighty to save and tender to care for those in need.

So, we bow to him joyfully. We bow to Christ to whom all things bow, for "God has put all things in subjection under his feet" (1 Corinthians 15:27). Even death will bow its knee to this King before it is banished from existence forever. Today, we hear the King's voice: "Do not harden your heart. Simply come." His hands can soothe our wounds. His hand is strong enough to save and guide.

FOR REFLECTION AND DISCUSSION

1. What images from Psalm 95 help you see the Lord as king?
2. How does this psalm point us toward the gospel?
3. What might it look like for you to bow before the Lord's strong and tender presence?

Acknowledgments

I'm grateful for the opportunity to write this book. I'm thankful most of all for God and his grace. I'm thankful for his kindness to me through my wife, Kelsey, and my children, Julian, Adrian, and Tatum. No book is a solo endeavor, so where my words are good and true, they share responsibility for such an accomplishment.

I give thanks to my mom for her prayers and support, along with my extended family. A major thank-you is due to Rob Berreth, Josh Kluth, and Heather Petersen for feedback on some early drafts. Thanks as well to Tom Carpenter for tracking down my Tim Keller citation and for always encouraging me in my ministry.

I'm extremely grateful to the entire team at WaterBrook & Multnomah for taking on this project and for the support of my editor, Jamie Lapeyrolerie. I also want to show love to my church, Church of the Resurrection in Charlottesville, Virginia, for keeping the Lord's time with me. Last but not least, I want to thank Jevon Bolden, my agent, for her guidance and encouragement.

Notes

Introduction

1. "The Great Vigil of Easter," Book of Common Prayer (Anglican Liturgy Press, 2019), 582, https://bcp2019.anglicanchurch.net/wp-content/uploads/2022/10/BCP-2019-MASTER-5th-PRINTING-05022022-3.pdf.
2. "Maundy Thursday," Book of Common Prayer, 560, emphasis added.
3. Annie Dillard, *The Writing Life* (Harper & Row, 1989), 32.
4. Robert E. Webber, *Ancient-Future Time: Forming Spirituality Through the Christian Year* (InterVarsity, 2004), 20.
5. Paul E. Miller, *A Praying Life: Connecting with God in a Distracting World* (NavPress, 2017), 52–54.
6. There are a variety of frameworks and names for these cycles or movements. Webber uses a twofold division: a cycle of light (Advent, Christmas, Epiphany) and a cycle of life (Lent, The Great Triduum, Easter, After Pentecost). I have followed the framework of Bobby Gross, who adapted Webber's model to more explicitly emphasize the missional dynamic of Ordinary Time, which is also called Trinitytide. See *Living the Christian Year: Time to Inhabit the Story of God* (InterVarsity, 2009).
7. Some traditions have two periods of Ordinary Time: one after Advent and the other after Pentecost.
8. Many of the Scripture readings align with Year A of the Revised Common Lectionary (Consultation on Common Texts, 1992), www.commontexts.org/wp-content/uploads/2015/11/RCL_YearA_Web.pdf.

9. Collect for the Second Sunday in Advent in "Collects of the Christian Year," Book of Common Prayer, 598.

Advent: The Lord Who Arrives Thrice

1. For ways to celebrate church seasons and feast days that include devotions, recipes, and crafts, see *Sacred Seasons* by Danielle Hitchen and The Liturgical Home series by Ashley Tumlin Wallace.

First Week: Light and Dark

1. Collect for the First Sunday in Advent in "Collects of the Christian Year," Book of Common Prayer (Anglican Liturgy Press, 2019), 598, https://bcp2019.anglicanchurch.net/wp-content/uploads/2022/10/BCP-2019-MASTER-5th-PRINTING-05022022-3.pdf.
2. Fleming Rutledge, *Advent: The Once and Future Coming of Jesus Christ* (Eerdmans, 2018), 251.
3. Brian Mansfield, "'We Are the World' at 30: 12 Tales You Might Not Know," *USA Today,* updated January 28, 2015, www.usatoday.com/story/life/music/2015/01/27/we-are-the-world-30th-anniversary/22395455/.
4. John Cassian, *The Conferences of John Cassian,* trans. Boniface Ramsey (Newman Press, 1997), 31.

Second Week: The Tree of Life

1. Collect for the Second Sunday in Advent, Book of Common Prayer, 598.
2. See Genesis 2:7–9; 2 Samuel 18:9–17; Psalm 92:12; Amos 7:14; Jonah 4:6–8; and Luke 19:4 to name just a few.
3. John Gill, "Revelation 22:2," *John Gill's Exposition of the Bible,* accessed January 30, 2025, https://johngill.thekingsbible.com/CommentaryVerse/66/22/2.
4. Kosuke Koyama, *Three Mile an Hour God: Biblical Reflections* (Orbis, 1979), 7.
5. Augustine of Hippo, *Saint Augustin: Expositions on the Book of Psalms,* ed. A. Cleveland Coxe, vol. 8 of *A Select Library of the Nicene and Post-Nicene Fathers of the Christian Church, First Series,* ed. Philip Schaff (New York, 1888), 133.

Third Week: The Judge Is at the Door

1. Collect for the Third Sunday in Advent, Book of Common Prayer, 599.

2. Ted Grimsrud, *Embodying the Way of Jesus: Anabaptist Convictions for the Twenty-First Century* (Wipf and Stock, 2007), 180.

Fourth Week: The Holy Family's Faith

1. Collect for the Fourth Sunday in Advent, Book of Common Prayer, 599.
2. Ruth Haley Barton, "Advent 4: Joseph and the Walk of Faith," Beyond Words (blog), December 19, 2010, https://transformingcenter .org/2010/12/advent-4-joseph-and-the-walk-of-faith/.

Christmastide: The Great Exchange

1. Ashley Tumlin Wallace, *A Thrill of Hope: Celebrating Advent at Home* (Anglican Compass, 2020).
2. C. S. Lewis, *Mere Christianity* (HarperCollins, 2009), 178.
3. St. Athanasius the Great from Alexandria, *On the Incarnation* (St. Vladimir's Seminary Press, 2011), 58–60.
4. Thomas F. Torrance, *Incarnation: The Person and Life of Christ* (InterVarsity, 2008), 87–88.
5. Bobby Gross, *Living the Christian Year: Time to Inhabit the Story of God* (IVP Books, 2009), 64.

Christmas Eve: The Manger Speaks

1. Collect for Christmas Eve, in "Collects of the Christian Year," Book of Common Prayer (Anglican Liturgy Press, 2019), 599, https://bcp2019.anglicanchurch.net/wp-content/uploads/2022/ 10/BCP-2019-MASTER-5th-PRINTING-05022022-3.pdf.
2. Bible Study Tools, "manger," accessed February 4, 2025, www .biblestudytools.com/dictionary/manger/.
3. Online Etymology Dictionary, "manger," updated November 15, 2018, www.etymonline.com/word/manger.
4. Ray Vander Laan, "Feeding the Flock," That the World May Know, accessed February 5, 2025, www.thattheworldmayknow .com/feeding-the-flock.
5. C. S. Lewis, *The Pilgrim's Regress* (HarperCollins, 2014), 234–36.
6. Dorothy Day, *The Duty of Delight: The Diaries of Dorothy Day,* ed. Robert Ellsberg (Marlowe & Company, 2008), 180.

Christmastide: For Us and for Our Salvation

1. Collect for Christmas Day, Book of Common Prayer, 600.
2. Dickinson to T. W. Higginson, August 16, 1870, in *Emily Dickinson: Selected Letters,* ed. Thomas H. Johnson (Belknap Press, 1971), 208.

3. I've adapted these searching questions from Rev. Lauren F. Winner, "Caminando with Jesus: The Queen Comes Down," Episcopal Diocese of North Carolina, December 29, 2019, www.episdionc.org/blog/caminando-with-jesus-the-queen-comes-down/.

4. C. S. Lewis, in *Mere Christianity*, uses a similar example of a human becoming a slug or crab.

5. The Nicene Creed, Book of Common Prayer, 109. For more on the Nicene Creed, see Justin S. Holcomb, *Know the Creeds and Councils* (Zondervan, 2014), chap. 2.

6. Sean Gilman (@TheEndofCinema), Twitter (now X), December 29, 2022, https://x.com/TheEndofCinema/status/1608470433569071106.

7. Athanasius, *On the Incarnation,* 55.

8. Athanasius, *On the Incarnation,* 55.

9. Athanasius, *On the Incarnation,* 58–59.

10. Charles Wesley, "Hark! The Herald Angels Sing," Hymnary.org, accessed February 6, 2025, https://hymnary.org/text/hark_the_herald_angels_sing_glory_to#instances.

Epiphany: The Light That the Darkness Cannot Overcome

1. Online Etymology Dictionary, "epiphany," updated December 29, 2023, www.etymonline.com/word/epiphany.

2. Lesslie Newbigin, *The Gospel in a Pluralist Society* (Eerdmans, 1989), 116.

3. Robert Webber, *Ancient-Future Time: Forming Spirituality Through the Christian Year* (InterVarsity, 2004), 91.

4. Christine Pohl, *Making Room: Recovering Hospitality as a Christian Tradition* (Eerdmans, 1999), 18.

5. *Brittanica,* "St. Valentine," last updated January 17, 2025, www.britannica.com/biography/Saint-Valentine.

First Week—The Baptism of Our Lord: He Enters the Waters

1. Collect for the Baptism of Our Lord, in "Collects of the Christian Year," Book of Common Prayer (Anglican Liturgy Press, 2019), 601, https://bcp2019.anglicanchurch.net/wp-content/uploads/2022/10/BCP-2019-MASTER-5th-PRINTING-05022022-3.pdf.

2. Erasmo Leiva-Merikakis, *Fire of Mercy, Heart of the Word: Meditations on the Gospel According to Saint Matthew,* vol. 1, *Chapters 1–11* (Ignatius, 1996), 130.

3. Fred Pratt Green, "When Jesus Came to Jordan," *The United Methodist Hymnal* (United Methodist Publishing House, 1989), 252, https://archive.org/details/unitedmethodisth0000unse/page/254/mode/2up?view=theater.

Second Week: The Fourfold Epiphany

1. Collect for the Second Sunday of Epiphany, Book of Common Prayer, 602.
2. Karl Barth, *Church Dogmatics,* vol. 4, *The Doctrine of Reconciliation, Part 1,* ed. G. W. Bromiley and T. F. Torrance (T&T Clark, 1988), 361, www.google.com/books/edition/Church_Dogmatics/9-feBAAAQBAJ?hl=en&gbpv=0.
3. Much of this section is based on Sayers's insights in *Rebuilders,* podcast, episode "Morality in the Grey Zone—the Sin Chart," July 20, 2022, https://creators.spotify.com/pod/show/red-church/episodes/Morality-in-the-grey-zone--The-sin-chart-e2t5cok, cited by Jake Meador, "Mark Sayers' 'Sin Chart,'" Mere Orthodoxy, September 16, 2022, https://mereorthodoxy.com/jake/mark-sayerss-the-sin-chart.

Third Week: A New Way to Fish

1. Collect for the Third Sunday of Epiphany, Book of Common Prayer, 602.
2. See also Jeremiah 16:16; Ezekiel 29:4–5; Habakkuk 1:14–17.
3. Malcolm Gladwell, *Outliers: The Story of Success* (Little, Brown, 2008), chap. 2.
4. Rich Villodas, *The Deeply Formed Life: Five Transformative Values to Root Us in the Way of Jesus* (WaterBrook, 2020), 179–80.

Fourth Week: Come and See

1. Collect for the Fourth Sunday of Epiphany, Book of Common Prayer, 602.
2. Louise Lerner, "The First Nuclear Reactor, Explained," UChicago News, accessed February 8, 2025, https://news.uchicago.edu/explainer/first-nuclear-reactor-explained.
3. Lesslie Newbigin, *The Gospel in a Pluralist Society* (Eerdmans, 1989), 116.
4. See books like *Dominion* by Tom Holland or the more accessible *The Air We Breathe* by Glen Scrivener.
5. Carson notes that "occasionally in rabbinic literature its shade is

associated with a place for meditation and prayer." While not under a fig tree, Jonah met with God in a profound encounter under a tree. D. A. Carson, *The Gospel According to John*, The Pillar New Testament Commentary (InterVarsity Press; W. B. Eerdmans, 1991), 161.

6. Mark Sayers, Day 1 of "Reappearing Church—a 3-Day Plan," YouVersion, accessed February 8, 2025, www.bible.com/reading -plans/16107-reappearing-church-a-3-day-plan/day/1.

Fifth Week—World Mission Sunday: Curing the Colonial Heart

1. Collect for World Mission Sunday, Book of Common Prayer, 604.
2. A form of this quote has often been attributed to Desmond Tutu, but the saying is rightfully credited to Jomo Kenyatta. "Corrections and Clarifications," *The Guardian,* April 17, 2009, www.theguardian.com/theguardian/2009/apr/18/corrections -clarifications.
3. See Thomas C. Oden, *How Africa Shaped the Christian Mind: Rediscovering the African Seedbed of Western Christianity* (InterVarsity, 2010).
4. Online Etymology Dictionary, "compassion," updated June 18, 2023, www.etymonline.com/word/compassion#etymonline_v _17258.
5. "How Much Would It Cost to End World Hunger?," World Food Program USA, August 10, 2022, www.wfpusa.org/articles/how -much-would-it-cost-to-end-world-hunger.
6. Alan Noble, *You Are Not Your Own: Belonging to God in an Inhuman World* (IVP, 2021), 5.
7. "Global Christianity Surges Beyond Projections in 2024," Frontier Partners International, March 15, 2024, www.frontierpartners.org/ global-christianity-surges.
8. Rebecca McLaughlin, "The Most Diverse Movement in History," Christianity Today, October 14, 2019, https://www .christianitytoday.com/2019/10/most-diverse-movement-history -mclaughlin-confronting/.
9. Aaron Earls, "5 Discouraging Trends in Global Christianity," Lifeway Research, February 5, 2024, https://research.lifeway.com/ 2024/02/05/5-discouraging-trends-in-global-christianity/.

Last Week—Transfiguration Sunday: The Transfiguration

1. Collect for Transfiguration, Book of Common Prayer, 604.
2. "St. Thomas Aquinas—at His Transfiguration," *Catholic Digest,* www.catholicdigest.com/from-the-magazine/quiet-moment/st -thomas-aquinas-at-his-transfiguration.

3. Jerome, *The Homilies of Saint Jerome (Homilies 60–96),* ed. Roy Joseph Deferrari, trans. Marie Liguori Ewald, vol. 2 of *The Fathers of the Church* (Catholic University of America Press, 1966), 166.
4. H. Richard Niebuhr, *The Kingdom of God in America* (Wesleyan University Press, 1988), 193.

Lent: A Bright Sadness

1. Ree Hines, "Mark Wahlberg Explains Why It's Important to Him Not to 'Deny' His Faith," Today.com, February 22, 2023, www .today.com/life/inspiration/mark-wahlberg-explains-important-not -deny-faith-rcna71761.
2. Joan Chittister, *The Liturgical Year: The Spiraling Adventure of the Spiritual Life* (Thomas Nelson, 2009), 113.
3. Richard Sibbes, *The Bruised Reed and Smoking Flax* (Edinburgh, 1878), 17, www.google.com/books/edition/The_Bruised_Reed _and_Smoking_Flax/45W7Se5darAC.
4. "Lenten Prayer of St. Ephrem," Orthodox Church of America, accessed February 11, 2025, www.oca.org/orthodoxy/prayers/lenten -prayer-of-st.-ephrem.
5. Jennifer Gregory Miller, "Laetare, Jerusalem! Rejoice!," Catholic Culture, March 29, 2019, www.catholicculture.org/commentary/ laetare-jerusalem-rejoice/.

Ash Wednesday: Our True Selves

1. Collect for Ash Wednesday, in "Collects of the Christian Year," Book of Common Prayer (Anglican Liturgy Press, 2019), 605, https://bcp2019.anglicanchurch.net/wp-content/uploads/2022/ 10/BCP-2019-MASTER-5th-PRINTING-05022022-3.pdf.
2. John Calvin makes this point in volume 1, book 1, chapter 1, of *Institutes of the Christian Religion,* trans. John Allen (Presbyterian Board of Publication and Sabbath-School Work, 1921), 46–48.
3. Psalm 51:3–4, as quoted in Book of Common Prayer, 546.

First Week: The Triple Temptation

1. Collect for the First Sunday in Lent, Book of Common Prayer, 605.
2. Oscar Wilde, Act 1 of *Lady Windermere's Fan* (New York, 1893), 10.
3. Christopher West, *Theology of the Body Explained: A Commentary on John Paul II's "Gospel of the Body"* (Pauline Books and Media, 2003), 22.

4. Joan Chittister, *The Liturgical Year: The Spiraling Adventure of the Spiritual Life* (Thomas Nelson, 2009), 113.

5. C. S. Lewis, *Mere Christianity* (HarperCollins, 2002), 142.

Second Week: The Hero's Journey

1. Collect for the Second Sunday in Lent, Book of Common Prayer, 605.

2. Michael S. Heiser, "The Tower of Babel Story: What Really Happened?," Logos, May 18, 2022, www.logos.com/grow/really-happened-tower-babel.

3. Stuart Fickler, "12—Go Out to Yourself," in *A Scientist's Journey Through Torah,* Chabad of Greater Dayton, accessed February 12, 2025, www.chabaddayton.com/templates/articlecco_cdo/aid/1150600/jewish/12-Go-Out-To-Yourself.htm.

4. Benedict XVI, "Address of His Holiness Benedict XVI, to the German Pilgrims Who Had Come to Rome for the Inauguration Ceremony of the Pontificate," April 25, 2005, Libreria Editrice Vaticana, transcript, www.vatican.va/content/benedict-xvi/en/speeches/2005/april/documents/hf_ben-xvi_spe_20050425_german-pilgrims.html.

Third Week: A World of Thirst

1. Collect for the Third Sunday in Lent, Book of Common Prayer, 606.

2. Oscar Wilde, *The Picture of Dorian Gray* (London, 1891), 25.

3. American Authors, "I'm Born to Run," track 2 on *What We Live For,* Island Records, 2016.

Fourth Week: The Gaze of Mercy

1. Collect for the Fourth Sunday in Lent, Book of Common Prayer, 606.

2. John Calvin and William Pringle, *Commentary on a Harmony of the Evangelists Matthew, Mark, and Luke* (Logos Bible Software, 2010), 263.

3. Frederick Dale Bruner, *Matthew: A Commentary,* vol. 1, *The Christbook: Matthew 1–12* (Eerdmans, 2004), 174.

4. This is a paraphrase of medieval theologian Thomas Aquinas. Aquinas, *Summa Theologica* 2.36.1.

Fifth Week: The Lord's Tears

1. Collect for the Fifth Sunday in Lent, Book of Common Prayer, 606.
2. Timothy Burke, quoted in W. David O. Taylor, "Boys Don't Cry—but God Does," W. David O. Taylor, March 12, 2024, www .wdavidotaylor.com/blog/boys-dont-crybut-god-does.

Holy Week: The Journey to Redemption

1. Collect for the Liturgy of Palm Sunday, "Passiontide and Holy Week," Common Worship, The Church of England, accessed February 12, 2025, www.churchofengland.org/prayer-and-worship/ worship-texts-and-resources/common-worship/churchs-year/times -and-seasons-2.
2. Online Etymology Dictionary, "Maundy Thursday," updated December 6, 2018, www.etymonline.com/word/Maundy%20 Thursday#etymonline_v_12450.
3. Stuart Townend, "How Deep the Father's Love," Thankyou Music, 1995, www.stuarttownend.co.uk/song/how-deep-the-fathers-love -for-us/.

Palm Sunday: God's Mighty Acts

1. "Palm Sunday: The Liturgy of the Palms," Book of Common Prayer (Anglican Liturgy Press, 2019), 555, https://bcp2019 .anglicanchurch.net/wp-content/uploads/2022/10/BCP-2019 -MASTER-5th-PRINTING-05022022-3.pdf.
2. Robert E. Webber, *Ancient-Future Time: Forming Spirituality Through the Christian Year* (InterVarsity, 2004), 117.
3. Russ Ramsey, "Easter Week in Real Time," The Gospel Coalition, April 10, 2017, www.thegospelcoalition.org/article/easter-week-in -real-time/.
4. From a sermon given on Palm Sunday when Thurman was installed as Honorary Canon at the Cathedral of St. John in New York City on Apr. 11, 1976. Accessed digitally through Pitts Theology Library at Emory University.
5. W. David O. Taylor, "Prayers for Lent and Eastertide," W. David O. Taylor, April 11, 2024, www.wdavidotaylor.com/blog/prayers -for-lent-and-easter.

Holy Monday: The Temple and the World

1. N. T. Wright, *Mark for Everyone* (Westminster John Knox, 2004), 151.
2. Wright, *Mark for Everyone,* 152.

3. Collect for Monday of Holy Week, in "Collects of the Christian Year," Book of Common Prayer (Anglican Liturgy Press, 2019), 607.

Holy Tuesday: The Cursed Tree

1. Donald English, *The Message of Mark: The Mystery of Faith* (Inter-Varsity Press, 1992), 187.
2. Collect for Tuesday of Holy Week, Book of Common Prayer, 607.

Spy Wednesday: Spying Hearts

1. *Pascal's Pensées,* 416–18 (E. P. Dutton, 1958), 110–11, https://archive.org/details/pascalspenses00pasc/page/110/mode/2up?view=theater.
2. Collect for Wednesday of Holy Week, Book of Common Prayer, 608.

Maundy Thursday: The Last Supper

1. Frederick Dale Bruner, *The Gospel of John: A Commentary* (Eerdmans, 2012), 766.
2. Collect for Maundy Thursday, Book of Common Prayer, 608.

Good Friday: The Twisted Truth

1. St. John Chrysostom, Homily 80 on the Gospel of Matthew, in *Nicene and Post-Nicene Fathers, First Series,* vol. 10, trans. George Prevost, 471–72.
2. Collect for Good Friday, Book of Common of Prayer, 608.

Holy Saturday: In the Silence

1. John Onwuchekwa (@jawn_o), "Tragedy doesn't ruin us; Hopelessness does. Hold on to hope, however you can," Threads, July 6, 2023, www.threads.net/@jawn_o/post/CuXBLYfugE9.
2. Collect for Holy Saturday, Book of Common Prayer, 609.

Easter: Resurrection Life

1. N. T. Wright, *Surprised by Hope: Rethinking Heaven, the Resurrection, and the Mission of the Church* (HarperOne, 2008), 256.
2. Jaroslav Pelikan, "In Memoriam," Yale Department of History Newsletter (Spring 2007), quoted in Dave Furman, *Kiss the Wave: Embracing God in Your Trials* (Crossway, 2018), 62.
3. Online Etymology Dictionary, "rogation," updated September 12, 2021, www.etymonline.com/word/rogation.

First Week: Called by Name

1. Collect for Easter Day, in "Collects of the Christian Year," Book of Common Prayer (Anglican Liturgy Press, 2019), 609–10, https://bcp2019.anglicanchurch.net/wp-content/uploads/2022/10/BCP-2019-MASTER-5th-PRINTING-05022022-3.pdf.
2. Greg McKinzie, "Selection from Athanasius, Festal Letter 10," Scripture and Mission (blog), March 15, 2019, https://scriptureandmission.com/2019/03/15/selections-from-athanasius-festal-letter-10.

Second Week: Resurrection Faith

1. Collect for the Second Sunday of Easter, Book of Common Prayer, 612.
2. Timothy Keller, *The Reason for God: Belief in an Age of Skepticism* (Dutton, 2008), 182–83.
3. William Barclay, *The Gospel of John: Volume 2* (Edinburgh, 2001), 322.
4. Bruce Milne, *The Message of John: Here Is Your King!: With Study Guide,* The Bible Speaks Today (InterVarsity Press, 1993), 303.

Third Week: Resurrection Community

1. Collect for the Third Sunday of Easter, Book of Common Prayer, 612.
2. Karl Barth, *Church Dogmatics,* vol. 2, *The Doctrine of God, Part 1,* ed. G. W. Bromiley and T. F. Torrance (T&T Clark International, 1957), 669.
3. Christine Pohl, *Living into Community: Cultivating Practices That Sustain Us* (Eerdmans, 2012), 56.

Fourth Week: Good Shepherd Sunday

1. Collect for Good Shepherd Sunday, Book of Common Prayer, 612.
2. Augustine, *Confessions*, trans. Edward B. Pusey, Christian Classic Ethereal Library, https://ccel.org/ccel/augustine/confess.v.i.html#:~:text=For%20what%20am%20I%20to,the%20food%20that%20perisheth%20not%3F.
3. William McClure Thomson, *The Land and the Book; or, Biblical Illustrations Drawn from the Manners and Customs, the Scenes and Scenery of the Holy Land* (Dark, 1985), 203.

Fifth Week: Transformed by the Resurrection

1. Collect for the Fifth Sunday of Easter, Book of Common Prayer, 612–13.
2. James Clear, *Atomic Habits: Tiny Changes, Remarkable Results* (Avery, 2018), chap. 2.
3. J. I. Packer, *Knowing God* (InterVarsity, 1973), 188.
4. Howard Thurman, *Jesus and the Disinherited* (Beacon, 1996), 39.
5. Saint Anselm, *Basic Writings*, trans. S. W. Deane (Open Court, 1962), 4.
6. Packer, *Knowing God,* 182.

Ascension Day: Completion and Beginning

1. Collect for Ascension Day, Book of Common Prayer, 613.
2. Michael Reeves (@mike_reeves), X, May 9, 2024, https://x.com/ mike_reeves/status/1788512989433176489.

Pentecost: The Wind and the Room

1. Collect for Pentecost, Book of Common Prayer, 614.

Ordinary Time: Walking the Way of Christ

1. Some liturgical traditions divide Ordinary Time into two periods: first, the weeks between the end of the Christmas season and Ash Wednesday, and second, the weeks between Pentecost and the first Sunday of Advent.
2. Laura Kelly Fanucci, "The Gift of Ordinary Time," The Christian Century, January 26, 2015, www.christiancentury.org/blogs/ archive/2015-01/gift-ordinary-time.
3. Gerard Manley Hopkins, "As Kingfishers Catch Fire, Dragonflies Draw Flame," Poets.org, accessed February 16, 2025, https://poets .org/poem/kingfishers-catch-fire-dragonflies-draw-flame.
4. Aaron Damiani, *Earth Filled with Heaven* (Moody, 2022), 70.
5. In the Roman Catholic Church, this feast is known as the Triumph of the Cross. In the Eastern church, it is called the Exaltation of the Holy Cross.
6. Some traditions believe and celebrate that during this period, Helena found fragments of the cross on which Jesus died when she traveled to the Holy Land.
7. Tai French, "All Saints' Day: A Rookie Anglican Guide," Anglican Compass, October 21, 2019, https://anglicancompass.com/all -saints-day-a-rookie-anglican-guide.

First Week: Trinity Sunday

1. Collect for Trinity Sunday, in "Collects of the Christian Year," Book of Common Prayer (Anglican Liturgy Press, 2019), 615, https://bcp2019.anglicanchurch.net/wp-content/uploads/2022/10/BCP-2019-MASTER-5th-PRINTING-05022022-3.pdf.
2. Dorothy L. Sayers, *The Greatest Drama Ever Staged* (Hodder and Stoughton, 1938), 6.
3. Karl Barth, *Church Dogmatics*, ed. G. W. Bromiley and T. F. Torrance, vol. 2, *The Doctrine of God: Part 2* (T & T Clark, 2004), 780.

Second Week: Mercy or Sacrifice?

1. Collect for Proper 5, Book of Common Prayer, 616.
2. This section draws from Dale Bruner's insights in *Matthew: A Commentary,* vol. 1, *The Christbook: Matthew 1–12* (Eerdmans, 2004), 417–23.
3. Although this quote is often attributed to Mark Twain, it likely originated with psychoanalyst Theodor Reik. "Quote Origin: 'History Does Not Repeat Itself, but It Rhymes,'" Quote Investigator, January 12, 2014, https://quoteinvestigator.com/2014/01/12/history-rhymes/.

Third Week: The Serious Surprise of Discipleship

1. Collect for Proper 6, Book of Common Prayer, 616.
2. Dallas Willard, *The Divine Conspiracy: Rediscovering Our Hidden Life in God* (HarperSanFrancisco, 1998), 282.
3. Andrew Delbanco, *The Death of Satan: How Americans Have Lost the Sense of Evil* (Farrar, Straus and Giroux, 1995), 3.

Fourth Week: Measures of Fear and Rejection

1. Collect for Proper 7, Book of Common Prayer, 617.

Fifth Week: The Terms of Allegiance

1. Collect for Proper 8, Book of Common Prayer, 617.
2. Alex Hern, "Thousands Sign Up to Clean Sewage Because They Didn't Read the Small Print," *The Guardian,* July 14, 2017, www.theguardian.com/technology/2017/jul/14/wifi-terms-and-conditions-thousands-sign-up-clean-sewage-did-not-read-small-print.
3. Chelsey Harmon, "Matthew 10:24–39 Commentary," Center for

Excellence in Preaching, June 25, 2023, https://cepreaching.org/commentary/2023-06-19/matthew-1024-39-3.

4. Charles E. Moore, comp. and ed., *Provocations: Spiritual Writings of Kierkegaard* (Orbis, 2003), 86.

Sixth Week: Freedom Time

1. Collect for Proper 9, Book of Common Prayer, 617.
2. *"The Usual Suspects:* Quotes," IMDb, accessed February 16, 2025, www.imdb.com/title/tt0114814/quotes/?ref_= tt_dyk_qu.
3. Saint Bernard, letter to Oger, regular canon, circa A.D. 1126, Bible Hub, accessed February 16, 2025, https://biblehub.com/library/bernard/some_letters_of_saint_bernard_abbot_of_clairvaux/letter_xxiv_circa_a_d_1126.htm.
4. Frederick Buechner, *Wishful Thinking: A Theological ABC* (Harper & Row, 1973), 2.

Seventh Week: The Great Seeker

1. Collect for Proper 10, Book of Common Prayer, 617.
2. Blue Letter Bible, "Zacchaeus," accessed February 16, 2025, www.blueletterbible.org/lexicon/g2195/esv/mgnt/0-1/.
3. Pastor Tim Keller often used a variation of the phrase, "everything sad will come untrue," drawn from the Lord of the Rings novels. Keller explains, "He [Christ] is going to make it [all suffering] come untrue. He is going to incorporate even the worst things that have ever happened to you. They will be taken up into the glory that is to come in such a way that they make the glory better and greater for having once been broken." "Everything Bad Is Going to Come Untrue," *Christianity Today,* October 2023, https://www.christianitytoday.com/2023/08/tim-keller-september-11-sermon-everything-bad-come-untrue/.
4. C. S. Lewis, *The Problem of Pain* (HarperSanFrancisco, 1996), 130.
5. See the chapter on "Chewing and Belching" in Hans Boersma, *Pierced by Love: Divine Reading with the Christian Tradition* (Lexham, 2023).
6. Graham Greene, *The Power and the Glory* (Viking Press, 1970), 177.

Eighth Week: Lamenting Losses

1. Collect for Proper 11, Book of Common Prayer, 618.
2. Mark Vroegop, *Weep with Me: How Lament Opens a Door for Racial Reconciliation* (Crossway, 2020), 37.

3. Psalm 60:6 can also be translated "The Lord speaks in his sanctuary." However, the sanctuary is the place of his holy presence, so
the point still stands.
4. Michael Wilcock, *The Message of Psalms: Songs for the People of God*,
ed. J. A. Motyer, vol. 1 of The Bible Speaks Today (InterVarsity
Press, 2001), 217.

Ninth Week: A Mixed Body

1. Collect for Proper 12, Book of Common Prayer, 618.
2. "What Does Matthew 13:30 Mean?," BibleRef.com, accessed February 16, 2025, www.bibleref.com/Matthew/13/Matthew-13-30
.html.

Tenth Week: The Ripple Effects of the Mustard Seed

1. Collect for Proper 13, Book of Common Prayer, 618.
2. Leon Morris, *The Gospel According to Matthew*, Pillar New Testament Commentary (Eerdmans, 1992), 351.

Eleventh Week: The Economy of Attention

1. Collect for Proper 14, Book of Common Prayer, 618–19.
2. Mary Oliver, *Upstream: Selected Essays* (Penguin, 2019), 8.
3. Michael Wilcock, *The Savior of the World: The Message of Luke's
Gospel* (InterVarsity, 1979), 137.
4. Andrew A. Bonar, *Memoirs and Remains of the Rev. Robert Murray
M'Cheyne* (Edinburgh, 1883), 252.

Twelfth Week: Exclusion and Embrace

1. Collect for Proper 15, Book of Common Prayer, 619.

Thirteenth Week: The Grand Question

1. Collect for Proper 16, Book of Common Prayer, 619.
2. Ray Vander Laan, "Caesarea Philippi," That the World May Know,
accessed February 17, 2025, www.thattheworldmayknow.com/
caesarea-philippi.
3. Ray Vander Laan, "Gates of Hell," That the World May Know, accessed February 17, 2025, www.thattheworldmayknow.com/gates
-of-hell-article.
4. Erasmo Leiva-Merikakis, *Fire of Mercy, Heart of the Word: Meditations
on the Gospel According to Saint Matthew, Chapters 1–25* (Ignatius,
1996–2012), 516.
5. Ulrich Luz, *Studies in Matthew* (Eerdmans, 2005), 165.

6. William Barclay, "Commentary on Matthew 16," *Barclay's Daily Study Bible,* StudyLight.org, accessed February 17, 2025, www .studylight.org/commentaries/eng/dsb/matthew-16.html.

7. "The Community Built on This Foundation Will Prevail (16:18)," IVP New Testament Commentaries, BibleGateway, accessed February 17, 2025, www.biblegateway.com/resources/ivp-nt/ Community-Built-on-This-Foundation-Will.

Fourteenth Week: The Body Tells the Story

1. Collect for Proper 17, Book of Common Prayer, 619.

2. Bill Bryson, *The Body: A Guide for Occupation* (Doubleday, 2019), 49.

3. Alasdair MacIntyre, *After Virtue: A Study in Moral Theory* (Bloomsbury Academic, 2013), 250.

4. John R. W. Stott, *The Message of Romans: God's Good News for the World* (InterVarsity, 2001), 322.

Fifteenth Week: The Song of Jesus

1. Collect for Proper 18, Book of Common Prayer, 619.

2. Alister E. McGrath, *Thomas F. Torrance: An Intellectual Biography* (T & T Clark, 2006), 74.

3. Irenaeus, *Against Heresies*, 4.6.6.

4. Betrand Russell, *A Free Man's Worship* (Mosher, 1927), 7.

5. Timothy Keller, *The Prodigal God: Recovering the Heart of the Christian Faith* (Dutton, 2008), 119.

Sixteenth Week: Scripture as Divine Encounter

1. Collect for Proper 19, Book of Common Prayer, 620.

2. Blue Letter Bible, *"Menō,"* accessed February 17, 2025, www .blueletterbible.org/lexicon/g3306/esv/mgnt/0-1/.

3. Augustine, *Sermons* 22.7, quoted in Trevin Wax, "Don't Miss the Main Point of Bible Study," The Gospel Coalition, March 24, 2022, www .thegospelcoalition.org/blogs/trevin-wax/main-point-bible-study/.

Seventeenth Week: Resurrecting Literacy

1. Collect for Proper 20, Book of Common Prayer, 620.

2. Paul Lee Tan, *Encyclopedia of 7700 Illustrations: Signs of the Times* (Bible Communications, 1996), 309.

Eighteenth Week: The Posture of Grace

1. Collect for Proper 21, Book of Common Prayer, 620.
2. William Barclay, *The Gospel of Luke* (Westminster John Knox Press, 2001), 266.
3. Barclay, *The Gospel of Luke,* 266.
4. Evelyn Underhill, *The Spiritual Life* (First Ariel Press Edition, 2000), 53.
5. Klyne R. Snodgrass, *Stories with Intent: A Comprehensive Guide to the Parables of Jesus* (Eerdmans, 2008), 9.
6. Lesslie Newbigin, *The Gospel in a Pluralist Society* (Eerdmans, 1989), 234.
7. "4 Ways to Turn Good Posture into Less Back Pain," Harvard Health Publishing, April 18, 2020, https://www.health.harvard .edu/pain/4-ways-to-turn-good-posture-into-less-back-pain.

Nineteenth Week: Endurance Wisdom

1. Collect for Proper 22, Book of Common Prayer, 620–21.
2. Flavius Josephus, *The Wars of the Jews, or History of the Destruction of Jerusalem,* trans. William Whitson, 5.5.6 (Project Gutenberg, 2013), www.gutenberg.org/files/2850/2850-h/2850-h.htm #link52HCH0005.
3. Sarah McCammon, Michael Levitt, and Kathryn Fox, "America's Christian Majority Is Shrinking, and Could Dip Below 70% by 2070," NPR, September 15, 2022, www.npr.org/2022/09/15/ 1123289466/americas-christian-majority-is-shrinking-and-could -dip-below-50-by-2070.

Twentieth Week: The Good Life

1. Collect for the Sixth Sunday of Epiphany, Book of Common Prayer, 603.
2. Augustine, *Sermons,* 22.7, quoted in Trevin Wax, "Don't Miss the Main Point of Bible Study," The Gospel Coalition, March 24, 2022, www.thegospelcoalition.org/blogs/trevin-wax/main-point-bible -study.

Twenty-First Week: More Grace

1. Collect for Proper 23, Book of Common Prayer, 621.
2. Michael S. Horton, "Grace," *Modern Reformation,* June 29, 2007, www.modernreformation.org/resources/articles/grace.

All Saints' Day: The Grace of Blessed Examples

1. Collect for All Saints' Day, Book of Common Prayer, 622.
2. Robert W. Jenson, *Systematic Theology*, vol. 2, *The Works of God* (Oxford University Press, 1999), 368.
3. *Brittanica*, "All Saints' Day," accessed February 18, 2025, www .britannica.com/topic/All-Saints-Day.
4. Kendrick Lamar, "FEEL.," track 5 on *DAMN.*, Top Dawg Entertainment, 2017.
5. Andrew A. Bonar, *Memoirs and Remains of the Rev. Robert Murray M'Cheyne* (Edinburgh, 1883), 158.

Christ the King Sunday: The Hands of the King

1. Collect for Christ the King Sunday, Book of Common Prayer, 623.

About the Author

CLAUDE ATCHO is an ordained priest in the Anglican Church in North America and an award-winning author. He serves as the pastor of Church of the Resurrection in Charlottesville, Virginia, having previously pastored in Boston, Massachusetts, and Memphis, Tennessee. Deeply passionate about multidisciplinary perspectives, he speaks and writes regularly at the intersection of faith, culture, and theology. He is the author of *Reading Black Books: How African American Literature Can Make Our Faith More Whole and Just,* and his writing has been featured in *Christianity Today* and *Think Christian,* as well as on The Witness: A Black Christian Collective.

About the Type

This book was set in Bembo, a typeface based on an old-style Roman face that was used for Cardinal Pietro Bembo's tract *De Aetna* in 1495. Bembo was cut by Francesco Griffo (1450–1518) in the early sixteenth century for Italian Renaissance printer and publisher Aldus Manutius (1449–1515). The Lanston Monotype Company of Philadelphia brought the well-proportioned letterforms of Bembo to the United States in the 1930s.